THE
INNKEEPERS
COLLECTION
COOKBOOK

ALSO FROM BERKSHIRE HOUSE PUBLISHERS

How to Open and Successfully Operate a Country Inn
C. Vincent Shortt

The Red Lion Inn Cookbook
Suzi Forbes Chase

Apple Orchard Cookbook
Janet M. Christensen and Betty Bergman Levin

Best Recipes of Berkshire Chefs
Miriam Jacobs

THE
INNKEEPERS
COLLECTION
COOKBOOK

C. VINCENT SHORTT

BERKSHIRE HOUSE PUBLISHERS
Stockbridge, Massachusetts

Edited by Constance L. Oxley
Cover design by Catharyn Tivy
Book design and page layout by Jane McWhorter
Production services by Ripinsky & Company

Color photographs and other illustrations used by permission of individual innkeepers.

Front cover photograph by Michael Cunningham.

Library of Congress Cataloging-in-Publication Data

Shortt, C. Vincent.
The Innkeepers collection cookbook / C. Vincent Shortt.
         p.   cm.
Includes index.
ISBN 0-936399-57-0 : $16.95
1. Cookery, American. Hotels—United States—Guidebooks. 3. United States—Guidebooks. I. Title.
TX715.S5589   1993
641.5973—dc20   93-32983

ISBN 0-936399-57-0, paper

10 9 8 7 6 5 4 3
Printed in the United States of America

This book is dedicated to the uniquely talented people who:

Treat guests in their home as honored members of their extended family,
Derive their ultimate reward each day from serving others,
Place more importance on the joy of creating memories for others
than sharing memories of their own,
Strive for excellence in all that they do to pamper people they have never met,
Unselfishly share their "best kept secrets" with cookbook authors and editors,
And ask only that we return again soon and often. . . .

. . . The Keepers of The Inn

Contents

NOTE: When this symbol ❖ appears next to a recipe, that recipe is from a specialty cookbook produced by the inn. We encourage you to write or call the inns for information about purchasing their unique cookbooks. (See the Appendix for complete addresses.)

Color Photographs
(following page 150)

This labor of love would not have been possible without the generous support and encouragement of my editor, Constance L. Oxley, who never stopped believing it would be great, my publisher, Berkshire House, who shares my enthusiasm for this wonderful segment of the hospitality industry, and Karen McGill, our transcriber, who made sure the recipes in this collection were accurate to the last teaspoon.

The love for this labor, I owe to the best chef I have ever met. Her unerring eye for palate-pleasing recipes and superb sense of good taste are reflected on every page of this collection...and reflected daily in everything we do as partners in life . . . my wife, Ann.

C.V.S.

Introduction

Country inns have long had a reputation for providing fine food to their guests—hearty breakfasts and fine country dinners. In this remarkable collection of recipes from inns throughout the country, we have gathered a tantalizing selection of original and delectable recipes, from favorite, traditional, home-style country fare to sophisticated, elegant recipes from French and European cuisines.

Our goal was to collect from regional country inns their best recipes, from appetizers to salads, soups to entrées, from breads to desserts. Innkeepers from Camden, Maine, to Santa Monica, California, generously shared their cherished recipes, and award-winning chefs included their culinary secrets and techniques for a truly delicious adventure in American regional cuisine. There is an entire chapter devoted to recipes for that wholesome breakfast or magnificent brunch for that special gathering of family and friends. Many innkeepers also contributed recipes from their own specialty cookbooks.

We hope this book will stand as an invaluable addition to your home-cooking library. Cookbooks should capture the imagination with their creativity, whet the appetite with their appeal, and be organized in such a way that makes the book easy to read and as comfortable to use as a favorite old kitchen utensil. We hope we have met our own criteria, and we wish you many gratifying hours of culinary enjoyment as you "taste your way" through the bills of fare of America's most celebrated country inns.

CHAPTER 1

Beverages

Iced Victorian Tea❖

1 cup water
2 tablespoons granulated sugar
3 whole cloves
1 cinnamon stick
2 tea bags
2 cups apricot nectar
2 tablespoons undiluted frozen orange juice concentrate
Club soda
8 ounces light rum
Grand Marnier liqueur
8 fresh orange slices
8 fresh whole strawberries, washed with stems

In a small saucepan, combine the first five ingredients and stir well. Simmer for 5 minutes, then steep for 15 minutes.

Strain the tea into a glass container and add the apricot nectar and orange juice concentrate. Mix together and let cool. Chill.

Pour the tea over ice in a brandy snifter and add the soda to each glass. Add 1 ounce of the rum and a splash of the liqueur to each glass. Garnish each glass with an orange slice and a strawberry and serve.

Yield: 8 servings, or about 1 quart

THE GOVERNOR'S INN
Ludlow, Vermont

Honeyed Peach & Ginger Brandy❖

4 very ripe peaches, peeled and chopped
Juice of ½ lemon
3 tablespoons ginger-flavored brandy
3 tablespoons honey
Pinch ground ginger
Pinch ground mace
2 cups plain yogurt
4 – 6 fresh mint sprigs

THE GOVERNOR'S INN

Here's your chance to visit one of those little gems of country innkeeping, which has literally reached "celebrity" status in its field. Deedy and Charlie Marble have earned about every distinction available to innkeepers, including the Mobil Four-Star Inn of The Year and Inn of The Decade, "Best Apple Pie in Vermont," as well as being featured on boxes of Uncle Ben's Rice.

The Governor's Inn was built in 1890 by Vermont governor, William Wallace Stickney, as a wedding present for his bride, Elizabeth Lincoln. From the moment you enter through the scented and polished front alcove and into the parlor, you begin to sense something special in the air. You've entered the comfortably elegant country home of someone you look forward to meeting . . . and it is 1890 all over again.

Eight distinctively and delightfully decorated guest chambers are furnished in period heirloom and Marble family antiques, oriental rugs, and highly polished brass beds. House guests enjoy six-course dinners and full English breakfasts, prepared, of course, by the innkeepers and served at elegant place settings that feature whimsical, antique sterling knife rests and rare fine china tea sets, which have been collected by the innkeepers through the years.

The gourmet kitchen turns out award-winning guest surprises, such as Bluefish Flambé with Gin & Juniper Berries, Oyster Newberg under Glass, Pear Bread & Apple Butter and for breakfast, Rum Raisin French Toast with Rum Raisin Ice Cream and warm Vermont maple syrup. Delicious!

In a blender, puree the first six ingredients. Add the yogurt and whip just to blend. Chill overnight.

Pour into chilled brandy snifters and garnish each with a mint sprig. Serve immediately.

THE GOVERNOR'S INN
Ludlow, Vermont

WESTWAYS RESORT INN

Of the more than 500 properties that were evaluated by the American Bed and Breakfast Association in 1992, Westways was one of the top-ranking four percent to receive the coveted ABBA Four-Crown rating as outstanding.

Gourmet breakfasts and creatively executed afternoon snacks are part of the daily hospitality extended at this contemporary, southwestern and mediterranean-styled, six-guest room inn. If your idea of "roughing" it includes a big screen satellite TV, diving pool, fitness room, and country club privileges, topped off with Darrell Trapp's gracious hospitality, then you'll think that you've died and gone to heaven here in the valley of the sun.

Arizona Citrus Mint Cooler

1 cup fresh lemon juice (about 6 lemons)
1 cup fresh orange juice (about 3 medium oranges)
1 ½ cups water
Granulated sugar to taste
10 sprigs fresh mint
One 32-ounce bottle ginger ale
Water
14 – 16 fresh lemon or orange slices

In a large saucepan, stir together the first five ingredients. Bring to a boil, stirring frequently until the sugar dissolves. Remove from heat, cover, and steep until cool. Strain. Cover and chill.

Fill tall, frosted glasses or a pitcher with equal amounts of the chilled fruit juice, ginger ale, and water. Add ice and garnish with a slice of lemon or orange on the edge of each glass. Serve.

Yield: 14 to 16 servings

WESTWAYS RESORT INN
Phoenix, Arizona

Mast Farm Inn Breakfast Frappé❖

1 banana, sliced
1 – 1 ½ cups fresh fruit
½ – 1 cup vanilla yogurt
Fresh orange juice
Fresh orange or lemon slices
Fresh mint leaves

In a blender, combine the banana, fruit, and yogurt. Add enough orange juice to reach the 4 ½-cup measure of a 5-cup blender. Blend on high until smooth.

Pour into chilled glasses and garnish with the fruit slices and mint leaves. Serve.

Yield: 4 servings

MAST FARM INN
Valle Crucis, North Carolina

All ingredients should be very cold, especially if using fresh instead of frozen fruit. If unsweetened fruit is used, sweeten with a little honey or sugar. Freeze leftover frappé in ice cube trays to use in future servings.

Hot Cranberry Cup❖

1 ½ cups apple cider
1 ½ cups cranberry juice
12 whole cloves
12 whole allspice
4 sticks cinnamon

In a small saucepan, mix together the first four ingredients and bring to a boil. Reduce heat, cover, and simmer for 20 minutes.

Pour into mugs and garnish with the cinnamon sticks. Serve.

Yield: 4 servings

GRANT CORNER INN
Santa Fe, New Mexico

Knock-Out Champagne Punch❖

One 6-ounce can frozen lemonade concentrate, thawed and undiluted
One 46-ounce can pineapple juice
2 liters champagne
2 liters white wine

CAMPBELL RANCH INN

The spectacular view from Mary Jane and Jerry's hilltop home is one of the extra-added treats, which comes with being a guest on this beautiful 35-acre ranch in the heart of the Sonoma Valley wine country. Beautiful rolling vineyards and a sea of colorful flowers in Mary Jane's garden provide the perfect backdrop for a delightful home-cooked breakfast on the terrace.

A visit to the Campbell Ranch Inn comes with a few amenities not often found in your more traditional inn, such as a professional tennis court, 20 x 40-foot swimming pool, hot tub spa, table tennis, horseshoes, and satellite dish-fed television. And if that were not pampering enough, Mary Jane is ready and waiting for you with fresh baked apple pie and steaming hot coffee when you return from enjoying dinner at one of the many excellent restaurants in the valley.

2 medium oranges, thinly sliced

Up to one hour before serving, combine the lemonade concentrate, pineapple juice, champagne, and wine in a large punch bowl and mix together well.

Float an ice ring on top and add the orange slices for color. Serve.

Yield: Variable servings, about 1 ½ gallons

CAMPBELL RANCH INN
Geyserville, California

THE OAKS HISTORIC BED & BREAKFAST COUNTRY INN

Margaret and Tom Ray have recently converted The Oaks into a bed and breakfast country inn, catering to both leisure and business travelers. Nestled among giant three-century-old namesake oaks, the inn epitomizes the luxury, charm, and tranquility of yesteryear.

Major W. L. Pierce built the magnificent Queen Anne Victorian in 1889 for his wife and seven children. The moment you step from the spacious porch into the expansive entry hall with its high ceilings, stained glass windows, and grand staircase, you begin to feel your spirits soar.

Breakfast each morning in the formal dining room, served by Margaret personally, is a delightful blend of tried-and-true, southern gourmet recipes and homemade breads and jellies.

Perky Porch Punch

**Two 12-ounce cans orange juice concentrate, thawed and
    undiluted**
1 liter club soda
1 lime, very thinly sliced
Vodka
1 – 2 pints lemon sherbet
Fresh mint sprigs

In a large pitcher, mix together both cans of the concentrate and substitute the club soda for half the water amount on package directions. (If package directions require 4 cans of water per 12-ounce can, use 2 cans club soda.) Stir until thoroughly mixed. Add the lime slices and stir again.

Fill frosted goblets half full with crushed ice and add 1 ounce of vodka to each goblet. Add a small scoop of the sherbet and fill with the prepared orange juice. Garnish each goblet with a mint sprig, add cocktail straws, and serve immediately.

Yield: 8 to 10 servings

THE OAKS HISTORIC BED & BREAKFAST COUNTRY INN
Christiansburg, Virginia

Fearrington House Fruit Punch❖

8 cups fresh orange juice
1 cup fresh raspberries
2 cups granulated sugar
4 cups water
2 quarts soda water
Two 46-ounce cans pineapple juice
One 46-ounce can grapefruit juice

Remove the pulp from the orange juice by pouring through a strainer. Press the raspberries through a fine-mesh sieve to remove the seeds. Set aside.

In a large saucepan, combine the sugar and the 4 cups water. Bring to a boil, stirring frequently until the sugar is dissolved. Remove from heat and cool.

Add the remaining ingredients to the cooled mixture and chill.

Pour into a very large punch bowl and serve.

Yield: Variable servings, about 2 ½ gallons

THE FEARRINGTON HOUSE
Chapel Hill, North Carolina

Golden Nectar Punch❖

One 6-ounce can frozen orange juice concentrate
One 6-ounce can frozen lemonade concentrate
One 12-ounce can apricot nectar
One 46-ounce can pineapple juice
2 quarts lemon-lime soda

Prepare the frozen juices according to package directions. Combine with the remaining juices, stirring well. Chill.

Place the chilled juices in a large punch bowl and mix in the soda. Add an ice block and serve.

Yield: Variable servings, about 1 ½ gallons

CAMPBELL RANCH INN
Geyserville, California

CHAPTER 2

Appetizers

Blackberry Scallop Seviche❖

1 ½ cups olive oil
1 cup blackberry juice
1 cup fresh orange juice
¾ cup fresh lemon juice
¾ cup fresh lime juice
1 medium red onion, julienned
4 shallots, minced
1 teaspoon minced garlic
⅛ cup chopped anise hyssop
½ teaspoon salt
½ teaspoon black pepper
½ teaspoon cayenne pepper
3 pounds fresh sea scallops
2 cups *Blackberry Marinated Onions* (see recipe below)
1 cup *Blackberry Catsup* (see recipe below)
Fresh anise hyssop

In a large shallow bowl, combine the first twelve ingredients and mix together well. Add the scallops, cover, and marinate in the refrigerator for 8 hours or overnight.

Remove from the refrigerator and reserve the marinade.

Make nests of the marinated onions on each serving plate. Place equal amounts of scallops in the center of each plate and spoon the reserved marinade over the top. Garnish with the catsup and the hyssop and serve.

Blackberry Marinated Onions

2 cups blackberry or raspberry vinegar
½ cup honey
4 medium red onions, very thinly sliced

In a medium-sized bowl, mix together the vinegar and honey. Add the onion slices, cover, and marinate overnight at room temperature. (The onions will become a vibrant pink color!)

If do not use immediately, cover, and refrigerate until ready to serve. Makes 4 cups. (The onions can be stored in the refrigerator for two weeks.)

Blackberry Catsup

8 cups fresh blackberries

2 shallots, minced
1 medium onion, chopped
2 teaspoons dried tarragon
2 teaspoons dried marjoram
1 teaspoon dried rosemary
Juice and zest of 1 lemon
¾ cup balsamic vinegar
½ cup granulated sugar
1 teaspoon salt
½ teaspoon pepper

In a large saucepan, mix together the first nine ingredients. Cover and bring to a boil. Reduce heat and simmer for 10 minutes.

Cool slightly, then puree in a blender or food processor. Strain through a medium-mesh sieve into another saucepan, pressing to retrieve as much puree as possible.

Add the salt and pepper and reduce over low heat to 4 cups. If do not use immediately, cover, and refrigerate until ready to serve. Makes 4 cups. (The catsup can be stored in the refrigerator for at least six months.)

Yield: 8 to 10 appetizer servings

SHELBURNE INN/THE SHOALWATER RESTAURANT
Seaview, Washington

Chilled Shrimp Spring Rolls

8 jumbo black tiger shrimp (10 – 15 count)
⅓ cup pickling spice
¼ cup lightly chopped mung bean sprouts
¼ cup lightly chopped red leaf lettuce
4 tablespoons finely chopped fresh cilantro
Rice paper, cut into eight 6-inch rounds
1 recipe *Spicy Kiwi-Mustard Sauce* (see recipe below)
1 pint fresh raspberries, pureed
4 sprigs celery heart leaves
4 lemon rind "roses"

In a large saucepan, boil the shrimp in the pickling spice for 2 – 2 ½ minutes, or until all of the shrimp float to the top. Remove from heat and drain. Peel and devein the shrimp. Set aside and chill for 25 – 30 minutes.

Dice the reserved shrimp into medium-sized pieces. In a small bowl, mix together the shrimp pieces, sprouts, lettuce, and cilantro and set aside.

Dampen the rice paper rounds in water. Shake off excess water and place on a large cutting surface. Place one-eighth of the shrimp mixture on the front of each rice paper round. Roll the front edge of the rice paper over the shrimp mixture enough to cover it. Then fold in the left and right sides of the rice paper to enclose the mixture and continue to roll forward until completely wrapped. These should be completely cylindrical and look like small egg rolls. Place on a nonstick baking sheet and cover with plastic wrap. Chill, while making the mustard sauce.

To serve, place three ounces of the mustard sauce in a ring around the well of each serving plate. Spread evenly. Zig-zag one ounce of the raspberry puree, back and forth, across the top of the mustard sauce on each plate. Place two spring rolls in the center of each plate, side by side. Place one celery leaf sprig just beside the two spring rolls, with the leaves pointing out to the top left fourth of the plate. Place one lemon "rose" atop the leaf stem and serve.

Spicy Kiwi-Mustard Sauce

5 – 6 kiwi, pureed (1 cup)
¼ cup oyster sauce*
1 tablespoon tamari soy sauce
1 teaspoon dry mustard
1 tablespoon white wine vinegar

In a small bowl, mix together all of the ingredients and blend well. Cover and refrigerate until ready to use. Makes 1 ½ cups.

*Oyster sauce is available in Asian markets or in specialty gourmet food shops.

Yield: 4 appetizer servings

RICHMOND HILL INN
Asheville, North Carolina

RICHMOND HILL INN

The grand Victorian mansion known as Richmond Hill was built in 1889 as the private residence of Richmond Pearson, former congressman and ambassador, who was renowned for his political service to the nation. The impressive Queen Anne-style home with the gracious wraparound porch was designed by James G. Hill, the supervising architect for the United States Treasury buildings in Washington D.C.

Richmond Hill was one of the most elegant and innovative private residences of its era—with running water, its own communications system, and even a pulley-operated elevator for transporting heavy baggage and luggage from one floor to the next. The mansion had a grand entrance hall, which soared overhead in rich native oak paneling from the oak floor to the exposed oak beams in the ceiling twelve feet above.

Today, after complete renovation, which included moving the massive structure six hundred feet east to its present site, owners Jake and Margaret Michel and their innkeeper/daughter, Susan Michel-Robertson, have succeeded in restoring the mansion's once all-but-lost luster and elegance. Popular chef John Babb presides over the award-winning and highly praised food and beverage presentations at Richmond Hill. Such delights as Sautéed Veal Sweetbreads Napoleon, wrapped in crispy puff pastry and served with a wild mushroom and merlot wine demi-glace or Applewood-Smoked

Salmon with a roasted red pepper aioli and chive butter sauce are typical first-course surprises in Richmond Hill's glass-walled dining room, Gabrielle's. This is one inn you will visit again and again.

THE BIRD & BOTTLE INN

From 1761, when it was known as Warren's Tavern, The Bird and Bottle Inn has had a colorful and romantic history. Warren's Tavern immediately became a popular resting place for the New York and Albany stages when it opened in 1761. While the horses were being changed, the colonial ladies and gentlemen were refreshed at Warren's tables with food and drink.

Today, innkeeper Ira Boyar continues to welcome travelers with traditional Hudson River Valley hospitality. This authentic old country inn is internationally renowned for its gourmet cuisine and comfortable, cozy rooms with woodburning fireplaces, four-poster or canopied beds, and colonial furnishings, of course.

Grilled Garlic Shrimp with Yellow Pepper Vinaigrette

20 jumbo shrimp (16 – 20 count), peeled and deveined, tails on
1 tablespoon olive oil
4 cloves garlic, minced
1 recipe *Yellow Pepper Vinaigrette* (see recipe below)
4 lemon slices
4 small sprigs fresh dill
1 small red bell pepper, finely chopped

In a medium-sized shallow bowl, mix together the shrimp, olive oil, and garlic and marinate in the refrigerator for 1 hour. Prepare the vinaigrette.

Make sure the marinated shrimp are encrusted with garlic and grill on high for 2 minutes on each side.

Pour the vinaigrette on the bottom of each small plate and place five shrimp on top of the vinaigrette, tails up. Garnish each serving with the lemon slices, dill, and red bell pepper and serve.

Yellow Pepper Vinaigrette

2 large yellow bell peppers, roasted, seeded, and peeled
1 shallot, peeled
1 tablespoon champagne
1 tablespoon champagne vinegar*
1 teaspoon Dijon mustard
¼ teaspoon white pepper
1 cup vegetable oil

In a food processor, combine the bell peppers, shallot, champagne, vinegar, mustard, and white pepper and process for 4 minutes. While processing, slowly add the oil in a steady stream and blend well. Set aside until ready to serve.

*Champagne vinegar is available in specialty gourmet food shops.

Yield: 4 appetizer servings

THE BIRD & BOTTLE INN
Garrison, New York

Grilled Spicy Shrimp

1 – 1 ¼ cups tequila
½ – ¾ cup olive oil
3 teaspoons ground cumin
2 teaspoons minced fresh rosemary
3 – 4 cloves garlic, minced
½ cup crushed peppers packed in vinegar
¼ teaspoon cayenne pepper
32 jumbo shrimp (16 – 20 count), peeled and deveined, tails on

In a medium-sized bowl, mix together all of the ingredients, except the shrimp.

In a shallow glass baking pan, place the shrimp and cover with the marinade. Marinate in the refrigerator for 6 – 24 hours. (The longer the shrimp are marinated, the better the results.)

Remove the shrimp from the marinade and place on short bamboo skewers, 4 shrimp per skewer. Grill on high for 2 minutes on each side. Baste often with the remaining marinade.

Serve the shrimp on the skewers with spicy-hot cocktail sauce on the side.

Yield: 8 appetizer servings

CHARLES HINCKLEY HOUSE
Barnstable, Massachusetts

Chafing Dish Crabmeat*

½ cup (1 stick) sweet butter
1 medium onion, chopped
½ bunch celery, chopped
One 4-ounce jar pimientos, chopped
1 pound fresh crabmeat
3 ounces cream cheese
2 cups sour cream
¼ teaspoon each: dried oregano, Worcestershire sauce, ground red pepper, garlic powder, ground paprika, curry powder, dried marjoram
½ pound Vermont cheddar cheese, grated

In a large skillet, melt the butter and sauté the onion and celery

CHARLES HINCKLEY HOUSE

This quaint, appealing four-guest room inn is considered by some to be one of the best bed and breakfast experiences in all of New England. Miya and Les Patrick's superb and tasteful restoration of this 1809 colonial building is matched only by the thoughtful and attentive service shown to their guests.

At breakfast, you will invariably find fresh-cut flowers arranged at your place setting—Miya's obsession with the inn's welcoming profusion of wildflowers is legendary. On weekends and holidays, dinner is served by reservation only and only for guests of the inn. Four-Vegetable Puree Soup and Veal with Morels are frequently requested inn favorites. Don't be surprised if you find a special gift in your room. Miya is a hopeless romantic who admits to a slight affinity for shopping and gift giving!

until the onion is translucent, about 4 – 6 minutes. Stir in the pimientos and crabmeat. Keep warm.

Place the cream cheese, sour cream, herbs, and spices in a blender or food processor and blend until just mixed. Add the cream cheese mixture and the cheddar cheese to the warm crabmeat mixture and cook over low heat until the cheddar cheese has melted. (If the mixture seems too thick, thin with a little light cream.)

Place in a warmed chafing dish and serve with assorted crackers. Makes about 4 cups.

Yield: Variable servings

THE GOVERNOR'S INN
Ludlow, Vermont

THE ROBERT MORRIS INN

The Robert Morris Inn is located on two acres of waterfront property with private beach. The water-bound village of Oxford was once Maryland's largest port of call and is still an important center for boat building and yachting. Many of the rooms in the inn's Sandaway Lodge have porches overlooking the water.

The inn was built prior to 1710 by ship's carpenters, and the son of the original owner, Robert Morris, helped finance the Revolutionary War, counted George Washington as a friend, and was a signer of the Declaration of Independence, the Articles of the Confederation, and the United States Constitution.

In the last few years, the inn has established a reputation of consistently serving noteworthy food with excellent service. To quote *The American Auberge,* "The dining room serves an ethereally light version of crab cakes and features equally deft handling of other Chesapeake fish." This historic country inn's innkeeper, Jay Gibson, invites you to sample the catch of the day.

Oysters A La Gino

2 tablespoons butter
⅓ cup all-purpose flour
1 tablespoon ground paprika
½ teaspoon monosodium glutamate
½ teaspoon garlic powder
½ teaspoon Chesapeake Bay-style seafood seasoning
½ teaspoon white pepper
1 cup milk
2 tablespoons Worcestershire sauce
2 tablespoons dry sherry
6 – 8 ounces lump crabmeat, cooked and shredded
24 fresh oysters on the half shell
6 slices bacon, stacked and cut into 4 pieces

Preheat oven to 375° F. In a large saucepan, melt the butter over low heat and mix in the flour and dry seasonings. Stir in the milk and Worcestershire sauce and whisk until smooth. Cook for 5 minutes or until thickened, stirring constantly.

Remove from heat and add the sherry. Cool for 20 minutes, then gently mix in the crabmeat.

Arrange the oysters in a shallow baking pan and top each with 1 tablespoon of the crab mixture. Place one piece of bacon atop each and bake for 10 – 12 minutes, or until the bacon is crisp. Serve immediately.

Yield: 6 to 8 appetizer servings

THE ROBERT MORRIS INN
Oxford, Maryland

Oysters Chelsea

12 fresh oysters on the half shell, loosened
½ pound (2 sticks) butter, softened
3 cloves garlic, minced
1 large shallot, minced
1 tablespoon chopped fresh parsley
½ teaspoon prepared mustard
¼ teaspoon fresh lemon juice
¼ cup sliced blanched almonds

Preheat oven to 400° F. Arrange the oysters in a shallow baking pan. In a small bowl, mix together the remaining ingredients, except the almonds, and blend well until smooth.

Place a mounding teaspoon of the butter mixture on each oyster and sprinkle with about five almond slices. Bake for 10 minutes, or until the almonds begin to brown. Serve immediately.

Yield: 4 appetizer servings

THE 1661 INN/HOTEL MANISSES
Block Island, Rhode Island

Oysters Palantine

2 tablespoons butter
2 quarts fresh spinach, cleaned and stemmed
Salt to taste
White pepper to taste
20 fresh oysters, shucked
1 ¼ cups *Curry Hollandaise* (see recipe below)

In a medium-sized saucepan, melt the butter on low heat. Add the spinach, salt, and white pepper and cook slowly until tender, about 3 – 5 minutes. Cool.

Preheat oven to 450° F. Place the oysters in a baking pan.
Spread each with the cooled spinach mixture until lightly coated

THE 1661 INN AND HOTEL MANISSES

The 1661 Inn, named after the year Block Island was settled by colonists from New England, is truly a "family affair." The Abrams family, Joan, Justin, Rita, Mark, and Rick, discovered the property in the late 1960s while on one of their family sailing adventures. All of the nine beautiful and sophisticated guest rooms come complete with antique furnishings, private baths, refrigerators, and most have an ocean view and private sun deck.

Scarcely two years after opening their 1661 Inn, the Abrams family stepped forward in 1972 and saved one of the most prestigious summer hotels on the east coast from almost certain demise. The Hotel Manisses, built in 1870, has now been thoroughly restored and is once again a nineteenth-century showpiece of hospitality and charm.

All seventeen Victorian-decorated guest rooms at the Hotel Manisses have private baths, and many have Jacuzzis as well. In the parlors, a past-century top shelf bar and beautiful stained glass windows reflect old-fashioned flower gardens, outdoor fountains, and Victorian-style patio furniture. Dinners in the Manisses' dining room are masterfully prepared and range from ocean fresh shellfish and catches of the day to luscious homemade desserts. Brandy in the serenity of the Library Room, then an early morning visit to the Hotel's own petting zoo complete a memorable visit to Block Island.

and bake for 5 minutes.

Remove from the oven and top each oyster with 1 tablespoon of the hollandaise. Place immediately under a hot broiler until golden brown, about 30 seconds. Serve immediately.

Curry Hollandaise

2 egg yolks
Dash cayenne pepper
3 tablespoons white wine
1 ¼ cups clarified butter
1 lemon, halved
Salt to taste
½ teaspoon curry powder

In the top of a double boiler, whip together the egg yolks, cayenne, and 1 tablespoon of the wine over a steam bath until thick and foamy. Do not scramble.

Slowly add ¾ cup of the butter, ¼ cup at a time, to the egg foam and whip constantly. Add the remaining wine and squeeze in the juice of half the lemon. After ¾ cup of the butter has been added, adjust the seasoning, then add the remaining butter. Adjust again, then add the salt and curry.

Yield: 4 appetizer servings

THE 1661 INN/HOTEL MANISSES
Block Island, Rhode Island

Duck Liver Pâté❖

½ cup heavy cream
1 tablespoon black pepper
1 cup brandy
10 ounces duck livers
10 ounces chicken livers
20 ounces pork fatback
10 ounces pork, ground
½ cup port wine
½ cup crème fraîche
4 eggs
½ teaspoon crushed juniper berries
1 teaspoon ground allspice
1 teaspoon ground ginger

1 teaspoon kosher salt
1 teaspoon white pepper
1 cup fresh blueberries
1 cup fresh cranberries
Chutney

In a medium-sized shallow glass bowl, combine the cream, black pepper, and ½ cup brandy. Add the duck and chicken livers and marinate overnight.

Thinly slice 10 ounces of the fatback. Line the bottom and sides of a 4 x 13 x 4-inch mold with the slices, pressing firmly in place. Chill. (Be sure there are enough slices remaining to cover the top of the pâté.)

Finely dice the remaining fatback and blend with the ground pork in a food processor until smooth and creamy. Blend in the remaining brandy, the port, crème fraîche, and eggs. Add the spices, salt, and white pepper. Blend, but do not over process. Rinse the livers and add to the forcemeat, blending well.

Preheat oven to 350° F. Alternate layers of the forcemeat and the berries in the mold. Finish with a layer of the fatback slices. Cover with aluminum foil and weight the top with pie weights. Place in a hot water bath that comes two thirds up the sides of the mold and bake for 1 ½ – 2 hours, or until the pâté has shrunk slightly from the sides of the mold and the liquids are a clear yellow.

Let the pie weights remain and chill the pâté overnight.

Remove the weights and unmold only when completely chilled. Thinly slice into twenty pieces. Place two thin slices on each small serving plate and serve with the chutney.

Yield: 10 appetizer servings

SHELBURNE INN/THE SHOALWATER RESTAURANT
Seaview, Washington

Crêpes Katrina

¾ cup all-purpose flour
2 large eggs
¾ cup milk
1 teaspoon salt

SHELBURNE INN

The Shelburne Inn on Washington's southwest coast is surrounded by some of the most stunning scenery in the country. Willapa Bay, located just east of the inn, is a haven for waterfowl, and Ilwaco's nearby docks provide unsurpassed sport fishing.

Built in 1896, the Shelburne Inn is the oldest continuously running hotel in the state of Washington. The inn has been extensively renovated over the past decade by David Campiche and Laurie Anderson, who have owned the inn since 1977. Easily the most photographed feature of the Shelburne is the stained glass windows, which preside over the entry of The Shoalwater Restaurant.

The *New York Times* raves that the Shoalwater has "superb Northwest cuisine." Ann and Tony Kischner own The Shoalwater Restaurant, and Ann does all the baking and heads the dessert department. Delicious and unique breakfasts, which have been featured in *Gourmet* magazine, are the specialty of innkeepers, David and Laurie.

¼ teaspoon pepper
2 tablespoons butter

Filling:
1 pound ricotta cheese
4 ounces freshly grated Asiago or Parmesan cheese
1 large tomato, diced
2 tablespoons chopped fresh basil
2 eggs
Salt and pepper to taste

Mushrooms:
2 tablespoons olive oil
1 pound fresh mushrooms, quartered
1 medium tomato, diced
½ cup sherry
Salt and pepper to taste

In a large bowl, place the flour and make a well in the center. Add the eggs, milk, salt, and pepper to the well. With a whisk, starting at the center and working slowly outward, blend together until the batter is smooth. Add the butter and whip until thoroughly blended and no lumps remain. Let stand for 1 hour at room temperature.

Heat a 5-inch teflon pan until a drop of water on the surface sizzles. Ladle ⅛ cup of the batter into the pan, rapidly tipping and moving the pan in a figure-eight motion so the batter is evenly and thinly covering the bottom and slightly up the sides. Brown on one side for 40 seconds. Turn and brown the other side. Remove and use the same procedure to make eleven more crêpes. As each crêpe is prepared, stack and set aside.

In a medium-sized bowl, beat together all of the filling ingredients with an electric mixer until well blended. Set aside.

In a medium-sized skillet, heat the oil to the smoking point. Add the mushrooms and lightly brown. Stir in the tomato and sherry and simmer until the raw sherry flavor is gone. Season with the salt and pepper and set aside. Keep warm.

Preheat oven to 375° F. Lay out the crêpes, brownest side down. One-third down from the top of the crêpe, spoon one-fourth of the reserved filling 1 inch high and 1 inch wide across the crêpe. Starting at the top, roll the crêpe around the filling. Repeat the procedure for the remaining crêpes.

Place the filled crêpes on a baking sheet and heat in the oven for

5 – 7 minutes. Serve immediately whole or cut in half on the reserved mushrooms. (The crêpes can be made up to a day in advance.)

Yield: 6 appetizer servings, 2 crêpes per person

BARROWS HOUSE
Dorset, Vermont

Montrachet & Tomato

½ cup all-purpose flour
Salt and pepper
Eight ½-inch thick slices Montrachet goat cheese
½ cup egg wash
8 ounces sliced almonds
Twelve ¼-inch thick slices tomato
1 cup *Strawberry-Orange Vinaigrette* (see recipe below)
Assorted fresh herbs
Edible flower blossoms

Season the flour with the salt and pepper and coat two slices of the goat cheese with the flour. Gently roll in the egg wash, then in the almonds. Repeat the procedure three more times. Chill until ready to serve.

Preheat oven to 450° F. Place the breaded goat cheese in a buttered ovenproof skillet and bake for 10 minutes, or until the almonds begin to brown.

Place three tomato slices on each of four small plates. Pour ¼ cup of the vinaigrette over the tomatoes and place the baked cheese portions on top. Garnish with the herbs and flowers and serve.

Strawberry-Orange Vinaigrette

¾ cup unsweetened frozen strawberries, thawed, pureed, and
   juice strained
Juice and zest of 1 orange
¼ cup olive oil
¼ cup red wine vinegar
⅛ cup granulated sugar
½ teaspoon salt
½ teaspoon pepper

In a small bowl, mix together all of the ingredients and blend

THE WHITE INN

The White Inn was built around 1868 on the homesite of the county's first physician. Robert Contiguglia and Kathleen Dennison now operate a twenty-three guest room oasis in this elegant mansion with its prominent 100-foot-long veranda.

Period antiques and reproductions are present everywhere, and the Inn's reputation for spectacular cuisine has enabled it to serve not only its own inn guests, but also lucky local folks as well. The White Inn also has the distinction of being a charter member of the Duncan Hines Family of Fine Restaurants. Nearby the Chautauqua Institution offers varied cultural programs and a variety of aquatic recreation awaits on Lake Erie. Antiquing, touring local wineries, and attending summer band concerts are also popular with White Inn guests.

well. Chill for 1 hour. Makes about 1½ cups.

Yield: 4 appetizer servings

THE WHITE INN
Fredonia, New York

THE BURN

The Burn, one of Natchez's most historic homes, was built in 1832 and is a superb example of pure Greek Revival architecture. The three-story mansion is especially noted for its semispiral stairway, unique gardens, and exquisite collection of museum-quality antiques.

The Burn was used as headquarters by the Federal troops and later in the Civil War became a hospital for Union soldiers. Today the innkeeper of The Burn, Loveta Byrne, pampers overnight guests with a seated plantation-style breakfast, private tour of the home, and abundant southern hospitality.

Special magnolia seated dinner parties beneath the gaslight glow of an antique crystal chandelier are presented on Old Paris China. The Empire dining table is complemented by matching Regency servers. One bedroom features a massive four-poster bed and furniture by Prudent Mallard, hand-carved in New Orleans. Aubusson carpets and Belgian lace-trimmed draperies complete the spectacular effect of an inn, not soon forgotten.

Green Tomato Tart

1 ¾ cups packaged baking mix
¼ teaspoon chopped fresh thyme
½ cup milk
¼ cup melted butter

Filling:
1 teaspoon granulated sugar
2 tablespoons chopped fresh basil
2 tablespoons chopped fresh garlic chives
1 teaspoon salt
1 teaspoon pepper
6 medium green tomatoes, peeled and sliced
1 medium mild onion, thinly sliced

Topping:
1 ½ cups homemade or commercial mayonnaise
⅔ cup grated sharp cheddar cheese

In a medium-sized mixing bowl, mix together the first four ingredients and press into a greased 10-inch tart pan.

Preheat oven to 350° F. In a small bowl, combine the sugar, basil, chives, salt, and pepper. Layer the tomatoes, onion slices, and the sugar mixture in the crust.

In another small bowl, mix together the mayonnaise and cheese and spread over the tart. Bake for 45 minutes. Let set for 10 minutes, then cut into wedges. Serve warm or at room temperature.

Yield: 8 appetizer servings

THE BURN
Natchez, Mississippi

Artichoke Hearts Romano❖

Two 14-ounce cans artichoke hearts
½ cup grated Romano cheese
6 ounces cream cheese
4 tablespoons (½ stick) butter

Preheat oven to 350° F. Cut the artichoke hearts into fourths and divide equally into small ramekins. In a food processor, process both cheeses and the butter until well blended.

Spread the cheese mixture evenly over the artichokes and bake for 20 – 25 minutes, or until the cheese is slightly browned. Serve immediately.

Yield: 8 to 10 appetizer servings

THE HIDDEN INN
Orange, Virginia

Spicy Yam Cakes

2 cups grated raw yams
1 egg, beaten
1 ½ tablespoons all-purpose flour
½ teaspoon salt
½ teaspoon pepper
½ teaspoon cayenne pepper, or to taste
Vegetable oil
Salt to taste

In a medium-sized bowl, combine the first six ingredients and mix well. Set aside.

Pour at least 1 inch of the oil in a large skillet and heat until very hot. With two forks, about 1 tablespoon at a time, place the reserved yam mixture into the hot oil, using forks to keep the cakes in a rounded shape. Cook until golden and crunchy.

Drain on paper towels and sprinkle with the salt. Serve hot.

Yield: 4 to 6 appetizer servings

THE REDBUD INN
Murphys, California

Chilled Walnut & Cheese-Stuffed Mushrooms❖

4 slices thick bacon (or 5 – 6 thin slices)
1 pound fresh mushrooms (about 30 – 40 medium-sized)
3 tablespoons butter
½ cup minced celery
¼ cup minced green onions (include tops)
2 tablespoons minced shallots
1 clove garlic, minced
5 tablespoons minced fresh parsley
2 ounces walnuts, toasted and chopped
2 teaspoons Worcestershire sauce
2 ounces cream cheese
3 – 4 tablespoons blue cheese
¾ – 1 teaspoon dried rosemary

In a small skillet, cook the bacon until crisp. Drain on paper towels and finely mince. Set aside. Wash and stem the mushrooms.* Set the caps aside and mince the stems.

In a medium-sized skillet, melt the butter and sauté the mushroom stems, celery, green onions, shallots, and garlic for 3 – 4 minutes, or until soft and most of the moisture has evaporated. Remove from heat.

Preheat oven to 400° F. Set aside 2 tablespoons of the parsley and one-fourth of the reserved bacon. Add the remaining parsley and bacon, Worcestershire sauce, cream cheese, blue cheese, and rosemary to the mushroom mixture and combine well. Adjust the seasonings.

Fill the mushroom caps and place on an ungreased baking sheet. In a small bowl, mix together the reserved parsley and bacon and garnish the tops of the stuffed mushrooms. Bake for 10 minutes.

Cool to room temperature. Chill until ready to serve.

Yield: 8 to 10 appetizer servings

STEAMBOAT INN
Steamboat, Oregon

*Washing mushrooms: Many times mushrooms need more than just wiping off. Place the mushrooms in a plastic bag, add water, and shake gently several times, changing the water if necessary. Drain, lay out the mushrooms on a kitchen towel, and pat dry.

Stuffed Pea Pods❖

2 quarts fresh edible-pod peas, washed
3 ounces cream cheese
½ cup cottage cheese
¼ cup fresh watercress, washed and patted dry
¼ pound almonds, chopped
1 tablespoon chutney
3 tablespoons chopped fresh chives
Fresh radishes, sliced
Edible flower blossoms

Set aside the washed peas. In a blender or food processor, blend together the cream cheese, cottage cheese, watercress, almonds, and chutney until smooth. Add the chives and mix together well. Chill for 30 minutes.

With a pastry bag, pipe the cream cheese mixture into opened pea pods and garnish each pod with three radish slices. Serve with the flower blossoms.

Yield: Variable servings

DAIRY HOLLOW HOUSE
Eureka Springs, Arkansas

Spicy Cold Sesame Noodles❖

1 pound linguine or thin spaghetti
3 tablespoons peanut oil
¾ cup sliced radishes
3 scallions, finely chopped
3 cloves garlic, minced
1-inch slice peeled fresh gingerroot
2 teaspoons crushed red pepper flakes, or to taste
½ cup soy sauce
½ cup rice vinegar
1 tablespoon granulated sugar or honey
4 scallions
¼ cup peanut oil
3 tablespoons sesame oil
1 teaspoon hot chili oil
½ cup peanut butter or sesame tahini
Lemon zest
Toasted sesame seeds

BLUEBERRY HILL

Tony Clark's completely restored 1813 farmhouse is truly "another world." Whether you're the type who prefers to quietly enjoy your morning coffee while basking in the sun in the tranquility of the garden, or the sort who wants to be up at the crack of dawn to pick blueberries, you'll be at home at Blueberry Hill.

At the end of the day, soak away your well-earned exhaustion from your hike up Hogback Mountain in your private bath, before nibbling hors d'oeuvres during the predinner social hour. Dinner at "The Hill" is a family affair. Guests are seated with new found friends for a splendid, candlelit four-course repast of simple, yet sophisticated cuisine—Blueberry Hill style! Relax, you have finally found your thrill!

In a large pot, bring 5 quarts of salted water to a full boil. Cook the pasta until *al dente*. Drain well and toss with the 3 tablespoons peanut oil. Place in a large bowl and mix in the radishes and the 3 chopped scallions. Set aside.

In a food processor, combine all of the remaining ingredients, except the lemon zest and sesame seeds, and process until very smooth and well blended.

Pour the sauce over the reserved noodle mixture and toss well. Cover and chill for 4 hours.

Before serving, toss again and let the noodles come to room temperature. Garnish with the lemon zest and sesame seeds and serve.

Yield: 8 to 10 appetizer servings

BLUEBERRY HILL
Goshen, Vermont

Pat's Chunky Salsa ❖

2 large firm tomatoes, coarsely chopped
$2/3$ cup roasted, peeled, and chopped fresh green chilies
$1/2$ cup tomato sauce
1 small onion, finely chopped
3 tablespoons finely chopped fresh cilantro
2 tablespoons finely chopped fresh parsley
2 teaspoons red wine vinegar
1 teaspoon fresh lemon or lime juice
1 small hot dried chili, crushed

In a medium-sized porcelain or glazed earthenware bowl, mix together all of the ingredients and let stand at room temperature for 2 hours to blend flavors. Makes about 4 cups.

Serve with fresh tortillas and guacamole on the side.

Yield: Variable servings

GRANT CORNER INN
Santa Fe, New Mexico

Sun-Dried Tomato Spread

12 – 14 sun-dried tomatoes
½ cup olive oil
1 tablespoon dried basil
1 tablespoon dried oregano
1 tablespoon dried marjoram
1 tablespoon dried thyme
1 small bay leaf
2 green onions, trimmed
1 ½ pounds cream cheese, cut into 2 ½-inch pieces
Fresh dill sprigs

Rehydrate the tomatoes.*

In a shallow glass bowl, mix together the oil, basil, oregano, marjoram, thyme, and bay leaf and set aside.

After the tomatoes are rehydrated, place in the reserved marinade and marinate overnight in the refrigerator.

Remove the tomatoes from the marinade and place the tomatoes and green onions in a food processor and thoroughly chop. In a medium-sized bowl, combine the tomato mixture and the cream cheese with an electric mixer, in small batches, until smooth.

Place the spread in two small glass bowls and garnish with the dill sprigs. Serve with a variety of colorful crudités or crisp wafers. Makes 4 cups. (The remaining marinade can be stored in a covered container in the refrigerator for one week.)

Yield: Variable servings

STAFFORD'S BAY VIEW INN
Petoskey, Michigan

*To rehydrate sun-dried tomatoes, spread them on a baking sheet and spray with hot water. Let stand for 15 – 20 minutes; spray again. Repeat this procedure until the tomatoes have plumped to the thickness of fresh tomatoes. This will take about 1 hour.

RIVERTOWN INN

The Rivertown Inn, built in 1882 by a prominent 33-year-old lumberman named John O'Brien, serves as a stately three-story Victorian monument to a time gone by. The historic charm and turn-of-the-century atmosphere of the Rivertown Inn today is a far cry from the rough and tumble logging days on the St. Croix River.

The Inn is adorned with the gracious furnishings once reserved for the enjoyment of only the wealthy, privileged few. Guests at the Rivertown Inn are transported back in time to the days when Teddy Roosevelt's address was 1600 Pennsylvania Avenue and Queen Victoria sat on England's throne.

When you step into Chuck and Judy Dougherty's Rivertown Inn, you enter to the strains of classical violin music and the aroma of fresh baked homemade goodies lovingly prepared to please the palate and pamper the spirit.

Warm Blue Cheese Dip with Garlic & Bacon

8 ounces cream cheese, at room temperature
$\frac{1}{4}$ cup heavy cream
4 ounces blue cheese, crumbled
7 slices bacon, cooked and crumbled
2 cloves garlic, chopped
2 tablespoons chopped fresh chives
3 tablespoons sliced almonds

Preheat oven to 350° F. In a medium-sized bowl, beat the cream cheese until smooth. Add the cream and blend together well. Stir in the remaining ingredients, except the almonds, and place in an ovenproof dish. Top with the almonds and bake for 20 – 30 minutes.

Serve warm with toast points. Makes about 2 ½ – 3 cups.

Yield: Variable servings

RIVERTOWN INN
Stillwater, Minnesota

Roquefort Wafers❖

7 tablespoons Roquefort cheese
7 tablespoons butter
4 teaspoons heavy cream
Pinch salt
1 egg yolk
Cayenne pepper to taste
1 cup all-purpose flour

In a small bowl, mix together all of the ingredients and roll into a dough. Let stand for 20 minutes.

Either thinly roll the dough, about ⅛ inch thick, and cut into oval shapes, or form the dough into an oblong log and refrigerate, slicing very thinly later.

When ready to serve, preheat oven to 400° F. Place the wafers on an ungreased, rimless baking sheet and bake for 8 – 10 minutes, watching closely.

Remove the wafers from the sheet with great care, as they are extremely delicate. Serve with any hors d'oeuvre.

Yield: 2 ½ dozen

DAIRY HOLLOW HOUSE
Eureka Springs, Arkansas

Blue Cheese Crisps❖

¼ **pound blue cheese, crumbled**
⅓ **cup butter, at room temperature**
⅛ **teaspoon cayenne pepper**
⅔ **cup all-purpose flour**
¼ **cup poppy seeds**

In a small bowl, cream together the blue cheese and butter until smooth. In another small bowl, mix together the cayenne and flour and add to the cheese mixture. Blend well.

Divide the mixture in two and wrap each half in plastic. Chill for 30 minutes.

Preheat oven to 350° F. Roll each ball of dough into a 1-inch thick oblong log, then roll each log in the poppy seeds, coating well. Cut the logs into ¼-inch slices. (They will slice better if slightly frozen.)

Place on an ungreased baking sheet and bake for about 15 minutes or until golden brown. Serve warm or at room temperature with any hors d'oeuvre.

Yield: 2 ½ dozen

SHELBURNE INN/THE SHOALWATER RESTAURANT
Seaview, Washington

CHAPTER 3

Soups

Black Bean & Butternut Squash Soup

Black Bean Soup:
1 pound black turtle beans
1 medium onion, chopped
1 medium carrot, chopped
1 stalk celery, chopped
6 cloves garlic, chopped
2 tablespoons chopped fresh cilantro
2 tablespoons chopped fresh thyme
2 tablespoons chopped fresh parsley
2 tablespoons whole black peppercorns
1 large ham bone, or 1 cup ham scraps
2 – 3 quarts chicken stock
1 tablespoon ground cumin
2 teaspoons chili powder
4 tablespoons unsweetened cocoa
Crème fraîche
4 – 6 fresh sprigs cilantro
Homemade salsa

Butternut Squash Soup:
2 large butternut squash
1 large onion, chopped
4 cloves garlic, chopped
1 medium carrot, chopped
1 stalk celery, chopped
¾ cup white wine
¾ cup champagne vinegar
4 cups heavy cream
Salt to taste
White pepper to taste

To make the black bean soup: In a large, heavy pot, soak the beans overnight in cold water.

Drain the beans and add the next ten ingredients. Cover and bring to a boil. Skim off excess fat. Reduce heat and simmer slowly, loosely covered, until the beans are tender, about 2 hours. Add more stock if necessary to keep the liquid level with the beans. Stir frequently so the beans cook evenly and do not burn.

Place the bean mixture, by batches, in a food processor and puree. Return the pureed mixture to the pot and blend in the cumin, chili powder, and cocoa. Keep warm.

CARTER HOUSE/HOTEL CARTER

Even though you might have to plan to get to this delightful, remote northern California town of 24,000 people, when you get there, you'll be very pleasantly surprised by what you find—a lovely historic community. But *planning* was not exactly what led Mark and Christi Carter into the inn business.

What happens when a young man with a penchant for carpentry and a love for beautiful buildings discovers a nineteenth-century detailed drawing of a splendid Victorian home, which was destroyed in the 1906 San Francisco earthquake? If you're Mark Carter, you take the next sixteen months of your life and build your dream home.

Faced with the need to generate some extra money to help pay for their new home, the Carters began accepting overnight guests. Before long, they both knew they had chanced upon the true love of their lives—innkeeping. According to Mark, the best part of the business is pampering their guests, something he and Christi do very well with unsurpassed hospitality and "the best breakfast in the state."

To make the butternut squash soup: Preheat oven to 350° F. Place the squash in a baking pan with ½ inch of water. Cover the pan with aluminum foil and bake until very soft, about 1 hour.

Cool. When cool, puree the squash in a food processor for about 5 minutes. Set aside.

In another large pot, mix together the onion, garlic, carrot, celery, wine, and vinegar. Reduce over high heat until there are just a few tablespoons of liquid remaining in the pot. Add the cream and reduce over lowered heat to about 3 cups. (It should be creamy, but not too thick.) Mix in the reserved squash puree, salt, and white pepper. Keep warm.

To serve the soups: Take one small ladle of the squash soup and one small ladle of the bean soup and pour them slowly into opposite sides of each soup bowl at the same time. The dark soup and the light soup should remain separate, filling the soup bowl evenly and forming a distinct line down the center of the bowl.

Garnish each serving with a dollop of the crème fraîche, one cilantro sprig, and a touch of the salsa. Serve.

Yield: 4 to 6 servings

CARTER HOUSE/HOTEL CARTER
Eureka, California

Lentil Soup

3 – 4 ham shanks
2 quarts water
One 1 – 1 ½-pound flank steak, cubed
2 large carrots, shredded
1 large onion, chopped
2 stalks celery, chopped with leaves
1 bay leaf
2 – 3 cloves garlic, quartered
6 complete grinds black pepper
1 teaspoon salt
1 pound dried lentils, washed and sorted
Shredded cheddar cheese

In a large saucepan, boil the ham shanks in the water for 20 – 30 minutes. Cool. Skim fat and remove the ham from the bones. Set aside the water, ham, and bones.

In a large pot, brown the flank steak. Remove the meat and set aside. Drain the fat. Place the remaining ingredients, except the lentils and cheese, in the pot and roast in a little water until well browned, but not overcooked.

Return the reserved water, ham, bones, and flank steak to the pot and add the lentils. Cover with water and bring to a boil. Reduce heat and simmer for 2 – 4 hours.

Cool and skim fat. Remove the bones and bay leaf and discard.

Reheat and add water to desired amount of liquid. Garnish with the cheese and serve hot.

Yield: 8 to 10 servings

BLUE HARBOR HOUSE
Camden, Maine

Red & White Potage❖

4 tablespoons good-quality olive oil, divided
2 large heads cauliflower, cut into florets
2 medium onions, chopped and divided
8 cups chicken stock, divided
¼ teaspoon ground nutmeg
Pinch white pepper
2 pounds beets, peeled and diced
2 tablespoons balsamic vinegar
1 tablespoon granulated sugar
Black pepper to taste

Note: Make the two soups at the same time in separate saucepans.

In a large saucepan, heat 2 tablespoons of the oil and sauté the cauliflower and half of the chopped onions for 8 – 10 minutes. Do not brown. Add 4 cups of the chicken stock and nutmeg and bring to a boil. Reduce heat and simmer for 1 hour.

In a food processor, puree the hot cauliflower mixture, in batches, until smooth. Return the mixture to the saucepan and add the white pepper. Keep warm.

In another large saucepan, heat the remaining oil and add the beets, remaining onions, remaining chicken stock, vinegar, and sugar and bring to a boil. Reduce heat and simmer for 45 minutes.

In the food processor, puree the hot beet mixture, in batches, until smooth.

In each of six soup bowls, pour both soups at the same time. Create a design with the two contrasting colors by swirling a toothpick around in the soup. Serve hot.

Yield: 6 generous servings

THE GOVERNOR'S INN
Ludlow, Vermont

Six-Onion Soup❖

½ cup (1 stick) butter
1 large yellow onion, sliced
1 large red onion, sliced
1 bunch leeks, cleaned thoroughly and sliced (white part only)
2 shallots, minced
4 cloves garlic, minced
2 tablespoons finely chopped fresh chives
½ teaspoon kosher salt
1 teaspoon ground nutmeg
1 teaspoon dried thyme
½ teaspoon ground paprika
4 cups heavy cream
4 cups chicken stock
1 ½ teaspoons Worchestershire sauce
Crisp-fried onions

In a large saucepan, melt the butter and sauté both onions, leeks, shallots, garlic, and chives over medium-high heat until golden and soft. Add the salt, nutmeg, thyme, and paprika and continue cooking for 5 minutes more, stirring gently to combine.

Add the cream, stock, and Worcestershire sauce and bring to a boil. Reduce heat and simmer, uncovered, for 45 minutes.

Serve in warm bowls and and top with the crisp-fried onions.

Yield: 6 to 8 servings

SHELBURNE INN/THE SHOALWATER RESTAURANT
Seaview, Washington

SHELBURNE INN and
THE SHOALWATER
RESTAURANT

Zucchini Soup❖

6 pounds zucchini, peeled and sliced
2 large onions, sliced
8 medium carrots, sliced
2 cups chicken broth
Salt and pepper to taste
Fresh parsley, chopped

In a large pot, place all of the ingredients, except the parsley, and
cook until the vegetables are soft, about 25 – 30 minutes.

Puree the vegetable mixture, in batches, in a blender or food
processor. (If the soup is too thick, add more chicken stock.)

Garnish with the parsley and serve hot.

Yield: 8 to 10 generous servings

TRAIL'S END
Wilmington, Vermont

Mushroom Bisque❖

1 pound fresh mushrooms, well cleaned
1 medium onion, chopped
1 quart chicken stock
6 tablespoons (¾ stick) butter
6 tablespoons all-purpose flour
3 cups hot milk
1 cup heavy cream
White pepper to taste
Dash Tabasco sauce
2 tablespoons sherry

In a food processor, very finely chop the mushrooms. In a large
pot, combine the mushrooms, onion, and stock and simmer,
covered, for 30 minutes.

In a large saucepan, melt the butter and whisk in the flour. Add
the milk, whisking constantly, until thick and smooth. Add the
cream and blend well. Combine the cream sauce with the mushroom mixture and stir in the white pepper and Tabasco sauce.

TRAIL'S END

Innkeepers Bill and Mary Kilburn
are always ready with a warm welcome at this cozy inn located in
the heart of Deerfield Valley—just
five miles from Mount Snow and
Haystack.

Tucked away literally at the end of
a serene country road, Trail's End
combines traditional New England
hospitality with a variety of enjoy-
able facilities, including an outdoor
swimming pool, clay tennis court,
fully stocked trout pond, lovely English flower gardens, and when the
snow falls, sleigh rides through the
Deerfield Valley countryside.

Reheat and add the sherry just before serving. Serve hot.

Yield: 8 to 10 servings

WINDHAM HILL INN
West Townshend, Vermont

MADRONA MANOR

Madrona Manor is distinguished by a sense of homey elegance, combined with the graciousness one might feel at a friend's home. The inn is located in the celebrated Sonoma Valley wine country of California.

The heart of Madrona Manor is the three-story Victorian mansion built in 1881. The mansion has a music room graced by an original rosewood piano and a lovely fireplace, which is a delightful area for getting acquainted with other guests. Eight beautifully landscaped and wooded acres surround the Manor.

Innkeeper Carol Muir offers elegant candlelight dinners in three dining rooms. "This isn't your ordinary run-of-the-mill backyard country inn," says the *San Francisco Examiner*. "... Internationally acclaimed executive chef, Todd Muir, oversees a staff of twelve, who serve exclusively fresh ingredients. All breads, pastries, ice creams, pastas, smoked and cured meats, and fish are prepared on site."

Goat Cheese-Wonton Soup

4 tablespoons goat cheese
1 tablespoon chopped fresh chives
Salt and pepper to taste
12 wonton skins
Egg wash
4 cups chicken consommé
2 tablespoons cooked egg whites
2 tablespoons small-dice red bell pepper
2 tablespoons sliced shiitake mushrooms
1 tablespoon diagonally sliced green onions
8 paper-thin slices garlic
8 strands orange zest
8 slivers fresh gingerroot
Hot pepper oil to taste

In a small bowl, mix together the goat cheese, chives, salt, and pepper. Place 1 teaspoon of the cheese mixture in the center of a wonton skin, and moisten the edges with the egg wash. Fold corner to corner to form a triangle, then fold two corners around a finger and press to hold together. Use this procedure for the remaining wonton skins.

In a medium-sized saucepan, heat the consommé. In a large saucepan, poach the wontons in simmering salted water for 3 minutes.

Place three wontons in each soup bowl and pour the hot consommé over the wontons. Garnish each serving with the remaining ingredients, divided among the servings. Serve immediately.

Yield: 4 servings

MADRONA MANOR
Healdsburg, California

Potage de Vermont❖

2 tablespoons sweet butter
½ cup chopped carrots
½ cup chopped onions
½ cup chopped fresh dill
½ cup chopped celery
5 tablespoons unbleached all-purpose flour
5 cups chicken stock
3 cups grated Vermont cheddar cheese
2 cups half-and-half
Salt to taste
Freshly ground white pepper to taste
Toasted sesame seeds

In a large saucepan, melt the butter and sauté the carrots, onions, dill, and celery. Sprinkle in the flour, 1 tablespoon at a time, stirring after each addition. Stir in the stock. Bring to a boil over medium heat and cook for about 5 minutes.

Strain the vegetables and puree in a food processor. Return the pureed vegetables to the stock and continue to cook over medium heat until the soup boils. Reduce heat and simmer slowly for 15 minutes more.

Add the cheese, stirring constantly with a large whisk until melted. Slowly add the half-and-half and stir until well blended. Add the salt and white pepper.

Ladle into soup bowls and garnish with the sesame seeds. Serve immediately.

Yield: 8 servings

BLUEBERRY HILL
Goshen, Vermont

Cheddar Cheese Soup with Sun-Dried Tomatoes

6 tablespoons (¾ stick) unsalted butter
1 cup diced onions
¾ cup diced celery
½ cup diced carrots

RABBIT HILL INN

In a world filled with inns that call themselves "romantic hideaways" it's a genuine treat to come across one that really and truly is! John and Maureen Magee are living their fantasy. This splendid white-columned 1795 mansion is a complete package of historic presence, superb cuisine, gracious unpretentious service, and all of it carefully wrapped in romantic whimsy. Whether you're overnighting in the spacious antique organ-equipped Music Chamber or cozied into the queen-sized canopy bed in Caroline's Chamber, the thoughtful attention to detail in this inn will amaze you.

On the dresser you may find antique grooming accessories or century-old love letters. Leave your chamber for a leisurely stroll down to the Connecticut River, and you're likely to be greeted by a personalized "surprise" left in your room by the staff. Tiny hand-crocheted heart-shaped pillows with silk ribbons serve as a discreet "do not disturb" sign on your door at Rabbit Hill, and they are yours to keep when you must reluctantly bid farewell to this oasis midway between Montreal and Portland, Maine.

2 teaspoons minced garlic
4 tablespoons all-purpose flour
4 cups chicken stock
1 pound Vermont cheddar cheese, grated
1 teaspoon dry mustard
1 cup heavy cream
1 cup chopped sun-dried tomatoes
Salt and pepper to taste
1 teaspoon Worcestershire sauce

In a large pot, melt the butter and sauté the onions, celery, carrots, and garlic for 5 – 7 minutes. Sprinkle the flour on top and stir constantly for 5 minutes more.

Add the chicken stock, 1 cup at time, blending well each time. Bring to a boil. Reduce heat and simmer for 45 minutes.

Strain the soup through a medium-mesh strainer into another large pot, pushing through as much vegetable and liquid as possible. Place on very low heat and stir in the cheese, mustard, cream, and tomatoes, blending well. Season with the salt, pepper, and Worcestershire sauce and serve immediately.

Yield: 8 to 10 servings

RABBIT HILL INN
Lower Waterford, Vermont

Reuben Soup

1 cup diced carrots
1 cup diced celery
1 cup diced onions
1 cup vegetable oil
1 cup all-purpose flour
1 quart hot chicken stock
2 cups cooked shredded corned beef
2 cups well-rinsed sauerkraut
1 cup grated Swiss cheese
One 6-ounce bottle Russian dressing
1 cup tomato sauce
Dark rye croutons

In a large pot, steam sauté all of the vegetables in the oil over low heat until tender, about 5 – 7 minutes. Add the flour, ¼ cup at a time, and make a roux. Stir in the hot stock, 2 cups at a time, and bring to a boil. Reduce heat and whisk until smooth.

Add the corned beef, sauerkraut, cheese, dressing, and tomato sauce and mix together well.

Pour into soup bowls and garnish with the croutons. Serve immediately.

Yield: 6 to 8 servings

ASA RANSOM HOUSE
Clarence, New York

Lemon Chicken Soup❖

5 cups chicken stock
¼ cup fresh lemon juice
¼ cup shredded carrots
¼ cup chopped onions
¼ cup chopped celery
2 teaspoons salt
1 teaspoon white pepper
2 tablespoons butter, softened
2 tablespoons all-purpose flour
4 egg yolks
½ cup heavy cream
¼ cup cooked long grain white rice
½ cup cooked diced chicken
Fresh lemon slices

In a large saucepan, combine the stock, lemon juice, carrots, onions, celery, salt, and white pepper and bring to a boil over high heat. Reduce heat, partially cover, and simmer until the vegetables are tender, about 20 minutes.

In a small bowl, blend together the butter and flour until smooth. Add to the hot soup, a bit at a time, stirring constantly. Simmer for 10 minutes, continuing to stir.

In a large bowl, beat the egg yolks with the cream with an electric mixer until blended. Reduce the speed and mix in the hot soup, a bit at a time. Return the soup to the saucepan and bring to a low boil. Add the rice and chicken and stir well. Season to taste.

Ladle into soup bowls and garnish with the lemon slices.

ASA RANSOM HOUSE

In 1799, the Holland Land Company offered "lots" ten miles apart in what is now Clarence, New York. Fortunately for history-loving inn-goers everywhere, an enterprising and eager young silversmith named Asa Ransom was the first to accept the company's generous offer. Within two years, Mr. Ransom had built a combination log cabin home and tavern and had completed a sawmill nearby on the banks of the creek that bears his name. In 1803, he added a grist mill to his holdings, the first in what is now Erie County.

Bob and Judy Lenz, proprietors of Asa Ransom House, have lovingly created an elegantly casual six-guest room and three-suite inn, which preserves the eighteenth-century character of Mr. Ransom's tavern. Dinners at Asa Ransom reflect the bounty of western New York farmland, complemented by an added flair for contemporary culinary creativity. Country Inn Veal, Raspberry Chicken, Smoked Corned Beef with Apple-Raisin Sauce, and Steak & Kidney Pie are regularly served in the inn's two contrasting dining rooms. Pick the one which suits your mood: The Ransom Room for country-formal occasions or The Clarence Hollow Room for the more country-rustic traveler.

After dinner, you might wish to accept the challenge of the giant jigsaw puzzle of the day, which always awaits you in the library, while you plan your excursion to Niagara Falls, only twenty-eight miles from the front door of the inn.

Yield: 4 to 6 servings

SHELBURNE INN/THE SHOALWATER RESTAURANT
Seaview, Washington

Seafood-Mushroom Soup with Sherry

4 tablespoons (½ stick) butter
4 tablespoons all-purpose flour
3 cups light cream or half-and-half
2 cups milk
1 ½ cups chopped seafood (cod, haddock, shrimp, lobster, or any type or combination)
½ cup diced fresh mushrooms
½ teaspoon grated lemon rind
¼ teaspoon white pepper
½ teaspoon granulated sugar
2 teaspoons salt
4 tablespoons Harvey's Bristol Cream Sherry
1 hard-cooked egg, yolk finely chopped
Fresh chives, chopped

In the top of a double boiler, melt the butter and blend in the flour to make a roux. Add the cream and milk and blend with a wire whip. Stir in the seafood, mushrooms, lemon zest, white pepper, sugar, and salt and cook for about 25 minutes.

Add the sherry 5 minutes before removing from heat. Ladle into hot soup bowls. Garnish with the chopped egg yolk and chives and serve immediately.

Yield: 6 servings

CHALET SUZANNE
Lake Wales, Florida

New England Clam Chowder ❖

2 ½ cups warm water
14 fresh clams in the shell
½ teaspoon salt
⅛ teaspoon white pepper

⅛ teaspoon Worcestershire sauce
1 ¼ cups potatoes, peeled and diced
2 ounces salt pork, diced
½ cup chopped onions
1 tablespoon all-purpose flour
1 ½ cups scalded milk
½ cup light cream
1 tablespoon butter

In a large pot, combine the water, clams, salt, white pepper, and Worcestershire sauce and bring to a boil. Boil until the clams open, about 12 – 18 minutes. Discard any clams that do not open. Strain and set aside the clam stock. Remove the meat from the clam shells and mince. Set aside the minced clams.

In a large saucepan, combine the potatoes and half of the reserved clam stock and gently simmer for 10 minutes, or until the potatoes are cooked, but still firm. Drain and reserve separately the clam stock and potatoes.

In a heavy soup pot, sauté the salt pork until partially rendered, about 5 minutes. Remove and set the pork aside. Remove half of the melted fat and discard. In the remaining fat, sauté the onions over medium heat until translucent, about 5 minutes. Add the flour and blend thoroughly to make a roux. Cook over medium heat for 5 – 6 minutes, stirring constantly.

Add the reserved clam stock and stir until hot and smooth. Add the reserved clams, potatoes, and pork, the milk, and cream. Heat through. Adjust the seasoning. Add the butter just before serving, stirring until melted. Serve hot.

Yield: 6 servings

THE RED LION INN
Stockbridge, Massachusetts

Great Lakes Chowder

1 ¼ pounds walleye, skinned, boned, and diced
½ pound whitefish, skinned, boned, and diced
¼ pound smoked whitefish
2 quarts water
5 cups heavy cream
5 tablespoons medium-dice smoked bacon
½ cup (1 stick) butter

STAFFORD'S BAY VIEW INN

Located on Michigan's northwestern shoreline, Stafford's Bay View Inn offers guests one of this country's few remaining active chautauquas. Antique furnishings and period-style decorating contribute wonderfully to the charm of this inn, owned by the Stafford Smith family.

The inn was constructed in 1886 and opened the summer of 1887. The original building was a small "rooming house," which has been incorporated into the existing structure. The wallpaper, furnishings, and costumed staff never fail to place the guest in Victorian times. Sunday brunch at the Stafford is a crowded affair. The "Sunday Brunch at the Stratford" tradition is enjoyed by thousands of hungry brunchers each year, who have elevated tomato pudding to a northern Michigan institution.

5 tablespoons thinly sliced leeks
1 ⅔ cups medium-dice onions
Flour
6 cups diced and cooked potatoes
⅛ cup clam stock
1 bay leaf
Old Bay Seasoning, white pepper, ground coriander, dried thyme, and salt to taste

In a large pot, slowly boil the walleye and both whitefish in the water until thoroughly cooked, about 30 – 35 minutes. Remove the fish from the stock, strain, and cool. Reserve the stock and keep warm.

Add the cream and the cooled fish to the reserved stock and mix together well.

In a small skillet, cook the bacon until crisp. Add the butter, leeks, and onions and cook until the onions are transparent, about 3 – 5 minutes. Add the bacon mixture to the stock mixture and thicken as desired with the flour.

Stir in the potatoes, stock, bay leaf, and seasonings and simmer until heated through. Serve immediately.

Yield: 8 generous servings

STAFFORD'S BAY VIEW INN
Petoskey, Michigan

Lobster Stew

Two 1 ¼-pound lobsters (about 2 cups meat)
2 quarts salted water
4 medium red potatotes
2 cups water
6 teaspoons butter
½ cup chopped onions
½ cup chopped celery
½ cup grated carrots
¼ cup chopped scallions
¼ cup chopped leeks
¼ cup chopped red bell pepper
¼ cup chopped green bell pepper
One 12-ounce can evaporated milk
2 cups whole milk

1 cup sherry
1 teaspoon sesame seeds
Salt and pepper to taste
6 – 8 fresh parsley sprigs

BLUE HARBOR HOUSE

In large stock pot or lobster pot, boil the lobsters in the 2 quarts water until cooked, about 20 minutes. Discard the water and let the lobsters cool.

Remove the meat and tomalley* from the shells and set aside. Reserve the tail and claw shells.

In a medium-sized saucepan, cook the potatoes in the 2 cups water until completely cooked and very soft, about 25 – 30 minutes. Drain and reserve the water. Cut the potatoes into quarters and set aside.

In a large nonreactive pot, melt 4 teaspoons of the butter and sauté the onions, celery, carrots, scallions, leeks, and both bell peppers over medium heat for 4 – 6 minutes. Add the evaporated and whole milk, sherry, and the reserved potato water and potatoes. Lower heat to simmer and cook for 5 minutes.

Cut the reserved lobster meat into bite-sized pieces. In a medium-sized skillet, melt the remaining butter and sauté the lobster meat, tomalley, and the sesame seeds for 5 minutes. Add to the stew. In the same skillet, sauté the reserved shells for 5 minutes and add to the stew. (The shells will give the stew a roasted flavor.) Cook the stew over low heat for 1 hour 30 minutes.

Add the salt and pepper. Remove the shells and discard. Pour the stew into large soup bowls and garnish each serving with a parsley sprig. Serve immediately.

*Tomalley is the green-colored liver of the lobster and is considered very edible and delicious.

Yield: 6 to 8 servings

BLUE HARBOR HOUSE
Camden, Maine

Black Cherry Soup

1 cup pitted fresh tart cherries
1 cup pitted fresh sweet cherries

½ cup sun-dried cherries
1 ½ cups cherry yogurt
1 cup sour cream
1 cup heavy whipping cream
1 cup milk
Granulated sugar to taste
Brandy to taste

In a food processor, puree the tart and sweet cherries. Set aside and add the dry cherries to the puree.

In a large mixing bowl, combine the yogurt, sour cream, whipping cream, and milk and blend thoroughly. Stir in the reserved puree, the sugar, and brandy and mix well. Serve at room temperature or chilled.

Yield: 4 to 6 servings

STAFFORD'S BAY VIEW INN
Petoskey, Michigan

THE LORDS PROPRIETORS' INN

Arch and Jane Edwards established the Inn in 1982. Since then, the Inn has grown from eight guest rooms in a large brick, turn-of-the-century Victorian home to twenty elegant guest rooms in three restored homes on an acre and a half in the Historic District of Edenton, North Carolina.

Edenton has been described by the *New York Times* as "the South's prettiest town." Established in the late seventeenth century and incorporated in 1722, it is located on beautiful Edenton Bay at the head of the Albermarle Sound, about ninety miles southwest of Norfolk, Virginia.

James T. Yenckel, associate editor of the *Washington Post,* remarked, "The Lords Proprietors' Inn is one of the friendliest and best managed inns I have ever visited."

Martha's Famous Apple Soup❖

½ cup (1 stick) butter
6 Red Delicious apples, peeled, cored, and thinly sliced
6 Granny Smith apples, peeled, cored, and thinly sliced
2 cups finely chopped onions
2 teaspoons minced garlic
2 ½ quarts chicken stock
Salt and pepper to taste
3 cups whipping cream

In a large pot, melt the butter and sauté the apples, onions, and garlic for 5 – 7 minutes, or until the onions are transparent. Add the stock and cook, stirring occasionally, for 30 – 35 minutes, or until the apples are tender.

Add the salt, pepper, and cream and blend well. Heat through. Remove from heat and cool slightly. Serve at room temperature or chilled.

Yield: 8 generous servings

THE LORDS PROPRIETORS' INN
Edenton, North Carolina

CHAPTER 4

Salads and Salad Dressings

Rose Inn Salad

1 head Bibb lettuce, washed and well dried
2 medium tomatoes, cut into wedges
20 snow peas
4 whole artichoke hearts packed in water, drained
4 stalks hearts of palm, divided and cut into ¼-inch rounds
4 red bell pepper rings
4 yellow bell pepper rings
1 container fresh onion sprouts
4 fresh nasturtium flower blossoms
1 recipe *Raspberry Vinaigrette Dressing* (see recipe below)

Place the lettuce leaves flat on each salad plate in a circular pattern with the lettuce hearts toward the center. Fan the tomato wedges one on top of the other, pointing toward the outside of the plate.

Carefully cut the ends off the snow peas. In a medium-sized saucepan, blanch the peas in boiling water for 1 minute. Rinse under cold water and pat dry. Cut an X in the bottom of each artichoke heart. (Do not slice all the way through.)

Moving clockwise around the plate, place one sliced stalk of hearts of palm together next to the tomatoes. Fan out five blanched snow peas with the points facing toward the outside of the plate. Place one artichoke heart next to the snow peas. Place one red pepper ring, half over the artichoke heart and half in the center of the plate. Place one yellow pepper ring, half over the tomatoes and half in the center of the plate. (Pepper rings should overlap, forming a ring in the center.)

Cut the bottom ends off of the bunch of sprouts, so bottom is even. Pull apart a good-sized portion of the sprouts and place in the center of the pepper rings, pulling the sprouts slightly apart. Place one flower blossom in the center and serve the dressing on the side. Serve immediately.

Raspberry Vinaigrette Dressing

¼ cup raspberry vinegar
1 tablespoon Dijon mustard
1 tablespoon garlic salt
½ teaspoon freshly ground black pepper
2 teaspoons granulated sugar
4 sprigs fresh basil
1 egg yolk

ROSE INN

The Rose Inn is situated in a magnificent rural setting halfway between New York City and Niagara Falls, in the heart of New York's Finger Lakes. Just minutes from Cornell University and Ithaca College, Rose Inn guests relax in twenty beautifully landscaped acres of lawns and gardens.

Built in 1851, "The House with the Circular Staircase" is one of the wonders of the countryside. The Italianate Victorian decor is enhanced with rich mahogany. Innkeepers Charles and Sherry Rosemann are proud of their well-earned Four-Star, Four-Diamond inn. Breakfast offers a number of Sherry's temptations, including homemade jam and fresh picked apples. Charles has a specialty of his own—puffy Black Forest Apple Pie. The coffee at the Rose Inn is creatively blended by the innkeepers themselves. Their secret? Kona . . . maybe.

¾ cup olive oil

In a blender or food processor, combine all of the ingredients, except the oil and mix together well. While the blender is running, drizzle in the oil. Chill until ready to serve. Makes enough for 4 servings.

Yield: 4 servings

ROSE INN
Ithaca, New York

Overnight Layer Salad❖

½ head iceberg lettuce, shredded
½ cup sliced celery
½ cup chopped green bell pepper
¼ cup sliced green onions
5 ounces frozen peas, thawed under hot water and drained
½ cup sliced water chestnuts
¾ cup mayonnaise
1 ½ tablespoons granulated sugar
½ cup grated Vermont cheddar cheese
½ pound bacon, cooked and crumbled

In a large salad bowl, place all of the vegetables in layers in the order given above. Spread the mayonnaise over the water chestnuts and sprinkle the sugar over the mayonnaise. Sprinkle the cheese over the top. Cover tightly and chill overnight.

Before serving, add the bacon and toss together. Serve.

Yield: 8 to 10 servings

TRAIL'S END
Wilmington, Vermont

TRAIL'S END

Spectrum of Summer Salad❖

2 – 3 small heads red oakleaf lettuce, washed, patted dry, and left whole
2 – 3 small heads green leaf lettuce: combination limestone and butterhead, washed, patted dry, and torn
3 medium yellow bell peppers, roasted, peeled, and diced

3 medium tomatoes
Fresh basil leaves, rinsed
6 – 8 *Herbed Croquettes of Oklahoma Goat Cheese* (see recipe
  below)
1 recipe *Beet Vinaigrette* (see recipe below)
½ medium red onion, very thinly sliced

Chill six to eight large plates in the freezer for 1 hour.

Divide the lettuces among the chilled plates, laying down a bed
of the whole oakleaf covered with a mound of the limestone and
butterhead. Place a small amount of the bell peppers on each
plate. Overlap several tomato slices with a leaf of basil between
each slice on each plate.

Place one warm croquette in each salad and spoon a small
amount of the vinaigrette over the salad. Lightly sprinkle the
onion slices over the top and serve immediately with the remaining vinaigrette on the side.

Herbed Croquettes of Oklahoma Goat Cheese

1 pound Oklahoma or Montrachet goat cheese
3 cloves garlic
One 1 ½-inch sprig rosemary, leaves removed
¼ teaspoon freshly ground black pepper
1 leaf fresh basil, finely chopped
1 cup all-purpose flour
Salt and pepper
Pinch ground paprika
Dash cayenne pepper
1 egg, beaten
2 cups fresh bread crumbs
½ – 1 tablespoon vegetable oil

Note: Season and shape the cheese several hours or a day ahead,
but bread and brown immediately before serving, while preparing
the salad.

In a food processor, combine the cheese, garlic, rosemary, black
pepper, and basil and process until smooth. Form herbed cheese
into croquettes. Flatten into 2-ounce rounds, 2 ½ x ¼ inch thick.
(The mixture may be soft.) Place the croquettes on a baking
sheet covered with wax paper and chill overnight until very firm.

In a medium-sized bowl, combine the flour, salt, pepper, paprika,
and cayenne. Dip each firm croquette in the flour mixture, then
in the egg, then in the bread crumbs.

DAIRY HOLLOW HOUSE

What's not to like about an inn situated in a lovingly restored 1888 Ozark mountain farmhouse and run by two very creative innkeepers, who describe their fresh and seasonal cuisine as "nouveau zarks?"

Ned Shank and Crescent Dragonwagon enjoy serving people in a gracious and whimsical "Dairy Hollow" way. Whether its hot, cinnamon-scented, spicy cider by the fire on a chilly winter afternoon or a glass of white wine as you soak in your own private Jacuzzi, you quickly realize little has been left to chance here.

Dinner at the Dairy Hollow House is a very personal experience. A small, intimate dining room is the setting for the superb contrast of old-fashioned service and fashionably prepared food. Everything is, of course, made-from-scratch, and the menu reflects the best of the growing season. Local trout, game hen, and rabbit are all frequent selections of a constantly changing menu, which always features homegrown vegetables and herbs, raspberries, and fresh whipped cream. This frequently honored small inn of three suites and three guest rooms deserves a special place in the hearts, minds, and spirits of inn-goers everywhere.

In a large nonstick skillet, heat the oil and brown the croquettes, turning once. Drain on paper towels, blotting well. Serve on the salads. Makes 8 croquettes.

Beet Vinaigrette

1 medium fresh beet, unpeeled and well washed
⅓ cup fresh lemon juice
1 teaspoon freshly grated lemon rind
½ teaspoon salt
¼ teaspoon freshly ground black pepper
1 tablespoon honey
1 cup olive oil

Preheat oven to 350° F. Wrap the beet in oiled aluminum foil and bake for 35 minutes. Cool. Slip off peel and coarsely chop.

In a food processor, combine the chopped beet, lemon juice, lemon zest, salt, pepper, and honey and process until smooth. While processor is running, drizzle in the oil until well blended. Adjust seasonings. Makes 2 cups. (The vinaigrette may be made up to three days ahead and stored in the refrigerator.)

Yield: 6 to 8 servings

DAIRY HOLLOW HOUSE
Eureka Springs, Arkansas

Warm Salad of Baked Chèvre & Fresh Baby Greens with Fruit Vinaigrette

6 ounces hazelnuts, roasted and chopped
Six 2-ounce rounds chèvre cheese
1 pound fresh baby greens and lettuces, washed, patted dry, and torn
⅛ cup olive oil
Salt and pepper to taste
1 cup *Fruit Vinaigrette* (see recipe below)
Fresh edible flower blossoms

Preheat oven to 350° F. Press the roasted hazelnuts into the cheese rounds and place the rounds on a baking sheet. Bake for

10 minutes. Cool slightly until warm.

In a large bowl, toss together the greens and oil. Add the salt and pepper. Pour the vinaigrette in the bottom of each salad plate and place the greens on top. Place the warm chèvre over the greens and sprinkle with the flower blossoms. Serve immediately.

Fruit Vinaigrette

4 cups pureed and strained fruit: strawberries, raspberries, or nectarines
1 tablespoon chopped fresh dill
2 tablespoons Mendocino mustard, or other sweet mustard
2 egg yolks
2 ½ tablespoons red wine vinegar
Juice of 1 lemon
¼ – ½ cup granulated sugar (to taste)
2 cups vegetable oil
Salt and pepper to taste

In a blender, combine the fruit, dill, mustard, egg yolks, vinegar, lemon juice, and sugar at slowest speed. With the blender still at slowest speed, slowly drizzle in the oil, ¼ cup at a time. (The ingredients should only blend, not thicken. When blended, the dressing will have a slight sheen.) Add the salt and pepper and set aside until ready to use.

Yield: 6 servings

CARTER HOUSE/HOTEL CARTER
Eureka, California

Carter House
COUNTRY INN

Strawberry-Spinach Salad with Honey-Pecan Dressing❖

⅓ cup light vegetable oil
3 tablespoons honey
1 tablespoon fresh lemon juice
2 teaspoons white wine vinegar
1 teaspoon soy sauce
1 teaspoon dried dill
⅓ – ½ cup chopped pecans
2 tablespoons warm water
Few gratings lemon rind
2 cloves garlic, minced

1 pound fresh spinach, washed, trimmed, and torn into bite-
  sized pieces
1 pint fresh strawberries, washed, hulled, and sliced
¾ – 1 pound fresh mushrooms, sliced
5 – 6 slices bacon, cooked crisp and crumbled

In a blender, combine the first ten ingredients and blend until
smooth. Chill thoroughly.

Arrange the spinach, strawberries, mushrooms, and bacon on
salad plates and spoon the chilled dressing over the top. Serve
immediately. (Any remaining dressing can be stored in the
refrigerator for about two weeks.)

Yield: 6 to 8 servings

HEARTHSTONE INN
Colorado Springs, Colorado

Karen's Fresh Broccoli Salad❖

10 slices bacon
2 bunches fresh broccoli
½ cup raisins
1 medium red onion, finely chopped
1 cup mayonnaise
⅓ cup granulated sugar or honey
2 – 3 tablespoons white wine vinegar

In a large skillet, cook the bacon until crisp. Crumble and set aside.

Peel the broccoli stalks and slice horizontally. In a medium-sized
bowl, break the broccoli florets into bite-sized pieces and
stir in the raisins and onion. Chill.

In a small bowl, whisk together the mayonnaise, sugar, and
vinegar. Chill for at least 1 hour.

Before serving, toss together the reserved bacon, chilled broccoli
mixture, and chilled dressing. Serve.

Yield: 6 servings

MAST FARM INN
Valle Crucis, North Carolina

Chinese Pea Pod Salad❖

Two 6-ounce packages frozen snow peas
1 cup halved cherry tomatoes
2 green onions, chopped including tops
One 8-ounce can sliced water chestnuts, drained and well
  rinsed
⅓ cup vegetable oil
4 teaspoons fresh lemon juice
2 teaspoons white wine vinegar
Pinch garlic powder
½ teaspoon salt
1 tablespoon granulated sugar

In a large saucepan, cook the peas in a small amount of boiling water for 1 minute only. Drain and stir in the tomatoes, onions, and water chestnuts. Set aside.

In a medium-sized salad bowl, mix together the oil, lemon juice, vinegar, garlic powder, salt, and sugar. Add the reserved vegetables and toss well. Chill. Serve.

Yield: 6 servings

HEARTHSTONE INN
Colorado Springs, Colorado

HEARTHSTONE INN

Bright colors, exquisite antiques, color-coordinated linens, and superb gourmet breakfasts make Dot and Ruth Williams' Hearthstone Inn a restful, elegant, and friendly place from which to enjoy the sights and sounds of picturesque Colorado Springs.

Crescent's Wonderful Oriental Slaw❖

1 head green cabbage, cut into finely slivered long strands
1 stalk celery, finely chopped
1 medium green bell pepper, diced
1 medium carrot, grated
½ bunch green onions, diced
½ cup peanut oil
2 teaspoons sesame seed oil
1 tablespoon tamari soy sauce
4 tablespoons rice wine vinegar
⅓ cup honey
2 cloves garlic, pressed
One 1-inch piece fresh gingerroot, peeled and diced
¼ – ½ teaspoon hot red pepper sauce, or to taste

In a large salad bowl, toss together the first five ingredients and set aside.

In a blender or food processor, blend together the remaining ingredients and pour over the reserved slaw. Stir well and chill thoroughly. Serve.

Yield: 8 to 10 servings

DAIRY HOLLOW HOUSE
Eureka Springs, Arkansas

GRANT CORNER INN

New Mexico Patio Salad❖

8 boneless skinless chicken breasts
Juice of 1 lemon
4 ripe avocados, halved and pitted
16 small purple plums
6 ounces cream cheese, softened and whipped
8 bananas, peeled and halved
1 cup honey
1 ½ cups chopped pine nuts
2 pounds red seedless grapes
2 egg whites, slightly beaten
½ cup granulated sugar
1 head purple kale, washed, dried, and separated into leaves
1 pint fresh strawberries, washed with stems
1 recipe *Spicy Vinaigrette* (see recipe below)

Grill the chicken breasts over mesquite for about 20 – 25 minutes or until thoroughly cooked, turning often. Cut into diagonal strips and set aside. Keep warm.

Pour the lemon juice over the avocado halves. Make half slices through the plums (pitting them) and fill with the cream cheese. Roll the bananas in the honey, then in the pine nuts. Dip the grapes in the egg whites, then in the sugar.

Arrange the kale leaves on serving plates and place the avocado halves over the kale. Arrange the reserved chicken and all of the fruit around the avocado halves. Serve with the vinaigrette.

Spicy Vinaigrette

1 ¼ cups granulated sugar
2 teaspoons dry mustard

2 teaspoons ground chile powder
2 teaspoons celery seeds
½ teaspoon salt
⅔ cup strained honey
¾ cup white wine vinegar
2 tablespoons fresh lemon juice
2 teaspoons grated onions
2 cups olive oil

In a medium-sized bowl, mix together the first five ingredients. Add the honey, vinegar, lemon juice, and onions and mix well. Slowly pour the oil into the mixture and whisk. Make 4 cups.

Yield: 6 to 8 servings

GRANT CORNER INN
Santa Fe, New Mexico

Chicken-Tarragon Salad❖

4 cooked boneless skinless chicken breasts
1 stalk celery, diced
One 8-ounce can sliced water chestnuts, drained and well
   rinsed
2 tablespoons sliced almonds
1 cup mayonnaise
2 tablespoons dried tarragon
Salt and pepper to taste
Fresh greens, washed and patted dry

Cut the chicken into bite-sized pieces. In a large bowl, mix together the remaining ingredients, except the greens, and stir in the chicken pieces. Chill.

Serve the salad on a bed of fresh greens.

Yield: 4 to 6 servings

THE HIDDEN INN
Orange, Virginia

GRANT CORNER INN

You have just driven into beautiful Santa Fe, New Mexico, where virtually all of the homes and businesses are thick-walled buildings made of attractive, red adobe clay. But as you turn onto Grant Avenue, just a block or so from the Plaza, where Native Americans display their exquisite jewelry and history abounds, you come upon a colonial-style "railroad era," 1905 inn with a terra-cotta tile roof and a white picket fence. White Picket Fence? In Santa Fe? Yep. Welcome to the Grant Corner Inn. The surprises are just beginning.

As you come through the gate and the greenery surrounding the walk to the front porch, you suddenly feel as if you've been transported to some magic place far away. Go past the wraparound front porch and into the foyer, and you're in "Bunny Country." Everywhere there are whimsical bunnies—fat ones, wooden ones, stuffed bunnies, and stately bunnies. Louise Stewart, her husband Pat, and daughter Bumpy clearly love running one of Santa Fe's most successful country inns, and it shows everywhere you look.

One of the few inns in the Southwest that offers a truly gourmet breakfast, Grant Corner has become so widely respected for its creative combination of stylish southwestern cuisine and original recipes, they've been forced by public demand to offer brunch all weekend long. Reservations well in advance are a must.

Southwest Olé Salad

Three 6 ⅛-ounce cans water-packed solid white tuna, drained
¾ pound (18 cups) mixed salad greens (romaine, leaf, radicchio, savoy, endive)
3 cups diced tomatoes
⅓ cup diced avocados
¾ cup sliced black olives
1 ½ cups cooked chick-peas
1 ½ cups cooked chili beans
Six 1-ounce portions reduced-fat cheddar cheese, shredded
48 "light" ranch tortilla chips
1 ½ cups *Westways Dressing* (see recipe below)
1 ⅛ cups mild salsa

For each serving, arrange 3 cups of lettuce on each serving plate.

Layer on each bed of lettuce, 3 ounces tuna, ½ cup tomatoes, 1 tablespoon avocado, 2 tablespoons olives, ¼ cup chick-peas, and ¼ cup beans. Spoon 2 ounces of the dressing over each salad and sprinkle with 1 ounce of the cheese.

Garnish each salad with 8 tortilla chips and 2 – 3 tablespoons salsa. Serve immediately.

Westways Dressing

¾ cup buttermilk
¼ cup light mayonnaise
¼ cup light sour cream
⅛ cup chopped green onions
1 tablespoon chopped fresh cilantro
1 small clove garlic, crushed
¼ tablespoon fresh lime juice
Pinch black pepper
Pinch chili powder
Pinch salt

In a medium-sized bowl, stir together all of the ingredients and chill for at least 1 hour before serving. Makes 3 cups.

Yield: 6 servings

WESTWAYS RESORT INN
Phoenix, Arizona

Pasta with Bacon, Broccoli & Mozzarella❖

3 cups uncooked elbow macaroni
1 head broccoli, cut into florets
½ pound bacon, cooked crisp and crumbled
½ pound mozzarella cheese, shredded
1 cup shredded carrots
½ cup finely chopped red onions
1 tablespoon garlic powder
Salt and pepper to taste
1 teaspoon onion powder
1 ½ – 2 cups *Coleslaw Dressing* (see recipe below)

In a large saucepan, cook the macaroni in boiling salted water for 8 – 10 minutes or until tender. Drain thoroughly and set aside. Cool.

Blanch the broccoli florets by dropping into boiling water for 2 minutes. Drain and cool in ice water, then thoroughly drain again. Set aside.

In a salad bowl, combine the bacon, cheese, carrots, and onions and toss to mix well. Add the cooled pasta and toss again. Add the reserved broccoli and season with the garlic powder, salt, pepper, and onion powder.

Add the dressing, ½ cup at a time, until the salad is lightly dressed and bound together. Serve immediately.

Coleslaw Dressing

2 cups mayonnaise
6 tablespoons pure maple syrup
4 tablespoons white vinegar
2 teaspoons ground paprika
4 tablespoons light cream

In a small bowl, combine all of the ingredients and mix well. Cover and chill. Makes 2 ½ cups. (The dressing can be stored in the refrigerator for two to three days.)

Yield: 6 to 8 servings

THE RED LION INN
Stockbridge, Massachusetts

THE RED LION INN

You begin to realize how important this inn is to history and to its guests when you learn that it is the centerpiece of Norman Rockwell's painting, *Main Street in Stockbridge*. It is perfectly fitting that this beloved artist has saved for all time the image of The Red Lion Inn. The "Red Lion" has occupied the same site since 1773, first as a small way station for carriages moving between Boston and Albany or Hartford and now as a New England landmark of traditional hospitality. In 1774, the year after the soirée in Boston Harbor, the inn was the site of the Berkshire County delegation meeting, which pledged to boycott British goods.

With more than 100 guest rooms, the inn today is an extraordinary example of gracious hospitality and operating efficiency. John and Jane Fitzpatrick, the native Vermonters who purchased the inn in 1968, take great and justifiable pride in their roles as trustees of the "Red Lion Corner." Sooner or later, whether it's a visit to Tanglewood in the summer or a colorful fall weekend in the Berkshires, you owe it to yourself to spend an hour in a rocking chair on the front porch of this very special place.

Bow Ties with Ham, Peas & Parmesan Dressing❖

1 pound uncooked bow tie pasta
2 tablespoons shredded carrots
¼ cup cooked diced ham
¼ cup diced cheddar cheese
2 tablespoons thawed frozen peas
1 cup *Parmesan Dressing* (see recipe below)

In a large saucepan, cook the pasta in boiling salted water for 8 – 10 minutes or until tender. Drain well and cool thoroughly.

When cool, add the remaining ingredients and toss until well mixed. Serve immediately.

Parmesan Dressing

¼ cup grated Parmesan cheese
½ cup heavy cream
1 cup mayonnaise
2 tablespoons garlic powder
Salt and pepper to taste

In a small bowl, combine the cheese and cream and let stand for 10 minutes until the cheese has softened.

Stir in the mayonnaise, garlic powder, salt, and pepper and mix well. Makes 1 ¾ cups.

Yield: 4 to 6 servings

THE RED LION INN
Stockbridge, Massachusetts

Rice Salad Village Inn❖

¾ teaspoon dried basil
¾ teaspoon dried tarragon
½ teaspoon Dijon mustard
⅛ cup red wine vinegar
⅛ cup vegetable oil
Salt and pepper to taste

1 cup uncooked long grain white rice
Pinch salt
¼ cup (½ stick) sweet butter
Salt and pepper to taste
¼ cup toasted slivered almonds
3 ounces marinated artichoke hearts, drained and cut
   lengthwise into quarters
¼ cup cooked fresh peas
⅛ cup chopped pimientos
½ bunch scallions, thinly sliced
¼ pound marinated mushrooms, sliced*
¼ cup sliced black olives
¼ pound salami, diced
¼ cup chopped fresh parsley
Watercress
Cherry tomatoes

In a small bowl, mix together the first six ingredients and set
aside. In a large saucepan of boiling water, add the rice and
pinch of salt. Cover and cook over low heat for 18 minutes.

Preheat oven to 250° F. Drain the rice and rinse with warm
water. Return the rice to the saucepan and add the butter, salt,
and pepper. Dry the mixture in the oven for 30 minutes, stirring
occasionally with a fork.

Place the mixture in a large bowl and add the remaining ingredients, except the watercress and tomatoes. Add the reserved
dressing and mix well. Pack tightly into a small oiled ring mold
and chill overnight.

Unmold and garnish with the watercress and tomatoes. Serve
immediately.

*Marinated mushrooms are available in the delicatessen of any
supermarket, or use a favorite recipe.

Yield: 6 servings

THE GOVERNOR'S INN
Ludlow, Vermont

Cherry Vinaigrette Dressing

¼ cup granulated sugar
¼ cup raspberry vinegar

McNINCH HOUSE

This 1892 Victorian, in the shadow of Charlotte's imposing, central business district skyline, was originally home to Charlotte's mayor at the turn of the century, Sam McNinch. Although the McNinch House is not set up yet for overnight guests, it has earned a special place in this collection due to the inspired work of Chef/Proprietor, Ellen Davis.

Imagine a place where each table has a different place setting artistically orchestrated in colors and textures, from the place mats to the antique serving pieces to the fresh-cut flowers and napkin rings. Reservations are made not hours, but weeks ahead for those seeking Chef Davis' own brand of exquisite signature foods. The service begins at 7:00 P.M. each evening with the first of six courses from the fixed-price menu and spans a leisurely three and a half hours.

The first-course appetizer might be Dressed Shrimp in a Beggar's Bag of Phyllo Pastry. Following the shrimp, perhaps a Roasted Red Bell Pepper Soup served with jalapeño pepper corncakes. Next, a salad of several fresh lettuces with Orange Salad Dressing and a palate-cleansing sorbet. Entrées often include Roast Chicken Chesapeake with Seafood Stuffing, sautéed Filet of Tenderloin and Lobster Tail, Norwegian Salmon with Dill Sauce, or Quail with Crabmeat served with a warm blackberry sauce. You get the idea. As the saying goes, "The world's best restaurants are owned by the chef." McNinch House is certainly true to form.

½ cup heavy cream
¾ cup vegetable oil
¼ cup fresh dark sweet cherries, pitted and pureed*

In a medium-sized bowl, stir together the sugar and vinegar until the sugar is dissolved.

Add the cream and whip until the mixture starts to thicken. While whipping, slowly drizzle in the oil until thoroughly blended. Add the cherry puree and stir well.

Serve with choice of salad greens. (The dressing can be stored in a covered jar in the refrigerator for one to two days.)

*Can substitute raspberries, blueberries, or cranberries in season.

Yield: 2 cups

STAFFORD'S BAY VIEW INN
Petoskey, Michigan

Orange Salad Dressing

⅛ cup white wine vinegar
¾ cup vegetable oil
Juice of 2 oranges (about ¾ cup)
1 green onion, minced
1 tablespoon minced fresh parsley
1 tablespoon granulated sugar
¼ teaspoon pepper
¼ teaspoon minced garlic
½ teaspoon salt

In a small bowl, mix together all of the ingredients. Cover and chill overnight in the refrigerator.

Serve with choice of salad greens. (The dressing can be stored in a covered jar in the refrigerator for about one week.)

Yield: About 1 ½ cups

McNINCH HOUSE
Charlotte, North Carolina

CHAPTER 5

Entrées

Filet Mignon
with Jack Daniel's Sauce❖

4 tablespoons minced shallots
2 tablespoons red wine vinegar
7 teaspoons cracked black peppercorns
4 cups veal stock
2 cups chicken stock
Four 8-ounce filets mignon
1 teaspoon dried thyme
1 teaspoon dried rosemary
½ cup olive oil
2 tablespoons Jack Daniel's Whiskey

In a large saucepan, boil the shallots, vinegar, and 3 teaspoons of the peppercorns until reduced to almost no liquid. Add both stocks and reduce to 1 cup. Set aside.

Place the steaks in a shallow glass baking dish and rub the remaining peppercorns and herbs on all of the steaks. Pour the oil over the steaks and turn to coat. Cover and chill for 1 hour.

Remove the meat from the marinade and grill until done to choice. Heat the reserved sauce and add the whiskey. Pour the sauce over the steaks and serve immediately.

Yield: 4 servings

INTERLAKEN INN
Lake Placid, New York

Tournedos of Beef
with Port Wine Sauce

1 tablespoon virgin olive oil
1 shallot, chopped
1 ½ cups tawny port wine
½ tablespoon dried thyme
½ tablespoon dried rosemary leaves
½ cup veal or beef stock
2 sun-dried tomatoes, chopped
1 tablespoon cornstarch (mixed with a dash of cold water)
1 tablespoon butter

PROSPECT HILL PLANTATION INN

Imagine a splendid two-century-old Virginia manor house with its own adjacent carriage house, summer kitchen, smokehouse, and groom's quarters. Next paint your imaginary manor house a soft spring yellow and trim it neatly in white.

The sun filters through the gently fragrant magnolias, tall tulip poplars, and giant beech trees. Accommodations are in the restored outbuildings with their original hand-hewn beam ceilings, squeaking floors, and cozy fireplaces or in the manor house with its fine furnishings and quilts and a private veranda overlooking the ancient foothills of the Blue Ridge Mountains.

Your full country breakfast is served on a tray in your room if you wish, and afternoon tea is always hosted by one of the Sheehan family. When Michael, Bill, or Murielle rings the dinner bell, guests gather in candlelit dining rooms of the manor house for an unforgettable five-course culinary experience. Enjoy!

Four 6 – 8 ounce beef tenderloin steaks, trimmed, 1 inch thick, and 3 – 4 inches round

In a medium-sized saucepan, heat the oil and sauté the shallot over high heat until browned, about 3 minutes. Add the wine and bring to a medium boil, then add the thyme and rosemary. Reduce by one-third, adding the stock and tomatoes. Continue to reduce for 5 – 7 minutes more and remove from heat.

Strain the mixture into separate bowls, reserving the tomatoes, shallots, and herbs in the strainer. Return the liquid to the saucepan and bring to boil. Thicken the sauce with the cornstarch and water, then stir in the reserved tomato mixture. Keep warm.

In a large, hot cast-iron skillet, melt the butter and cook the steaks, searing both sides and turning often, until the steaks are done (usually rare to medium), about 7 – 10 minutes.

Place the tournedos on serving plates and pour the sauce over each. Serve immediately.

Yield: 6 servings

PROSPECT HILL PLANTATION INN
Trevilians, Virginia

Beef Tenderloins with Bourbon❖

Eight 3-ounce beef tenderloins
2 teaspoons coarsely ground pepper
2 tablespoons vegetable oil
4 green onions, chopped
¼ cup bourbon whiskey
½ cup (1 stick) plus 2 tablespoons butter
2 tablespoons grated Parmesan cheese
2 tablespoons grated Romano cheese
1 clove garlic, minced
2 teaspoons granulated sugar
1 teaspoon salt
¼ teaspoon dried sage
¼ teaspoon dried marjoram
¼ teaspoon dried oregano
¼ teaspoon dried thyme

¼ teaspoon ground paprika
Dash nutmeg
Fresh mushroom caps
Fresh parsley sprigs

Rub both sides of the tenderloins with the pepper. In a large
skillet, heat the oil and sauté the beef until done to choice (about
5 minutes each side for medium-rare). Transfer to a large platter
and keep warm.

In the same skillet, sauté the onions for 1 minute. Lower heat
and slowly add the whiskey, scraping up the brown bits in the
pan. Stir in the remaining ingredients, except the mushroom
caps and parsley, and sauté for 2 minutes more.

Pour the sauce over the reserved tenderloins and garnish with the
mushroom caps and parsley. Serve immediately.

Yield: 4 servings

TRAIL'S END
Wilmington, Vermont

Range Veal on Rosemary Brochette with Blueberry Sauce

12 fresh rosemary branches, 4 – 5 inches long
2 pounds range veal leg meat, cleaned of all fat and silver
    skin and cut into 1-inch cubes
1 tablespoon chopped fresh rosemary
½ cup olive oil
½ cup white wine
1 ½ teaspoons cracked black peppercorns
1 recipe *Blueberry Sauce* (see recipe below)
1 recipe *Pecan Wild Rice* (see recipe below)

Remove only the lower leaves from the rosemary branches,
leaving leaves at the top. In a small bowl, combine the remaining ingredients for a marinade.

Skewer three cubes of veal onto each branch and place the
skewers in a shallow baking dish. Pour the marinade over the
veal and marinate for 2 hours or more in the refrigerator.

Grill the veal skewers over mesquite charcoal, turning often, for 10 minutes or until done. Place two skewers on each serving plate and moisten with the blueberry sauce. Serve immediately with the wild rice.

Blueberry Sauce

1 cup whole fresh blueberries
¼ cup granulated sugar
1 ¾ cups beef broth
2 cups blackberry wine
Juice of 1 lemon, or to taste

In a blender or food processor, puree ½ cup of the blueberries and set aside.

In a small saucepan, caramelize the sugar, stirring until dark. Immediately add the broth, wine, and the reserved blueberry puree and reduce to 1 cup liquid. Add the remaining whole blueberries and the lemon juice and stir well. Makes about 4 ½ cups.

Pecan Wild Rice

2 tablespoons butter
2 tablespoons minced yellow onions
2 cups California wild rice
4 cups chicken stock
Salt and pepper to taste
1 cup toasted and coarsely chopped pecans

In a large saucepan, melt the butter and sauté the onions until translucent. Add the rice, stock, salt, and pepper and bring to boil. Reduce to simmer, cover, and cook just until the rice starts to burst open, about 25 minutes. (The rice should still be crunchy.) Mix in the pecans and serve.

Yield: 6 servings

MADRONA MANOR
Healdsburg, California

Pan-Roasted Loin of Veal with a Ragout of Virginia Shiitake Mushrooms

½ cup extra-virgin olive oil
2 tablespoons chopped garlic
3 sprigs fresh rosemary
1 tablespoon balsamic vinegar
2 pounds boneless veal loin
1 recipe *Ragout of Virginia Shiitake Mushrooms* (see recipe below)

In a small bowl, mix the oil, garlic, rosemary, and vinegar. Place the veal in a shallow dish and pour the marinade over the top. Marinate in the refrigerator for 1 hour, turning once.

Preheat oven to 400° F. Remove the veal from the marinade. In a ovenproof, heavy deep skillet, sear the veal on all sides over medium-high heat. Roast in the oven for 13 minutes. Let stand for 25 minutes before slicing. Serve with the ragout.

Ragout of Virginia Shiitake Mushrooms

2 tablespoons extra-virgin olive oil
2 cups finely chopped fresh shiitake mushrooms
½ cup diced shallots
1 cup dry red wine
1 teaspoon balsamic vinegar
1 tablespoon granulated sugar
1 teaspoon chopped fresh parsley
1 tablespoon freshly ground black pepper
2 cups veal demi-glaze
2 tablespoons each finely shredded red, yellow, and green bell peppers

In a medium-sized skillet, heat the oil and sauté the mushrooms and shallots until tender. Deglaze with the wine and vinegar. Add the sugar, parsley, and black pepper and reduce by half. Add the demi-glaze and simmer for 5 minutes. Stir in the bell peppers and keep warm until ready to serve.

Yield: 6 servings

CLIFTON, THE COUNTRY INN
Charlottesville, Virginia

CLIFTON, THE COUNTRY INN

This forty-eight-acre, historic southern plantation was once home to Thomas Jefferson's daughter, Martha. You'll find it difficult to climb out of your four-poster bed, particularly when the fireplace in your room has burned down to glowing embers, and the newly fallen snow glistens in the morning sun. The quiche of the day and hot, rich, freshly brewed Kona coffee await, so hurry.

Innkeepers Craig and Donna Hartman are the gifted young couple who combine Culinary Institute training with a genuine desire to serve people, to create a showpiece of hospitality.

Fresh seafood from the Chesapeake Bay, free-range veal, and an excellent selection of Virginia vineyard-harvested wines are among the reasons Clifton guests return often to this serene section of Virginia Hunt Country for the kind of dining experience you will enter in your diary.

Parmesan-Crusted Pork Loin with Caponata, Braised Fennel & Roasted Peppers

1 cup dried bread crumbs
1 cup grated Parmesan cheese
2 ½ pounds fresh boneless pork loin
Salt and pepper
Flour
3 eggs, slightly beaten
1 recipe *Caponata* (see recipe below)
1 recipe *Braised Fennel & Roasted Peppers* (see recipe below)
1 pound fresh fettuccine
⅛ cup butter
1 tablespoon chopped fresh fennel
Salt and pepper to taste
Reduced port stock or demi-glace, warmed

Preheat oven to 450° F. In a small bowl, mix together the bread crumbs and cheese and set aside.

Cut the pork into six equal portions, roughly 2 inches thick and season with the salt and pepper. Roll the portions in the flour, then the beaten eggs, and finally the reserved bread crumb mixture, coating well each time. Quickly deep-fry to set crust and lightly brown. Place on a baking sheet and bake until medium, about 8 minutes. Remove and keep warm.

Bring 4 quarts of water to a boil and cook the fettuccine until . Drain and toss with the butter and chopped fennel. Season with the salt and pepper.

Arrange a small portion of fettuccine at the top of each plate and a mound of the fennel and peppers to the left of the pasta. Slice the pork portion into three pieces and fan out against the fettuccine. Top the pork with the caponata and drizzle on the pork glaze. Serve immediately.

Caponata

1 medium eggplant, unpeeled and cut into ½-inch dice
Kosher salt
Olive oil
½ cup peeled ¼-inch dice celery
½ cup ¼-inch dice red onions

Salt and pepper to taste
½ cup ¼-inch dice bell peppers (combination of red, yellow, and green)
¼ cup drained capers
¼ cup pitted and coarsely chopped Niçoise olives
⅓ cup red wine vinegar
½ tablespoon granulated sugar, or to taste
2 tablespoons tomato paste
½ tablespoon chopped fresh basil
½ tablespoon chopped fresh thyme
½ tablespoon chopped fresh oregano
½ tablespoon chopped garlic

Lightly salt the eggplant with the kosher salt and place in a colander. Weight with a heavy plate and let drain for 1 hour.

In a large skillet, heat 1 tablespoon oil and quickly sauté the celery and onions until crisp-tender, about 5 minutes. Season with the salt and pepper. Add the bell peppers and cook until tender, about 3 – 5 minutes. Set aside.

Rinse the eggplant and squeeze dry. In another skillet, heat 1 – 2 tablespoons oil and sauté the eggplant, in small batches. Combine with the reserved celery mixture in a large pot and add the capers and olives.

In a small bowl, whisk together the vinegar, sugar, and tomato paste and add to the eggplant mixture. Heat gently and add the herbs and garlic. Adjust the seasoning. Serve warm or at room temperature.

Braised Fennel & Roasted Peppers

½ each red, yellow, and green bell peppers, seeded and deveined
1 tablespoon olive oil
Salt and pepper
1 tablespoon butter
1 ½ bulbs fennel, cut into ½-inch strips; tops finely chopped and reserved
Salt and pepper
¼ cup chicken stock

Halve the bell peppers again. Toss with the oil, salt, and pepper and broil skin-side up, until charred. Place in a bowl, cover with plastic wrap, and set aside for 15 minutes. Remove the skins and slice into ½-inch strips.

In a large skillet, melt the butter and sauté the fennel over medium heat and season with the salt and pepper. Add the

THE ASHBY INN

Barely sixty miles west of Washington D.C., lies one of the most hotly contested communities of America's Civil War, Paris, Virginia, (population 60). Directly across the street from one of George Washington's favorite "Paris" taverns, during his early days as a surveyor, is the 1829 ten-guest room inn owned and operated by John and Roma Sherman.

The Ashby Inn has been painstakingly restored to preserve its early architectural dimensions and furnished throughout with fine pieces dating back to the early nineteenth century. Hand-painted wardrobes, quilts and coverlets, rag and Oriental rugs, and antique blanket chests adorn virtually every guest room. But the heart of The Ashby Inn is its kitchen. The menu is clearly rooted in tradition rather than trend, with great attention paid to fresh seasonal food.

The inn's backfin crab cakes are regarded as the best in the region, and without exception, the breads and desserts are homemade. Much of the produce and herbs served in the inn are grown in its own gardens. If you happen upon The Ashby for Sunday brunch, you'll probably have your omelet made-to-order by Roma, and your baked ham carved to your specifications by John. But save room for chef Eric Stamer's superb evening selections. A typical seasonal dinner at The Ashby might include Parmesan-Crusted Pork Loin with Caponata, Braised Fennel & Roasted Peppers served with buttered fresh fettuccine or perhaps Sautéed Soft-Shell Crabs served with Artichoke & Sun-Dried Tomato Risotto . . . my, oh my!

chicken stock, cover, and braise slowly until tender. Add the roasted peppers and the reserved chopped fennel. Adjust the seasoning. Set aside and keep warm.

Yield: 6 servings

THE ASHBY INN
Paris, Virginia

WINDHAM HILL INN

Windham Hill Inn is nestled at the end of a tree-shrouded country lane above the tiny village of West Townshend. To get a mental image of the inn, simply picture the prototypical Vermont village postcard—and presto, you're at Windham Hill.

The inn passed through many owners before coming into the capable hands of Ken and Linda Busteed. The furniture of this spacious eighteenth-century house includes sleigh beds, gateleg and claw foot tables, and well-built heart pine dressers. You truly feel the essence of Americana at Windham Hill.

Named "Best Inn of the Year" in 1989 by Uncle Ben's, the inn has what Uncle Ben's calls "comfort food." Dinners at the inn are unhurried times that make guests feel as if they are at a dinner party that has been carefully and artfully planned to perfection.

Herb-Marinated Pork Tenderloin with Maple-Mustard Sauce❖

2 pork tenderloins (about 2 ¾ pounds)
5 bay leaves
1 teaspoon ground cloves
½ teaspoon cayenne pepper
1 teaspoon ground nutmeg
1 teaspoon ground thyme
½ teaspoon ground allspice
½ teaspoon ground cinnamon
½ teaspoon dried basil
½ teaspoon freshly ground black pepper
½ teaspoon salt
Good-quality olive oil
1 recipe *Maple-Mustard Sauce* (see recipe below)

Place the pork in a shallow glass baking dish and rub the next ten ingredients into the meat. Cover and chill for several hours.

Preheat oven to 375° F. Bring the meat to room temperature. Rub generously with the oil and roast for 1 hour, or until the internal temperature reaches 150°. Slice and serve with the sauce.

Maple-Mustard Sauce

¾ cup pure Vermont maple syrup
½ cup Dijon mustard

In a small bowl, whisk together the syrup and mustard and serve at room temperature with the pork.

Yield: 6 to 8 servings

WINDHAM HILL INN
West Townshend, Vermont

Rolled Pork Loin with Balsamic Mustard❖

2 tablespoons each fresh herbs: rosemary, thyme, oregano,
   and parsley
3 shallots, finely chopped
3 green onions, finely chopped
3 cloves garlic, minced
3 tablespoons butter, melted
2 cups dried bread crumbs
1 teaspoon salt
1 teaspoon pepper
2 pounds boneless pork loin
3 tablespoons olive oil
½ cup white wine
3 tablespoons *Balsamic Mustard* (see recipe below)
1 cup heavy cream
Salt to taste
White pepper to taste

In a small bowl, mix together the herbs, shallots, onions, garlic,
butter, bread crumbs, salt, and white pepper and set aside.

Trim the loin of all fat and silver skin. For the next step, work
slowly. (Or ask the butcher to flatten the loin.)

Place the loin on the cutting surface, pointing away from you
(perpendicular to the edge of the counter). Starting at the center
of the far end of the loin, with a sharp boning knife, slice down
its length so it leaves ¼ inch at the bottom intact. The loin is
now splayed into two connected halves ("butterflied") with the
cut making a kind of V-shape in the center of the loin.

Lay the knife in this V so that the blade is flat (parallel to the
table). Cut the left half in half, stopping before cutting all the
way through and leaving ¼-inch edge on the meat. Lay the knife
in the center V again and cut the right half of the loin the same
way. This should make the loin a large rectangle about ¼ inch
thick.

Spread the reserved stuffing on the pork in a thin layer and roll it
tightly, jelly-roll fashion. Tie the roll in six places, evenly spaced.
Cut between the ties to create six small roasts.

Preheat oven to 350° F. In a heavy saucepan, heat the oil and sear
each roast on all sides. Lay the roasts in a roasting pan and bake

for about 20 – 25 minutes, turning once, or until a meat thermometer registers 160°. Let the roasts rest for 10 minutes before slicing.

Deglaze with the wine and reduce to 2 tablespoons. Add the balsamic mustard and cream and reduce until thickened. Season with the salt and white pepper.

Divide the sauce among six serving plates. Slice each roast and fan out the slices on the sauce. Serve immediately.

Balsamic Mustard

1 cup dark mustard seeds
1 ½ tablespoons Coleman's dry mustard
¼ cup water
½ cup red wine
1 ½ teaspoons honey
½ cup balsamic vinegar
2 tablespoons apple cider vinegar
2 tablespoons granulated sugar
4 teaspoons salt
2 cloves garlic, minced

Grind the mustard seeds in a blender or coffee grinder to the texture of ground pepper. Add the dry mustard and blend well. Add the water and wine and mix until blended. Let stand for 1 – 4 hours or overnight.

Pour the mixture into a food processor and add the remaining ingredients. Process until well blended. Remove to a covered glass container and let stand for 1 – 3 days to develop the flavor. Makes 2 cups. (The mustard can be stored in the refrigerator for a hotter mustard or at room temperature for a mellow flavor; the mustard will keep indefinitely.)

Yield: 6 servings

SHELBURNE INN/THE SHOALWATER RESTAURANT
Seaview, Washington

Greek-Style Leg of Lamb✧

4 pounds boneless leg of lamb, or 6-pound bone-in
8 cups buttermilk
4 bay leaves
6 whole cloves

1 teaspoon crushed juniper berries
½ teaspoon crushed black peppercorns
3 teaspoons minced garlic
3 tablespoons dried oregano
6 cups cooked long grain white rice
12 ounces ham, cooked and diced
8 ounces chicken, cooked and ground
12 ounces feta cheese, crumbled
1 medium yellow onion, diced
2 tablespoons olive oil
¼ cup chopped fresh parsley
4 hard-cooked eggs, sliced
2 cups *Lemon Egg Sauce* (see recipe below)

(If the lamb is bone-in, remove the bone from the leg completely.) Lay the lamb flat between sheets of parchment paper to
prevent tearing or splattering. Using a mallet, pound the lamb to
an even thickness. Place the meat in a pan large enough to hold
the meat and marinade in one layer.

In a large bowl, combine the buttermilk, bay leaves, cloves,
juniper berries, peppercorns, garlic, and 1 tablespoon of the
oregano. Pour the marinade over the leg of lamb, cover, and
refrigerate overnight, turning occasionally.

In a large mixing bowl, mix together the rice, ham, chicken,
cheese, onion, oil, parsley, and remaining oregano. Remove the
lamb from the marinade and pat dry. Pat the stuffing evenly on
the lamb and space the egg slices lengthwise on top of the stuffing.

Preheat oven to 425° F. Roll up the meat firmly and tie securely
at 1-inch intervals with butcher's twine. Place in a roasting pan
and roast until done, about 1 hour and 30 minutes.

Let stand for about 15 minutes before slicing. Slice into six
portions and serve on top of the lemon egg sauce. Pass any
remaining sauce in a gravy boat.

Lemon Egg Sauce

1 tablespoon all-purpose flour
2 tablespoons softened butter
2 cups veal stock
2 teaspoons dried oregano
¼ cup fresh lemon juice
1 small onion, peeled and stuck with 2 whole cloves
¼ cup ouzo liqueur
2 egg yolks

In a small bowl, blend together the flour and butter and set aside.

In a medium-sized saucepan, combine the stock, oregano, lemon juice, and onion and bring to a boil. Reduce to 1 cup liquid. Remove the onion and discard. Add the liqueur and simmer for 10 minutes.

In a small bowl, beat the egg yolks, then add ¼ cup of the hot liquid in a thin stream, whisking constantly. Return the egg yolk mixture to the simmering liquid and continue stirring as the sauce begins to thicken. Add the reserved flour mixture, in bits, stirring constantly.

When the sauce has further thickened, keep warm over warm water until ready to serve. Makes 2 cups.

Yield: 6 servings

SHELBURNE INN/THE SHOALWATER RESTAURANT
Seaview, Washington

THE INN AT WEATHERSFIELD

This inn began serving stagecoach travelers while George Washington was still President. Innkeepers Ron and Mary Louise Thorburn have that wonderful ability to make every guest who arrives at the door feel like a member of the family.

The gourmet kitchen at Weathersfield is only one of the reasons the facility has been repeatedly honored with Mobil's Four-Star rating for hospitality excellence. The respect for tradition is apparent in the furnishings of the nine guest rooms and three suites, some with featherbed mattresses and down comforters. Also, the beehive oven still works, and the horse-drawn sleigh comes fully equipped with a lap robe.

But there are also many contemporary conveniences that have been added to this splendid inn, such as a fitness center and sauna, which provide a soothing break from tennis, skating, swimming, or hiking before you experience the elegant dinner of locally raised wild game, awaiting you in the dining room.

Roast Rack of Lamb with New Vegetables in Napa Cabbage Bundles

2 racks of lamb (about 7 pounds)
Seasoned salt
Coarsely ground black pepper
2 sprigs fresh rosemary, leaves removed and chopped
¼ cup red wine
1 ½ cups veal or chicken stock
2 tablespoons butter
¼ cup julienned baby carrots
¼ cup julienned red bell peppers
¼ cup julienned spring onions
¼ cup coarsely chopped fresh mung bean sprouts
¼ cup sliced fresh shiitake mushrooms
2 cloves garlic, coarsely chopped
Seasoned salt
1 teaspoon fresh lemon juice
1 head Napa cabbage
¼ cup melted butter

(When buying the lamb, ask the butcher to remove the chine

bone and crack the ribs.) Preheat oven to 425° F. Trim the surface fat from the lamb racks, leaving a thin fat coating. "French" the ribs by scraping the meat 1 ½ inches from the bone tips.

Place the racks in a large roasting pan and sprinkle with the salt, pepper, and rosemary. Prop the ribs against each other, fat-side out, allowing the bone tips to interlock. Insert a meat thermometer in the center and roast for 15 – 20 minutes, or until the thermometer reaches 110° . Remove the racks from the pan and let stand, covered, while preparing the sauce and vegetables. Keep warm.

Skim off all but 2 tablespoons of fat from the pan and deglaze with the red wine, scraping bits off the bottom of the pan. Add the stock and reduce, stirring frequently, until desired thickness. Adjust the seasoning. (The sauce should not be heavy.) Set aside and keep warm.

In a large skillet, melt the 2 tablespoons butter and sauté the carrots, bell peppers, onions, bean sprouts, mushrooms, and garlic. Sprinkle with the salt and lemon juice. Set aside and keep warm.

Preheat the oven to 350° F. Separate the cabbage leaves and blanch until wilted. Rinse in cold water and pat dry. Stuff the cabbage leaves with the reserved vegetable mixture and brush with the ¼ cup melted butter. Arrange the bundles in an oven-proof baking dish and bake for 10 minutes.

Pour the reserved warm sauce in the bottom of the serving plates and arrange the warm cabbage bundles on the sauce. Slice the roasts and place three or four ribs around the cabbage. Serve immediately.

Yield: 4 to 6 servings

THE INN AT WEATHERSFIELD
Weathersfield, Vermont

Rack of Lamb with Red Currant Sauce❖

Two 8-bone racks of Vermont lamb
2 tablespoons minced garlic
1 tablespoon finely chopped fresh parsley
4 tablespoons olive oil
1 recipe *Red Currant Sauce* (see recipe below)

(When buying the lamb, ask the butcher to remove the chine bone and crack the ribs.) Preheat oven to 400° F. Trim the surface fat from the lamb racks, leaving a thin fat coating. "French" the ribs by scraping the meat 1 ½ inches from the bone tips.

In a small bowl, mix together the garlic, parsley, and 2 tablespoons of the oil to make a paste. Rub the paste on the lamb. In a large skillet, heat the remaining oil and sear the lamb on all sides over medium-high heat. Place the lamb on a heavy rimmed baking sheet and roast in the oven for 15 minutes for medium-rare or longer until done to choice. Prepare the sauce while the lamb is roasting.

Slice the lamb. Divide the warm sauce among the serving plates and place four ribs on each plate. Serve immediately.

Red Currant Sauce

One 10-ounce jar red currant jelly
½ cup fresh red currants
3 tablespoons brandy

In a small saucepan, melt the jelly. Stir in the currants and brandy and mix together well. Keep warm until ready to use.

Yield: 4 servings

INTERLAKEN INN
Lake Placid, New York

INTERLAKEN INN

Grilled Lamb Chops with Green Peppercorn & Honey Mustard❖

1 cup olive oil
2 ½ cups red wine
2 teaspoons minced garlic
4 teaspoons dried rosemary
1 small green bell pepper, sliced
2 teaspoons black pepper
Six 6 – 8 ounce ¾-inch thick lamp chops
4 tablespoons (½ stick) butter
3 shallots, minced
1 ½ cups lamb stock
¾ cup *Green Peppercorn & Honey Mustard* (see recipe below)
1 ½ cups heavy cream

In a shallow glass baking pan, whisk together the oil, 2 cups of the wine, garlic, 3 teaspoons of the rosemary, bell pepper, and black pepper. Add the chops, cover, and marinate in the refrigerator overnight.

In a medium-sized sauté pan, melt 2 tablespoons of the butter and sauté the shallots until soft, about 3 – 5 minutes. Add the remaining wine and rosemary and the stock and boil until the liquid is reduced by half, stirring constantly. Strain the liquid into a clean sauté pan and add the mustard, whisking well to combine. Reduce again by half.

Add the cream and reduce until the sauce begins to thicken. Add the remaining butter and keep warm over warm water, while preparing the chops.

Remove the chops from the marinade and pat dry. Grill until resilient and barely pink. Serve with the mustard sauce.

Green Peppercorn & Honey Mustard

½ cup mustard seeds
3 tablespoons Coleman's dry mustard
½ cup water
2 small green bell peppers
2 tablespoons green peppercorns in water
¼ cup balsamic vinegar
¼ cup honey
2 teaspoons salt
2 tablespoons dried rosemary

In a blender or food processor, combine the mustard seeds, dry mustard, and water and process until the mixture resembles a coarse puree. Let stand, uncovered, for at least 3 hours at room temperature.

Roast the bell peppers under a broiler, turning until all sides have blackened and blistered. Place in a plastic bag to cool. Peel and seed the cooled peppers.

In a food processor, blend the roasted peppers, peppercorns, vinegar, honey, salt, and rosemary. Add the reserved mustard mixture and blend well. Cover and let stand overnight before serving. Makes 3 cups. (The mustard will keep indefinitely in the refrigerator or at room temperature.)

Yield: 6 servings

SHELBURNE INN/THE SHOALWATER RESTAURANT
Seaview, Washington

Loin of Venison with Bourbon & Mango Chutney Sauce

3 pounds venison loin
Olive oil
Black pepper
1 recipe *Bourbon & Mango Chutney Sauce* (see recipe below)

Preheat oven to 350° F. Rub all sides of the venison with the oil and roll in the pepper.

In a large ovenproof frying pan, brown the venison on all sides over medium heat, then bake for 15 – 20 minutes for medium-rare. Remove from the oven and place on a warm platter. Let stand, while preparing the sauce. Set aside the hot frying pan. Do not wash.

Slice the venison into thin slices. Divide the slices among warm serving plates and serve immediately with the warm sauce.

Bourbon & Mango Chutney Sauce

2 cups *Mango Chutney* (see recipe below)
½ cup bourbon whiskey
2 cups veal demi-glaze*
White pepper to taste

Wipe the reserved frying pan. Add the chutney, whiskey, and demi-glaze and bring to a boil, stirring frequently. Add the white pepper and reduce heat. Keep warm until ready to serve.

*Veal demi-glaze is available in specialty gourmet food shops.

Mango Chutney

½ pound mangos, peeled and cut into ½-inch dice
½ pound apples, peeled and diced
½ pound tomatoes, peeled and diced
2 medium onions, diced
1 large clove garlic, minced
½ pound golden raisins
1 ¼ cups cider vinegar
⅛ teaspoon ground mace
⅛ teaspoon ground apple pie spice
1 teaspoon ground ginger
1 ⅓ cups packed brown sugar

In a large pot, mix together all of the ingredients, except the brown sugar, and simmer for 30 minutes. Add the brown sugar and simmer until thick. Makes 1 quart. (The chutney will keep, tightly covered, for several weeks in the refrigerator.)

Yield: 8 servings

L'AUBERGE PROVENÇALE
White Post, Virginia

Sirloin of Venison with Red Wine Sauce❖

1 ½ pounds venison, cut into ¼ – ½-inch medallions
½ cup all-purpose flour
¾ cup (1 ½ sticks) butter
¾ cup fresh shiitake mushrooms, cleaned and stemmed
¾ cup fresh oyster mushrooms, cleaned and stemmed
2 teaspoons black peppercorns, cracked
4 tablespoons minced shallots
2 teaspoons chopped fresh thyme
¼ cup red wine
¼ cup *Glace de Viande* (see recipe below)

Dredge the venison in the flour. In a large skillet, melt ½ cup of the butter and sauté the venison over medium heat, turning once, until cooked to choice (rare, about 6 – 8 minutes). Remove from the skillet. Set aside and keep warm.

Slice the shiitake mushroom caps. Add all of the mushroom caps to the skillet and cook until the liquid evaporates, about 5 minutes. Add the cracked peppercorns, shallots, thyme, and wine and cook, stirring frequently, over high heat until reduced by half, about 3 minutes.

Add the glace and quickly stir in the remaining butter. Heat through, but do not boil. Pour the sauce over the reserved warm venison and serve immediately.

Glace de Viande

2 cups beef stock

In a medium-sized saucepan, heat the stock over high heat and bring to a boil. Reduce heat and simmer, stirring occasionally and skimming the fat, until reduced to a very thick, dark consistency, about 5 – 6 hours.

Use immediately or cool. The glace will have a rubbery texture. Makes ¼ cup. (The glace can be stored, tightly covered, in the refrigerator for up to three months.)

Yield: 4 servings

THE RED LION INN
Stockbridge, Massachusetts

Sauté Rabbit Chasseur

4 tablespoons vegetable oil
1 large Spanish onion, diced
4 large carrots, diced
4 cups canned whole plum tomatoes; reserve liquid
2 teaspoons salt
½ teaspoon pepper
6 sprigs fresh tarragon
½ teaspoon ground cloves
12 shallots
6 fresh mushrooms, halved
6 bay leaves
Two fresh 3 ½-pound rabbits, dressed and each cut into 7
    pieces (4 legs, 3 pieces of loin)
Flour
2 tablespoons butter
6 cloves garlic
2 cups white wine
3 cups veal stock
1 tablespoon tomato puree

In a medium-sized saucepan, heat 2 tablespoons of the oil and simmer the onion and carrots for 4 – 6 minutes or until tender. Drain the oil and remove the vegetables to a roasting pan.

In a food processor, puree the tomatoes, then add to the vegetables and spread evenly on the bottom of the pan. Add one-third of the reserved tomato liquid and the salt, pepper, tarragon, cloves, whole shallots, mushrooms, and bay leaves.

Dust the rabbit pieces in the flour. In a large frying pan, melt the butter with the remaining oil and sauté the pieces for 8 minutes on each side. During the last 4 minutes, add the garlic cloves. Remove the pieces and garlic and place on top of the

THE INN
SAWMILL FARM

vegetables. Drain the oil from the frying pan and deglaze with the wine. Bring to a boil and add the stock and tomato puree. Let boil for 4 minutes.

Preheat oven to 350° F. Pour the stock mixture over the rabbit, cover with aluminum foil, and bake for 1 hour 45 minutes. Serve.

Yield: 6 servings

INN AT SAWMILL FARM
West Dover, Vermont

Smoked Rabbit with Chanterelle Mushrooms

1 ½ cups olive oil
½ cup white wine vinegar
2 sprigs fresh tarragon, chopped
2 sprigs fresh thyme, chopped
6 cloves garlic, chopped
1 large onion, chopped
1 teaspoon salt
1 teaspoon pepper
Two 2 ½-pound rabbits
3 tablespoons butter
1 ½ cups fresh chanterelle or morel mushrooms
1 ½ cups heavy cream
Salt and pepper to taste
2 pounds fresh pasta, cooked, drained, and set aside

In a large baking dish, combine the first eight ingredients. Add the rabbits, cover, and marinate overnight in the refrigerator, turning two times.

Remove the rabbits from the marinade and place in a hot smoker. Smoke for 45 minutes, turning every 15 minutes. Allow the rabbits to cool after smoking. Debone the rabbits and cut the meat into bite-sized pieces. Set aside.

In a large frying pan, melt the butter and sauté the mushrooms for 8 – 10 minutes. Add the cream and reserved rabbit and bring to a boil. Reduce heat and cook, stirring constantly, until the cream thickens and coats a spoon. Sprinkle with the salt and pepper. Add the reserved pasta and heat through.

Place some rabbit pieces in the center of each serving plate and surround with the pasta. Pour the remaining mushroom sauce over the top and serve immediately.

Yield: 8 servings

L'AUBERGE PROVENÇALE
White Post, Virginia

Chicken Breasts in Phyllo with Dijon❖

4 tablespoons (½ stick) butter
3 whole boneless skinless chicken breasts, halved
1 cup sour cream
3 tablespoons Dijon mustard
1 tablespoon chopped fresh basil
9 sheets phyllo dough
Melted butter

In a large skillet, melt the 4 tablespoons butter and sauté the chicken, covered, over medium heat for 10 minutes. Remove from the skillet and set aside.

Into the skillet drippings, whisk and stir together the sour cream, mustard, and basil and set aside.

Preheat oven to 425° F. Lay out one sheet of phyllo dough and brush quickly with the melted butter. Repeat twice more, so there are three sheets of butter-brushed dough stacked one on top of the other.

Place one piece of the chicken in the center of the three-stacked sheets and top with ½ cup of the reserved sour cream mixture. Wrap the dough around the chicken and seal the edges with more melted butter. Repeat the entire procedure with the remaining five chicken pieces, using three sheets of dough plus melted butter for each.

Place seam-side down on a rimmed baking sheet and bake for 15 – 20 minutes. Serve immediately.

Yield: 6 servings

DAIRY HOLLOW HOUSE
Eureka Springs, Arkansas

Stuffed Chicken Breasts with Paprika Sauce❖

2 whole boneless skinless chicken breasts, halved
Salt and pepper to taste
8 whole pimientos
12 medium stalks fresh asparagus, cooked crisp-tender
3 – 4 quarts chicken stock
1 recipe *Paprika Sauce* (see recipe below)
Fresh orange nasturtium flower blossoms
Fresh watercress

Spread the chicken pieces skin-side down on a cutting surface and flatten slightly with a mallet. Season with the salt and pepper. Line each piece with two pimientos and lay three stalks asparagus lengthwise in the center of each piece. Roll up each piece in plastic wrap, twisting the ends together.

In a large saucepan, bring the stock to a boil. Place the wrapped chicken in the saucepan and simmer (poach) for about 15 minutes. While the chicken is simmering, prepare the sauce.

Remove the chicken bundles from the stock and unwrap. Slice on the diagonal, exposing the filling. Ladle about ⅛ cup sauce on each of four warmed serving plates and fan the chicken slices over the sauce. Garnish with the nasturtiums and watercress and serve immediately.

Paprika Sauce

1 teaspoon butter or olive oil
1 medium onion, minced
5 teaspoons ground paprika
⅛ cup red wine vinegar
1 ¾ cups heavy cream
2 teaspoons tomato paste
Salt and pepper to taste

In a medium-sized saucepan, melt the butter and sauté the onion. Sprinkle the paprika over the onion and deglaze with the vinegar. Simmer until almost dry. Stir in the cream, tomato paste, salt, and pepper. Set aside and keep warm.

Yield: 4 servings

THE GOVERNOR'S INN
Ludlow, Vermont

RALPH WALDO EMERSON INN

The Ralph Waldo Emerson Inn, named for its most famous guest, is one of Rockport's original summer hotels. Pigeon Cove is where Emerson "made acquaintance with the sea for seven days." At the Emerson, there are party boats for fishing, sight-seeing, and, of course, whale watching.

The family of the innkeeper, Gary Wemyss, acquired the inn in 1965 and restored this elegant historic hotel. Emerson's room, in the old section, lacked a private bath and telephone in his day, but if he could return to it now, he would feel quite at home.

The new section, built in 1912, houses the attractive dining room where breakfast is served daily. The dinner menu is extremely impressive, featuring many culinary delights under such descriptive headings as "hearty fare" and "poultry with a flair."

Gary and Diane Wemyss invite you to come visit their charming inn soon.

Baked-Stuffed Chicken Breast Boursin

Two 10-ounce whole boneless skinless chicken breasts, halved
1 cup Boursin cheese
Flour
4 eggs, well beaten
Dried bread crumbs
1 cup olive oil

Sauce:
1 ½ cups Chablis wine
½ cup (1 stick) butter
6 sun-dried tomatoes, sliced
12 fresh shiitake mushrooms, cleaned
½ cup chopped fresh chives
Fresh lemon juice to taste

Pound each piece of chicken until thin. Put ¼ cup of the cheese in each piece. Form a ball around the cheese and wrap each piece with plastic wrap to keep the form. Place the chicken in the freezer for 30 minutes or until slightly hard.

Coat each of the partially frozen pieces with the flour, then dip into the eggs. (This will form a paste.) Roll in the bread crumbs, coating each piece well.

Preheat oven to 350° F. In a large skillet, heat the oil and cook the chicken until brown on all sides. Remove and drain on paper towels. Place in a baking dish and bake for 20 – 30 minutes.

In a medium-sized saucepan, combine the wine, butter, tomatoes, and mushrooms and reduce by half over medium heat until thick. Stir in the chives and lemon juice and keep warm.

Divide the chicken amoung serving plates and top with the sauce. Serve immediately.

Yield: 4 servings

RALPH WALDO EMERSON INN
Rockport, Massachusetts

Chicken Breast Citron❖

6 half chicken breasts, deboned with skin intact
1 cup fresh lemon juice
1 cup fresh lime juice
¾ cup all-purpose flour
2 teaspoons ground paprika
Pepper
¾ cup chicken stock
2 tablespoons brown sugar
2 teaspoons *Herbes de Provence* (see recipe below)
1 lemon, thinly sliced

Place the chicken pieces in a large shallow baking dish. In a small bowl, combine both the juices and pour over the chicken. Marinate in the refrigerator for 12 hours, turning occasionally.

Preheat oven to 350° F. Remove the chicken from the marinade and set aside the remaining marinade. In a medium-sized bowl, combine the flour, paprika, and pepper and dredge the chicken. Place skin-side up in a shallow baking pan and bake for 25 minutes.

While baking, place the reserved marinade in a small saucepan and add the stock, sugar, and herbs. Heat to a boil and set aside.

After baking for 25 minutes, remove the chicken from the oven, lay one lemon slice on each piece, and pour the sauce over all. Return to the oven and bake for 20 minutes more. Serve immediately.

Herbes de Provence

¼ cup dried parsley
2 tablespoons dried basil
2 tablespoons dried oregano

In a small bowl, combine all of the ingredients. Store in a sealed container in a cool, dry place.

Yield: 6 servings

HIGH MEADOWS
Scottsville, Virginia

HIGH MEADOWS

Mary Jae Abbitt and Peter Sushka's splendid little place in history doesn't really know whether it wants to be a classic country inn, an inspired restaurant, or a dedicated prolific vineyard. So High Meadows is very simply—all of the above!

This nineteenth-century inn, which is in the National Register of Historic Places, consists of a 50-acre estate with two dwellings that were built in 1832 and 1882 and connected by a bilevel, longitudinal hall. The home, with its seventeen rooms, nine fireplaces, and original grained woodwork, is the only structure in Virginia displaying this unique architectural detail.

On weekdays, High Meadows presents the evening meal in a European-styled supper basket, overflowing with such treats as freshly herbed lasagnas, quiche, salads, and the inn's original recipe mousse. Splendid by every standard!

HIGH MEADOWS

Roast Chicken Chesapeake with Seafood Stuffing

One 7-pound roasting chicken, fat and giblets removed
1 recipe *Seafood Stuffing* (see recipe below)
Old Bay Seasoning

Preheat oven to 325° F. Rinse the chicken thoroughly inside and out. Stuff the chicken with the stuffing and sprinkle the outside with the seasoning. Place the chicken in a baking pan and bake for about 3 hours.

Slice the chicken and serve immediately.

Seafood Stuffing

¼ pound cooked fresh salad shrimp, chopped
¼ pound cooked fresh bay scallops, chopped
¼ pound cooked fresh crabmeat, shredded
1 egg
1 small green bell pepper, seeded and chopped
½ medium onion, diced
¼ cup (½ stick) butter, melted
½ teaspoon garlic powder
½ cup chicken broth
⅓ cup dried Italian bread crumbs
⅔ cup crushed seasoned croutons
1 teaspoon fresh lemon juice

In a large bowl, combine all the ingredients and mix together well.

Yield: 6 servings

McNINCH HOUSE
Charlotte, North Carolina

Mast Farm Inn Chicken with Parsley Dumplings❖

1 quart water
2 teaspoons salt
Dash pepper
1 carrot, cut into 1-inch chunks
1 stalk celery with leaves, broken in pieces

1 medium onion, quartered
One 4 – 5-pound stewing chicken, or two 2 – 2 ½-pound
    fryers, cut into pieces
1 cup milk
⅓ cup all-purpose flour
3 medium carrots, cut into ¼-inch rounds
1 cup fresh peas
1 recipe *Parsley Dumplings* (see recipe below)

In a large pot, heat the water to boiling and add the salt, pepper,
carrot chunks, celery, onion, and chicken. Cover and simmer
until the chicken is tender, about 25 – 35 minutes. Skim off fat.
Remove the chicken from the broth and set aside. Keep warm.
Strain the broth and add enough water to make 3 cups. Return
the broth to the pot and reheat.

In a small saucepan, cook the carrot rounds in a small amount of
water until almost tender, about 4 – 6 minutes and set aside.

In a blender, combine the milk and flour until smooth. Slowly
add the milk mixture to the hot broth, stirring rapidly with a
wire whisk, and cook for about 5 minutes. Stir in the reserved
chicken and carrot rounds and the peas. Keep warm, while
making the dumplings.

Drop the dumpling dough by tablespoons into the hot chicken
mixture and simmer for 10 minutes, uncovered. (If the broth
becomes too rich or thick, thin with a little chicken broth.)
Cover and simmer for 10 minutes more. Adjust the seasoning
and serve immediately.

Parsley Dumplings

2 cups all-purpose flour
1 tablespoon baking powder
1 teaspoon salt
¼ cup vegetable shortening
¼ cup minced fresh parsley
1 cup milk

In a medium-sized bowl, sift together the flour, baking powder,
and salt. Cut in the shortening and add the parsley. Add the
milk and mix, stirring as little as possible, to form a soft dough.
(Dumpling dough freezes well.)

Yield: 8 servings

MAST FARM INN
Valle Crucis, North Carolina

Chicken Pot Pie❖

4 whole chicken breasts
1 ½ quarts water
¼ cup white wine
½ teaspoon dried rosemary
1 clove garlic, crushed
2 small bay leaves
½ teaspoon chopped fresh thyme
¼ teaspoon chopped fresh tarragon
4 whole black peppercorns
¼ cup clarified butter
¼ cup all-purpose flour
2 medium carrots, diced
24 whole pearl onions, peeled
1 cup cooked frozen peas
6 warm *Buttermilk Biscuits* (see recipe below)

Butter six individual crocks or ramekins. In a large pot, combine the first nine ingredients and bring to a boil, skimming off any foam that rises to the surface. Reduce heat and simmer for 20 – 30 minutes, or until the chicken is tender. Remove the chicken from the pot and let cool slightly. Remove the skin and separate the meat from the bones. Set the meat aside and keep warm.

Return the chicken bones to the stock and simmer until reduced by half, about 15 minutes. Strain and return the stock to a boil.

In a small saucepan, melt the clarified butter over low heat. Stir in the flour and bring the roux to a slow boil. Cook without browning for 5 minutes. Add the roux to the stock and simmer for 10 minutes more. Adjust the seasoning and keep warm.

In separate saucepans, cook the carrots and onions in boiling salted water to cover until just tender, about 8 – 10 minutes for the carrots and 12 – 13 minutes for the onions. Drain and combine the carrots and onions in a large saucepan.

Dice the reserved chicken and toss together the chicken, peas, carrots, and onions. Divide the mixture among the prepared crocks and pour the sauce over the chicken. Top with a biscuit and serve immediately.

Buttermilk Biscuits

1 ¾ cups all-purpose flour
1 tablespoon plus 1 teaspoon baking powder

⅛ teaspoon salt
7 tablespoons butter
1 ¼ cups buttermilk
1 egg, well beaten
1 tablespoon water
2 tablespoons butter, melted

Preheat oven to 400° F. In a medium-sized mixing bowl, sift together the flour, baking powder, and salt. With a pastry blender, cut in the 7 tablespoons butter until the mixture resembles small peas. Add the buttermilk and mix well with hands. Shape the dough into a ball.

On a floured surface, roll out the dough to ½-inch thickness. Cut out the biscuits with a biscuit cutter and place on an ungreased baking sheet. In a small bowl, stir together the egg and water. Brush the egg wash on the biscuits and bake for 25 – 30 minutes or until golden brown.

Brush the hot biscuits with the melted butter. Makes 12 biscuits.

Yield: 6 servings

THE RED LION INN
Stockbridge, Massachusetts

THE RED LION INN
Stockbridge, Massachusetts

Roast Goose Grand Marnier

One 10 – 12-pound goose, excess skin, fat, neck, and giblets
   removed
1 recipe *Grand Marnier Sauce* (see recipe below)

Preheat oven to 425° F. Rinse out the cavity of the goose and place breast-side down in a roasting pan on a rack high enough to keep the goose from touching the fat that is released. Roast for 30 minutes.

Turn the goose breast-side up and reduce the temperature to 350° and roast for 3 – 3 ½ hours more, or until the legs can be twisted. Carve the goose and serve immediately with the sauce.

Grand Marnier Sauce

2 cups apple cider vinegar
2 cups granulated sugar
¾ cup (1 ½ sticks) melted butter

LONGFELLOW'S WAYSIDE INN

When you think of quaint New England towns, covered bridges, and New England clam chowder, it's difficult not to think about history. Robert Purrington's inn enjoys the unusual distinction of being immortalized in 1863 by poetic genius Henry Wadsworth Longfellow in his famous poem, *Tales of a Wayside Inn.*

While you wait to be seated for dinner, stop by the Red Stone School House next door. Even this little building has a special place in history; it is the source of the poem, *Mary's Lamb* by Sarah Hale, with the famous first line "Mary had a little lamb." You'll be interested to know this little school house was also the school with "all the rules, where the children laughed and played." Come and experience a bit of history.

1 cup all-purpose flour
6 cups hot chicken stock
1 teaspoon vegetable oil
2 medium oranges, each sliced and cut into sixths
5 ounces Grand Marnier liqueur
Dash Kitchen Bouquet seasoning

In a medium-sized saucepan, heat together the vinegar and sugar and reduce until sticky (test with a spoon). Set aside.

In a heavy saucepan, melt the butter and add the flour, mixing to form a paste-like roux. Cook for a few minutes, but do not brown or burn the roux. Add the hot stock to the roux and blend with a wire wisk until smooth. Add the reserved vinegar mixture.

In a small skillet, heat the oil and sauté the oranges for 2 – 3 minutes. Add the liqueur (Warning: This will flame!). When the flame dies down, add the liqueur mixture and the seasoning to the sauce and stir together well. Keep warm.

Yield: 4 to 6 servings

LONGFELLOW'S WAYSIDE INN
South Sudbury, Massachusetts

Roast Duck with Honey-Lime Sauce

Two 4 ½-pound ducks, excess skin, fat, neck, and giblets removed
Salt and freshly ground pepper
1 medium onion, sliced and divided
½ medium orange, unpeeled, sliced, and divided
1 lemon, unpeeled, sliced, and divided
½ cup honey
¼ cup fresh lime juice
1 ½ teaspoons grated lime rind
1 teaspoon cornstarch dissolved in ½ teaspoon water

Preheat oven to 450° F. Rinse out the cavities of the ducks and pat dry. Sprinkle the ducks inside and out with the salt and pepper. Stuff each duck with the onion, orange, and lemon slices. Prick the skin around the thighs, backs, and lower breasts. Place the ducks breast-sides up on racks in a large deep roasting pan and roast for 45 minutes.

Drain off fat from the ducks and continue roasting until the juices run clear when the thickest part of the thighs are pierced, about 45 minutes. Cool the ducks to room temperature.

Reduce the temperature to 400°. Split the ducks in half, cutting down the backs and through the breasts. Pull out all exposed bones and discard. Halve each piece by cutting between the breasts and thighs. Place the pieces skin-side up in another large roasting pan and roast until the skin is crisp, about 15 minutes.

Meanwhile, combine the honey, lime juice, and lime zest and bring to a simmer in a heavy small saucepan over medium heat, stirring frequently. Whisk in the cornstarch mixture, stirring constantly, until the sauce thickens and clears, about 30 seconds.

Arrange the duck on serving plates, crossing the wings and legs. Spoon the sauce over the duck and serve immediately.

Yield: 4 servings

OLIVER LOUD'S INN/RICHARDSON'S CANAL HOUSE
Pittsford, New York

RICHARDSON'S
CANAL HOUSE

Rose Inn Honey-Almond Duck

**One 4 ½ – 5-pound duck, excess skin, fat, neck, and giblets
  removed
Cooked wild rice**

**Glaze:
½ cup honey
¼ cup orange marmalade
½ cup sliced almonds
2 tablespoons Dijon mustard**

Preheat oven to 250° – 275° F. Rinse out the cavity of the duck and place the duck breast-side up in a roasting pan just big enough to hold snugly. Do not use a roasting rack. Cook for 5 – 6 hours. Drain off fat and let the duck cool. Remove the backbone and the rib cage, leaving only the leg and wing bones. Cut the duck into quarters and scrape off any bits of fat that still remain under the skin.

Increase the temperature to 450°. Place the duck pieces skin-side up in a lightly greased baking pan and cook for 10 – 15 minutes, or until the skin is crisp.

Reduce the temperature to 400° . In a small bowl, mix together all of the ingredients for the glaze. Spoon the glaze on top of each duck piece and cook for 6 – 10 minutes more, or until the almonds are toasted. Serve immediately with the wild rice.

Yield: 4 servings

ROSE INN
Ithaca, New York

Grilled Duck Breasts❖

1 ½ pounds ripe plums, pitted and chopped
4 cups chicken stock or duck stock
5 cups port wine
¼ cup brandy
2 tablespoons kirschwasser brandy
2 tablespoons raspberry wine vinegar
¼ cup heavy cream
¾ cup (1 ½ sticks) butter, chilled
½ pound fresh chanterelle mushrooms
Eight 6 – 8-ounce duck breasts

In a large saucepan, combine the plums and stock and bring to a boil. Reduce heat and simmer until the skins pop. Strain into a second saucepan, forcing the fruit through a strainer to puree. Add the port, both brandies, and vinegar to the puree and bring to a boil. Reduce heat and simmer, stirring frequently, until reduced by half. Add ⅛ cup of the cream and simmer, stirring frequently, until again reduced by half.

Add the remaining cream and simmer until the sauce begins to thicken and clarify. Add ½ cup of the butter, bit by bit, whisking continuously until thickened. Keep warm over warm water until ready to use.

In a medium-sized saucepan, melt the remaining butter and sauté the mushrooms until the butter is absorbed. Add the reserved plum sauce and toss with the mushrooms until coated. Keep the sauce warm over hot water, while cooking the duck.

Grill the duck breasts over a medium flame. The breasts should be resilient to the touch and still slightly pink when done.

Thinly slice the duck breasts. Ladle the sauce onto serving plates and fan the slices across the sauce. Serve immediately.

Yield: 8 servings

SHELBURNE INN/THE SHOALWATER RESTAURANT
Seaview, Washington

Cornish Game Hens with Spicy Sausage Stuffing & Red Chile-Pecan Sauce❖

1 cup fresh orange juice
⅛ cup chopped onions
½ teaspoon minced garlic
3 Rock Cornish hens, rinsed and fat and giblets removed
3 tablespoons butter
1 ½ tablespoons Worcestershire sauce
1 recipe *Red Chile-Pecan Sauce* (see recipe below)
1 recipe *Pat's Cranberry Salsa* (see recipe below)

Stuffing:
½ pound ground spicy sausage
3 tablespoons butter
½ medium white onion, chopped
3 slices day-old bread, cubed
1 tablespoon minced fresh parsley
½ teaspoon dried sage
½ teaspoon dried thyme
¼ cup chopped apples
¼ cup chopped pears
¼ cup red seedless grapes

In a small bowl, combine the orange juice, ⅛ cup chopped onions, and garlic. Place the hens in a large deep container and pour the orange juice mixture over the hens. Marinate in the refrigerator for 1 hour, reserving the marinade. Set aside the hens.

In a medium-sized skillet, cook the sausage until browned. Drain the fat and set aside.

For the stuffing: In a small saucepan, melt the butter and sauté the onion for 3 – 5 minutes or until golden. In a small mixing bowl, combine the bread, reserved sausage, and the herbs. Pour in the onion mixture and mix well with a large wooden spoon. Stir in the fruit.

Preheat oven to 425° F. Stuff each hen and place in a roasting pan. In a small saucepan, melt the butter and add the Worcestershire sauce and reserved marinade. Baste the hens with this mixture. Roast the hens for 10 minutes. Reduce the temperature to 350° and continue roasting, basting frequently, for 1 hour 15 minutes.

Cut the hens in half lengthwise and serve immediately with the pecan sauce and the salsa.

Red Chile-Pecan Sauce

5 Ancho chiles
5 mild Hatch green chiles
2 cups chicken broth
3 cloves garlic, minced
1 ½ teaspoons salt
4 tablespoons peanut oil
4 tablespoons olive oil
¼ teaspoon white wine vinegar
3 tablespoons pure maple syrup
⅔ cup fresh orange juice
1 cup chopped toasted pecans

Shake most of the seeds out of the chiles. In a medium-sized saucepan, bring the chiles and broth to a boil. Cover and simmer for 15 minutes, adding the garlic the last 5 minutes.

In a blender, puree the chile mixture (some small pieces of skin will remain). Add the salt. Return the puree to the saucepan and simmer on low heat, covered, for about 15 minutes.

In the blender, puree both oils, vinegar, syrup, orange juice, and pecans until smooth. Add to the chile mixture and heat through. Keep warm until ready to serve.

Pat's Cranberry Salsa

2 fresh kumquats, chopped
2 cups chopped dried cranberries
½ cup balsamic vinegar
3 green onions, chopped
2 medium white onions, chopped
1 bunch fresh cilantro, chopped

In a medium-sized bowl, stir together all of the ingredients. Chill for 1 hour before serving.

Yield: 6 servings

GRANT CORNER INN
Santa Fe, New Mexico

Breast of Pheasant Veiled in Port

Four 1 ½-pound young female pheasants
1 medium onion, chopped
2 cloves garlic, chopped
1 medium carrot, chopped
1 stalk celery, chopped
½ leek, chopped
1 bay leaf
Salt and pepper to taste
½ cup red wine
½ cup white wine
4 cups veal stock
2 cups chicken stock
5 ounces pork fatback, cut into ⅛-inch strips
10 tablespoons (1 ¼ sticks) butter
2 cups port wine

With a sharp knife, make an incision in the pheasants' necks. Oil your fingers and work them between the skin and flesh and pull off the skin. Cut off the legs and wings, leaving 1-inch wing bones attached to the breasts. Set aside the breasts.

Chop the wing tips and carcasses and roast in large deep saucepan. Add the onion, garlic, carrot, celery, leek, bay leaf, salt, and pepper and roast until golden in color. Add the red and white wines and reduce by three-fourths. Add both stocks and simmer for 3 hours, skimming the fat. Strain and set aside the stock.

Lard the breasts with the fatback.* In the saucepan, melt 4 tablespoons of the butter and sauté the breasts until golden. Cook until still pink inside, about 5 minutes more on each side. Remove the breasts and keep warm.

Deglaze the saucepan with the port wine. Set over high heat and reduce by two-thirds. Add the reserved stock and reduce until liquid becomes syrupy. Slowly stir in the remaining butter. Pass the sauce through fine-mesh sieve into another saucepan. Adjust the seasoning.

Place the breasts on serving plates and pour the sauce over each.

THE POINT

The Point is one of the "Great Camps" built by millionaires in the Gilded Age as vacation retreats. The Point still retains its quality as a superior getaway location. A unique part of American history, The Point has always been an exceptional example of Adirondack architecture with all that goes with being among the best—extremely romantic, wonderfully comfortable, and extraordinarily beautiful.

USA Today rated The Point #1 in American lakeshore resorts, and The Point is a member of the prestigious, Paris-based Relais & Chateaux Association. Owners David and Christie Garrett fell in love with the hotel in 1981 and acquired it in 1986. One of the Garretts' highest priorities is award-winning fine cuisine for their guests. They are advised by the Michelin three-star chef, Albert Roux of Le Gavrochein London. The Point is famous for its dinner party atmosphere, which the *New York Times* says "makes one feel like an old friend at a country house party."

The recipe for pheasant was created by former chef Neil Wigglesworth.

Serve immediately.

*To lard the breasts: Draw the fat strips through the breasts with a larding needle or thin knife and place the strips about ½ – 1 inch apart, at right angles to the breast bone.

Yield: 4 servings

THE POINT
Saranac Lake, New York

Baby Pheasant Sauté

Eight 1 ½-pound young pheasants
Salt and pepper
Flour
¼ cup vegetable oil
¼ cup chopped shallots
2 fresh sprigs each sage, thyme, and rosemary, leaves
**   removed and chopped**
½ cup dry white wine
2 cups sliced fresh mushrooms
½ cup chopped tomatoes
1 cup pheasant or chicken stock
Fresh parsley sprigs

Remove each pheasant breast, keeping the first wing joint attached. Cut the breasts in half and remove whole legs. Use the thighs and reserve the legs for hors d'oeuvres or another meal.

Sprinkle the breasts and thighs with the salt and pepper. Coat with the flour. In a 12-inch skillet, heat the oil over medium-high heat and lightly brown the pheasant, meat-side down, turning once.

Preheat oven to 400° F. Remove the pheasant from the skillet and place in a 15 x 10-inch jelly-roll pan. While preparing the sauce, bake the pheasant for 8 minutes.

Add the shallots and herbs to the skillet and cook, stirring constantly, for 2 minutes. Add the wine, stirring frequently, and reduce by half. Add the mushrooms, tomatoes, and stock and simmer for 5 minutes. Adjust the seasoning.

Arrange two breasts and two thighs on each warmed serving plate and spoon the sauce over the thighs. Garnish with the parsley and serve immediately.

Yield: 8 servings

THE INN AT WEATHERSFIELD
Weathersfield, Vermont

Roast Partridge Dijonnaise

Four 12 – 14-ounce partridges
Salt and pepper
¾ cup (1 ½ sticks) butter, melted
¼ cup chopped shallots
1 cup white wine
1 cup heavy cream
¼ cup Dijon mustard
8 slices bacon, cooked crisp and chopped

Preheat oven to 350° F. Cut all meat from the partridges, leaving wing bones and legs on half birds. Season the meat with the salt and pepper and place in a small roasting pan with 4 tablespoons of the butter. Roast for about 15 minutes.

Meanwhile, in a medium-sized saucepan, sauté the shallots in the remaining butter until tender, about 2 – 3 minutes. Add the wine and reduce in half, stirring frequently. Slowly stir in the cream and reduce until slightly thick, stirring constantly. Stir in the mustard and add the bacon.

Remove the partridge from the oven and place on serving plates. Pour the sauce over the partridge and serve immediately.

Yield: 4 servings

THE HERMITAGE
Wilmington, Vermont

Roasted Quail with White Wine & Cream

1 medium apple, peeled and cubed
3 small carrots, cubed
One 6-ounce package wild rice

THE HERMITAGE

Nestled into the base of southern Vermont's Green Mountains and surrounded by acres of lawns and fields, The Hermitage is a splendid all-season retreat. The inn began life in the eighteenth century as a simple farmhouse. Over the years, the farm became the summer estate of Bertha Eastman Berry, who once edited the renowned Social Register. Today the McGovern family are the owners of this beautiful country inn, which has twenty-nine guest rooms, each individually decorated with superior collections of New England antiquities.

The foundation of a superb country inn has always been fine dining in a gracious, relaxed manner. Over the years, the fame of the Hermitage restaurant has traveled far and wide. Game birds are an important part of the Hermitage heritage and are offered each evening as one of the chef's selections. Raised on the premises, of course, pheasant, goose, duck, and partridge are available year-round.

A 40,000-bottle wine cellar, a priceless collection of hand-carved decoys, and one of the largest collections of Michael Delacroix lithographs in existence are all clear evidence of the eclectic charm of The Hermitage.

12 young quail, dressed (2 per person)
3 tablespoons soy sauce
1 teaspoon garlic powder
1 teaspoon dried tarragon
$\frac{1}{8}$ teaspoon ground rosemary
1 cup all-purpose flour
$\frac{1}{4}$ cup grated Parmesan cheese
$\frac{1}{4}$ cup peanut oil
2 tablespoons chopped fresh parsley or other herbs

Sauce:
$\frac{1}{4}$ cup Chablis wine
1 teaspoon chicken stock base
$\frac{1}{8}$ teaspoon white pepper
2 cups heavy cream

In a medium-sized saucepan, combine the apple and carrot cubes and the rice and cook the rice according to package directions.

Season the quail inside and outside with the soy sauce and half of the garlic powder, tarragon, and rosemary. Stuff each bird with the cooked rice mixture. Set aside the remaining rice.

In a shallow bowl, mix together the flour, cheese, and remaining garlic powder and herbs. Roll each quail lightly in the flour mixture.

Preheat oven to 400° F. In a large ovenproof skillet, heat the oil and sauté the coated quail until light brown. Roast for 8 – 15 minutes, or until juices run clear when the breasts are pierced.

Arrange the reserved rice on a serving platter and place the quail on top. Keep warm. Pour off all but 2 tablespoons of oil from the skillet and add the wine, stirring to loosen pan drippings. Add the chicken base, white pepper, and cream and simmer until thickened, stirring frequently. Pour the sauce over the quail and garnish with the parsley. Serve immediately.

Yield: 6 servings

JORDAN HOLLOW FARM INN
Stanley, Virginia

Oyster & Walnut-Stuffed Lobster

Four 1 ½-pound Maine lobsters, steamed for 4 – 5 minutes
1 recipe *Oyster & Walnut Stuffing* (see recipe below)
6 tablespoons (¾ stick) melted butter

Preheat oven to 450° F. Lay each lobster on its back. Using an 8-inch French knife or small knife, insert the tip into the lobster's mouth and split down to the tail. Carefully open the lobster without breaking in half. Remove the brain located behind the lobster's eyes and fill all of the lobsters with the stuffing.

Place the lobsters in a large broiler pan, shell-side down, and divide the butter evenly over the top of the stuffing and bake for 10 – 15 minutes, or until the tail meat is cooked.

Oyster & Walnut Stuffing

8 ounces crackers
1 ½ cups chopped walnuts
½ pint fresh oysters, shucked and chopped; reserve juice
3 ounces dry sherry
½ teaspoon salt

In a medium-sized bowl, crush the crackers. Add the walnuts, oysters, reserved juice, and sherry and gently stir together. Season with the salt.

Yield: 4 servings

THE 1661 INN/HOTEL MANISSES
Block Island, Rhode Island

Jumbo Black Tiger Shrimp Stuffed with Lobster Mousse

20 jumbo (10 – 15 count) black tiger shrimp, peeled and
**   deveined, split belly, tail up**
1 ¼ cups *Lobster Mousse* (see recipe below)
1 ½ cups *Champagne Butter Sauce* (see recipe below)
4 teaspoons chopped fresh parsley
4 bundles fresh herb sprigs

Preheat oven to 425° F. Place the shrimp in a large baking pan with the tails fanned upward. With the chilled mousse in a pastry bag, pipe ½ ounce of the mousse into the center of each shrimp. Flash bake the shrimp for 8 minutes.

Place the butter sauce in the center well of four warmed serving plates and coat the plates well. On each plate, place five shrimp, clockwise, starting at right of center and sprinkle with the parsley. Place one herb bundle in the center of the shrimp and serve immediately.

Lobster Mousse

4 pounds cooked lobster meat
2 large eggs
3 cups heavy cream
Pinch salt
Pinch white pepper

Chill the lobster meat, food processor bowl, and blade in the freezer for 15 minutes. Place the lobster in the food processor bowl and finely chop. Chill for 30 minutes.

Remove from the refrigerator and using the pulse switch, add the eggs and heavy cream, in stages, to the lobster meat. Add the salt and white pepper. Control the consistency of the mousse by adjusting the amount of cream: too little cream, and the mousse will be rubbery; too much, and the mousse will break. Test by dropping a little mousse in boiling water and repeat, adding more cream until the desired texture is achieved.

Transfer the mousse to a glass bowl and chill for 1 hour before using. Makes 5 pounds (6 – 8 servings). (The mousse can be frozen for up to one month.)

Champagne Butter Sauce

1 ounce chardonnay wine
3 ounces champagne
⅛ cup minced shallots
10 whole black peppercorns
1 bay leaf
½ cup heavy cream
1 ½ cups (3 sticks) unsalted butter, at room temperature

In a medium-sized saucepan, combine the first five ingredients and reduce over medium heat until nearly dry, stirring frequently.

Remove from heat and add the cream. Return to heat and reduce by half, stirring constantly. Strain. Gradually whisk in the butter until thickened. Keep warm until ready to use. Makes 2 cups.

Yield: 4 servings

RICHMOND HILL INN
Asheville, North Carolina

Gulf Shrimp with Drambuie Cream Sauce

1 ½ tablespoons olive oil
12 large shrimp (12 – 20 count), peeled and deveined; reserve
  shells for stock
¼ cup Drambuie liqueur
¼ cup *Shrimp Stock* (see recipe below)
½ cup heavy cream
4 tablespoons (½ stick) unsalted butter, cut into bits
Pinch dried thyme
Salt to taste
Freshly ground pepper to taste
2 tablespoons vegetable oil
1 leek, thoroughly washed and julienned (white part only)
2 stalks celery, julienned
1 – 2 medium zucchini, julienned
Salt and pepper to taste

In a large saucepan, heat the olive oil and sauté the shrimp over medium heat for 2 minutes, or until the shrimp start to blush. Add the liqueur and flame. Immediately add the stock and cream, scraping up any bits that cling to the pan bottom. Reduce heat to simmer and cook for 2 minutes.

Add the butter, thyme, salt, and freshly ground pepper, shaking the pan constantly until the butter melts. Set the shrimp mixture aside and keep warm.

In a large skillet, heat the vegetable oil and sauté all the vegetables until tender, about 6 – 8 minutes. Season with the salt and pepper.

Divide the vegetables equally on four serving plates. Remove the shrimp from the sauce and fan out three shrimp alongside or on top of the vegetables on each plate. (The sauce may have to be reheated.) Pour the sauce over the shrimp and vegetables and serve immediately.

VERMONT MARBLE INN

The elegant Vermont Marble Inn commands a stately view of the village green in the fair town of Fair Haven, Vermont. Set on five acres of tastefully landscaped grounds, the inn is a quaint, sedate, and elegant retreat.

Built in 1867 of Vermont's own golden marble, this Victorian mansion features twelve-foot ceilings and carved moldings. A broad string staircase leads to the guest rooms, which are all named after English authors. Marble fireplaces, crystal chandeliers, and exquisite mahogany furniture adorn this old mansion.

Proprietors Rich and Bea Taube and Shirley Stein create an intimate and romantic atmosphere in their two stately dining rooms. The Breakfast Banquet is a tradition at the inn. The chef at the Vermont Marble Inn uses only fresh, hand-selected ingredients in all preparations. The baking is done personally by Bea, and the dining room flickers with elegance for your breakfast—by candlelight.

CHALET SUZANNE

The Hinshaw family has been making people feel welcome at their central Florida country inn and restaurant for more than fifty years. This enchanting thirty-room inn situated on a gracious seventy-acre estate is an oasis of serenity amidst the excitement of one of America's most popular tourist meccas.

The essence of the Chalet's reputation, however, is its glorious cuisine served in a unique setting of five quaint rooms on several levels overlooking Lake Wales—soups, which challenge the appetite, hot homemade potato rolls, relishes made from tropical fruits, and entrées of uncompromising excellence. Just as no two rooms are alike in the inn, no two tables are alike in the dining rooms, nor are the chairs, silver, or table settings. Enjoy dinner by candlelight, surrounded by fresh flowers with china selected from the family collection, composed of English or German porcelain, Italian pottery, or elegant Limoges.

Chalet Suzanne's ambience suggests a rich, eclectic combination of worldly tastes—Persian tiles, ornate Spanish ironwork, Egyptian copper pitchers. Every corner glows with antiques, stained glass, and old lamps from faraway places.

Shrimp Stock

4 cups water
Reserved shrimp shells

In a large saucepan, combine the water and shells and bring to a rapid boil. Boil for 1 hour, or until the liquid is reduce by half. Strain and reserve ¼ cup for sautéing the shrimp. (The remaining stock may be frozen.)

Yield: 4 servings

VERMONT MARBLE INN
Fair Haven, Vermont

Shrimp Curry Suzanne

⅓ cup butter
3 tablespoons all-purpose flour
1 – 2 teaspoons curry powder
½ teaspoon salt
¼ teaspoon ground paprika
Dash ground nutmeg
2 cups light cream
3 cups cooked shrimp
1 tablespoon finely chopped candied ginger
1 tablespoon fresh lemon juice
1 teaspoon cooking sherry
1 teaspoon onion juice
Dash Worcestershire sauce
Salt to taste

Preheat oven to 400° F. In a large saucepan, melt the butter and blend in the flour, curry, salt, paprika, and nutmeg. Gradually stir in the cream and cook until the mixture thickens, stirring constantly. Add the remaining ingredients and heat through.

Pour the mixture into a baking dish and bake for 10 minutes, or until the top is lightly browned. Serve immediately with choice of condiments: chutney, orange zest, flaked coconut, chopped roasted peanuts, watermelon pickles.

Yield: 4 servings

CHALET SUZANNE
Lake Wales, Florida

Scampi Mediterranean

2 teaspoons butter
Salt and pepper to taste
1 – 2 tablespoons chopped fresh parsley
2 cups cooked pasta acini di Pepe
1 teaspoon minced garlic
2 tablespoons Italian dressing
20 jumbo shrimp (10 – 15 count) peeled and deveined, tails on
4 tablespoons olive oil
40 pine nuts
2 ounces cognac or brandy
2 tablespoons chopped shallots
½ teaspoon curry powder
4 tablespoons tomato paste
½ teaspoon chicken stock base
1 cup white wine
1 cup heavy cream
Fresh parsley, chopped

Add the butter, salt, pepper, and the 1 – 2 tablespoons parsley to
the cooked pasta. Set aside the pasta and keep warm.

In a small bowl, stir together the garlic and dressing. Place the
shrimp in a shallow glass baking pan and pour the dressing
mixture over the shrimp. Turn to coat and marinate for 1 hour,
turning once.

ROSE INN

Arrange ½ cup of the reserved pasta on each of four warmed
serving plates, making a semicircle inside each plate. Cover and
place in a warm oven.

In a large sauté pan, heat the oil and brown the pine nuts.
Remove the nuts with a slotted spoon and drain on paper towels.
Set aside. Remove the shrimp from the marinade. In the same
hot sauté pan, sauté the marinated shrimp in the remaining hot
oil for 1 minute on one side. Turn the shrimp, add the cognac,
and flambé for 1 minute.

Remove the shrimp with a slotted spoon to the prepared plates,
arranging five shrimp per plate in a fan shape with the tails
pointing to the center of the plate. Cover and return to the oven.

Add the shallots and curry to the same pan, stirring constantly
with a wooden spoon for 30 seconds. Stir in the tomato paste,
chicken base, and wine, and bring to a rapid boil to reduce wine.
When the oil begins to separate from the sauce, stir in the cream

and reduce until desired consistency, stirring constantly. Pour the sauce over the shrimp and garnish with the toasted pine nuts and additional parsley. Serve immediately.

Yield: 4 servings

ROSE INN
Ithaca, New York

Shoalwater Seafood Fettuccine❖

6 tablespoons (¾ stick) unsalted butter
1 medium red onion, julienned
4 teaspoons minced garlic
8 ounces fresh crabmeat, shredded
1 ½ pounds small shrimp (8 ounces meat), peeled, deveined, and shredded
6 ounces ouzo liqueur
2 cups heavy cream
1 ½ pounds (6 cups) fresh fettuccine pasta, cooked
4 teaspoons dried parsley
2 teaspoons salt
1 teaspoon pepper
2 cups grated Parmesan cheese

In a medium-sized saucepan, melt the butter and sauté the onion and garlic for 3 – 5 minutes, or until the onion is translucent. Add the crabmeat and shrimp and toss to combine. Heat through.

Add the liqueur and reduce enough to evaporate the alcohol. Add the cream and pasta and stir once to combine, then cook until the sauce has thickened and darkened in color. Gently stir in the parsley, salt, pepper, and 1 ½ cups of the cheese and blend well.

Place the pasta on serving plates and top with the remaining cheese. Serve immediately.

Yield: 4 servings

SHELBURNE INN/THE SHOALWATER RESTAURANT
Seaview, Washington

Louisiana Rice & Shrimp❖

2 cups uncooked long grain white rice
1 cup (2 sticks) butter
1 cup chopped onions
4 stalks celery, chopped
1 medium green bell pepper, chopped
½ pound fresh mushrooms, sliced
½ cup all-purpose flour
1 ½ cups heated milk
¾ cup white wine or to taste
1 tablespoon chopped pimientos
¼ cup chopped fresh parsley
½ tablespoon Tabasco sauce
¾ teaspoon cayenne pepper
Salt to taste
1 ½ – 2 pounds cooked medium shrimp
¼ cup sliced almonds
½ pound grated cheddar cheese

Cook the rice according to package directions. Set aside.

In a large saucepan, melt the butter and sauté the onions, celery, bell pepper, and mushrooms for 4 – 6 minutes, or until the onions are translucent. Add the flour, blending well until the mixture forms a paste. Stir in the milk, wine, and pimientos and cook over low heat until the sauce is thick, about 5 – 8 minutes. Add the parsley, Tabasco sauce, cayenne, salt, and shrimp.

Preheat oven to 350° F. Remove the shrimp mixture from the heat and mix in the reserved rice and almonds. Spread the mixture in a greased 9 x 13-inch baking dish and cover with the cheese. Bake for 20 – 25 minutes, or until the cheese is completely melted. Serve immediately.

Yield: 8 servings

THE HIDDEN INN
Orange, Virginia

Baked Scallops❖

1 ¼ cups fresh bread crumbs
3 cloves garlic, minced
3 tablespoons finely minced onions

THE NEWCASTLE INN

The Newcastle Inn is a full-service inn overlooking the beautiful Damariscotta River, an ever-changing scene caused by daily tides. The inn is situated in a residential section of the town and is a ten-minute walk to the town center of Damariscotta, a picturesque four-season coastal village in midcoast Maine.

The Newcastle Inn is located in the heart of Native American history, which can be experienced first hand in the nearby town of Damariscotta. The Native American heritage and artifacts can be seen, heard, and felt throughout this enchanting coastal region.

Innkeepers Ted and Chris Sprague offer their guests five-course meals, which are prepared by Chris. *Food and Wine Magazine* calls Chris's breakfast, "not just another way to start the day." The cocktail hour is 6:00 P.M. at The Newcastle and, after cocktails, please be seated for a romantic candlelit dinner.

¼ cup chopped fresh parsley
¼ cup dry white wine
3 tablespoons fresh lemon juice
Salt to taste
Freshly ground pepper to taste
½ cup (1 stick) unsalted butter, melted
2 tablespoons olive oil
1 ½ pounds fresh bay scallops, gristle removed and patted dry
½ pound fresh mushrooms, thinly sliced
Salt to taste
Freshly ground pepper to taste

In a medium-sized bowl, mix together the bread crumbs, garlic, onions, parsley, wine, lemon juice, salt, and pepper. Pour the melted butter over the mixture and mix gently. Set aside.

Preheat the oven to 450° F. In a medium-sized skillet, heat the oil and briefly sauté the scallops and mushrooms, about 1 – 2 minutes. Drain well and season with the salt and pepper.

Fill a well-greased, shallow 2-quart baking dish with the scallops and mushrooms. Spoon the reserved bread crumb mixture over the top and bake for 8 minutes, or until the topping is golden brown. Serve immediately.

Yield: 6 servings

THE NEWCASTLE INN
Newcastle, Maine

Asian Crab Cakes❖

2 cups cracker meal; reserve 1 ½ cups
1 pound fresh crabmeat, drained well and shredded
1 green onion, finely chopped
½ medium red bell pepper, finely chopped
1 pound Gruyère cheese, grated
1 ½ teaspoons sesame oil
1 egg white
1 tablespoon sake (rice wine)
1 tablespoon soy sauce
1 tablespoon grated fresh gingerroot
½ teaspoon minced garlic
¼ teaspoon black pepper
Peanut oil

2 cups *Red Pepper & Ginger Mayonnaise* (see recipe below)
Fresh chive blossoms

In a large bowl, combine ½ cup of the cracker meal and the remaining ingredients, except the peanut oil and mayonnaise. Shape
into 2-inch diameter x ¼-inch thick patties, carefully forming the
edges. Coat with the reserved 1 ½ cups cracker meal and set aside.

Coat the bottom of a frying pan with a thin layer of the peanut oil.
Over medium-heat, sauté the cakes until golden on both sides.

Pour ¼ cup of the mayonnaise on each plate and top with two
cakes. Garnish with the chive blossoms and serve immediately.

Red Pepper & Ginger Mayonnaise

2 medium red bell peppers, roasted, peeled, and seeded
1 cup mayonnaise
2 ½ teaspoons sesame oil
3 tablespoons sake (rice wine)
1 teaspoon soy sauce
1 teaspoon minced garlic
2 tablespoons grated fresh gingerroot

In a blender or food processor, combine all of the ingredients and
puree until smooth. If prefer a smoother sauce, pass the
mixture through a fine-mesh strainer. Makes 2 cups.

Yield: 8 servings

SHELBURNE INN/THE SHOALWATER RESTAURANT
Seaview, Washington

Maine Crab Cakes Chesapeake Style

¾ cup mayonnaise
3 eggs, slightly beaten
4 slices fresh white bread, processed to medium-fine crumbs
1 tablespoon Old Bay Seasoning
1 tablespoon dry mustard
1 tablespoon chopped fresh chives
1 tablespoon chopped fresh oregano
1 tablespoon chopped fresh basil
2 tablespoons butter

BARROWS HOUSE

The new owners of the Barrows House are Linda and Jim McGinnis, and they both are very proud of their century-old country inn. This beautiful inn is a varied complex of eight buildings nestled exquisitely into eleven lushly wooded acres in Dorset, Vermont.

Built around 1804, the main building and seven other structures offer a range of accommodations from rustic to plush for groups as large as twenty-five people. With two full-time chefs, the Barrows House has earned a reputation for delectable and unusual dining and is a fine example of the best in American regional cuisine.

½ **medium red bell pepper, finely diced**
½ **medium Spanish onion, finely diced**
1 **pound fresh crabmeat, shredded**

In a medium-sized bowl, mix together the first eight ingredients until well blended. Set aside.

In a small skillet, melt 1 tablespoon of the butter and sauté the bell pepper and onion until tender, about 3 – 5 minutes. Add the bell pepper mixture to the mayonnaise mixture and gently fold in the crabmeat. Shape into 2-inch patties.

In a large skillet, melt the remaining butter and sauté the patties over medium-high heat until brown on both sides. Serve immediately.

Yield: 4 servings

BARROWS HOUSE
Dorset, Vermont

Red Snapper with Jalapeño-Lime Marinade❖

2 **fresh jalapeño peppers, seeded and chopped***
⅓ **cup chopped yellow onions**
1 **heaping tablespoon minced fresh gingerroot**
1 **teaspoon minced fresh rosemary**
1 **teaspoon salt**
¼ **cup fresh lime juice**
¼ **cup water**
1 ½ **pounds fresh red snapper fillets, bones removed and fat trimmed**
½ **cup** *Seasoned Flour* **(see recipe below)**
2 **teaspoons butter**
2 **teaspoons olive oil**
Fresh lime wedges

In a blender or food processor, puree the peppers, onions, gingerroot, rosemary, salt, lime juice, and water to make a thick marinade. Place the fish in a shallow glass baking pan and cover with the puree. Marinate for 1 – 2 hours in the refrigerator, turning occasionally.

Remove the fillets from the marinade and lightly dredge in the

seasoned flour, shaking off any excess. In a large skillet, melt the
butter and oil over medium heat and sauté the fillets for 3 – 4
minutes per side, or until the fish flakes easily with a fork.

Arrange the fillets on a serving platter and garnish with the lime
wedges. Serve immediately.

*When working with hot peppers, wear plastic gloves and keep
hands away from eyes and face.

Seasoned Flour

½ cup all-purpose flour
1 ¼ teaspoons dried rosemary
1 ¼ teaspoons dried marjoram
¼ teaspoon salt
¼ teaspoon black pepper
⅛ teaspoon cayenne pepper

In a small bowl, combine all of the ingredients and mix together
well. (The flour can be made in larger quantities and keeps well
in the refrigerator.)

Yield: 4 servings

STEAMBOAT INN
Steamboat, Oregon

Basil Tuna with Red Pepper Coulis

2 medium red bell peppers
1 tablespoon olive oil
3 cloves garlic, peeled
¾ cup fish broth or fish bouillon
3 tablespoons crème fraîche
Dash salt
Dash white pepper
1 recipe *Basil Tuna Steaks* (see recipe below)

Preheat oven to 425° F. Cut the peppers in half lengthwise.
Remove the stems and seeds and brush the skins with the oil.
Place the peppers, skin-side up, on a baking sheet and bake for 10
minutes.

Add the garlic cloves to the baking sheet and bake for about 10
minutes more, or until the skins of the peppers are charred.

Immediately place *only* the peppers in a paper bag and fold bag. (This steams the peppers and helps loosen the skin.) Set aside to cool.

When peppers are cool, peel and discard the skins. In a food processor, place the roasted peppers and garlic and process until smooth. Transfer the mixture to a small saucepan and stir in the broth. Bring to a boil. Reduce heat and simmer for about 5 minutes or until reduced to 1 ⅓ cups, stirring frequently. Whisk in the crème fraîche, salt, and pepper and blend well.

Place the tuna steaks on serving plates and spoon the coulis around the fish. Serve immediately.

Basil Tuna Steaks

Four ½-pound 1-inch thick fresh tuna steaks
2 tablespoons olive oil
2 tablespoons chopped fresh basil

Brush the tuna with the oil and sprinkle with the basil. Wrap in plastic wrap and chill for 1 hour.

To grill the fish, place the fish on a grill rack and grill on an uncovered grill directly over medium-hot coals for 4 – 6 minutes per ½-inch thickness, or until the fish flakes, turning once. Or to broil the fish, place the fish on the unheated rack of a broiler pan and broil 4 inches from heat for 4 – 6 minutes per ½-inch thickness, or until the fish flakes, turning once.

Yield: 4 servings

THE 1661 INN/HOTEL MANISSES
Block Island, Rhode Island

Flounder Picasso

1 ¾ pounds fresh flounder fillets
6 tablespoons all-purpose flour
6 tablespoons (¾ stick) butter
2 kiwis, peeled and coarsely chopped
1 banana, cut lengthwise and halved
8 whole strawberries, rinsed, hulled, and halved
¾ cup finely chopped fresh pineapple
¾ cup coarsely chopped apples
3 tablespoons Grand Marnier liqueur

Salt and pepper to taste

Lightly dredge the flounder in the flour. Shake off excess.

In a large sauté pan, melt the butter and slowly sauté the fillets over medium heat until the fish flakes easily with a fork. Remove and place on the serving plates. Keep warm.

Add all of the fruit to the sauté pan and stir over low heat for 3 minutes. Add the liqueur and flambé. Season with the salt and pepper. Top each serving of the fish with the fruit mixture and serve immediately.

Yield: 4 servings

THE 1661 INN/HOTEL MANISSES
Block Island, Rhode Island

Cedar-Planked Grouper with Lemon Vinaigrette

2 – 3 *untreated* cedar planks or shakes
Six 7-ounce fresh grouper fillets
⅓ cup olive oil
1 tablespoon minced garlic
1 ½ teaspoons cracked black peppercorns
Finely grated rind of 1 lemon
1 recipe *Lemon Vinaigrette* (see recipe below)

Soak the *untreated* planks in water the night before preparing the grouper. Partially dry the planks in a 200° oven for only 10 minutes.

In a small bowl, combine the oil, garlic, peppercorns, and lemon zest. Place the fillets in a shallow glass baking dish and rub the oil mixture on the fillets. Marinate for 1 hour.

Preheat broiler to 450° F. Place 2 – 3 marinated fillets on each untreated plank and place on the rack closest to the broiler. Broil for 5 minutes, then turn the fillets and broil 4 minutes more. (The planks will begin to blacken and release a small amount of smoke. This is the desired effect.)

Place the fillets on serving plates and drizzle the vinaigrette over the top. Serve immediately.

THE INN AT BLACKBERRY FARM

Blackberry Farm was built fifty years ago of mountain stone, shingles, and slate to ramble over its own special setting in the ancient Great Smokey Mountains — almost as if it grew from a sapling, like the trees that populate the surrounding 1,100 acres of protected woodlands.

Nowhere is Blackberry Farm's hospitality more evident than in the dining room. Imagine a crackling fire, flickering candlelight, and exquisite, freshly prepared cuisine, which is best described as elegantly classic New American with a southern flair.

Guests have been absolutely ebullient about their experiences at Blackberry Farm with comments ranging from ". . . a Ritz Carlton in the woods . . . a Cloister in the hills" to "If Nobel prizes were given to the best innkeepers, Gart and Bernadette Doyle would certainly be the winners."

Lemon Vinaigrette

½ cup fresh lemon juice
¼ cup rice wine vinegar
1 egg yolk
½ teaspoon salt
1 cup olive oil
2 tablespoons melted butter
1 tablespoon chopped fresh chives
2 teaspoons chopped fresh lemon thyme
½ teaspoon cracked black peppercorns

In a blender or food processor, blend together the lemon juice, vinegar, egg yolk, and salt. In a small bowl, combine the oil and butter and while still running, drizzle the oil mixture into the blender until the vinaigrette thickens.

Pour the vinaigrette into a small bowl and stir in the herbs and peppercorns. Makes 2 cups.

Yield: 6 servings

"Planking" fish is a cooking technique borrowed from Native Americans, some of whom would nail fish to cedar planks and roast their catch over an open fire. Warning: Only untreated cedar planks are to be used.

THE INN AT BLACKBERRY FARM
Walland, Tennessee

Morning Baked Bluefish

One 8 – 10-pound fresh bluefish, dressed
1 teaspoon salt
1 teaspoon pepper
½ bunch fresh dill, coarsely chopped
½ bunch fresh basil, coarsely chopped
½ bunch fresh parsley, coarsely chopped
2 large carrots, coarsely chopped
1 large onion, coarsely chopped
5 stalks celery, finely chopped
¼ cup white wine
¼ cup butter, melted

Season the bluefish inside and out with the salt and pepper. In a medium-sized bowl, mix together the herbs and vegetables.

Stuff the fish with the vegetable mixture and place the fish upright in a large baking pan. Place any remaining vegetable mixture around the fish. Pour the wine and butter over the fish and bake for 45 minutes, or until the fish flakes easily with a fork. Serve immediately.

Yield: 8 servings

THE 1661 INN/HOTEL MANISSES
Block Island, Rhode Island

Fresh Pacific Salmon with Olive Oil & Herbs

1 – 2 tablespoons extra-virgin olive oil
Six 6-ounce fresh salmon fillets
½ cup extra-virgin olive oil
Juice of 2 lemons
Juice of 2 limes
2 tablespoons chopped fresh Italian parsley
2 tablespoons chopped fresh cilantro
2 tablespoons chopped fresh dill
Salt and pepper to taste

Heat and brush a grill with the 1 – 2 tablespoons oil. Grill the fillets, skin-side up, for 4 minutes on each side.

In a small bowl, mix together the ½ cup oil, lemon juice, lime juice, herbs, salt, and pepper. Set aside.

Preheat oven to 350° F. Remove the grilled fillets and place in a large shallow baking pan. Brush the fillets with the reserved sauce and bake for 3 – 4 minutes, or until the fillets flake easily with a fork. Serve immediately.

Yield: 6 servings

CARTER HOUSE/HOTEL CARTER
Eureka, California

Hotel Carter
INTIMATE ACCOMMODATIONS
EXTRAORDINARY CUISINE

Cranberry-Blueberry Salmon❖

¾ cup dry white vermouth
1 ¼ cups white wine

¾ cup *Cranberry-Blueberry Mustard* (see recipe below)
¾ cup (1 ½ sticks) butter, chilled and cut into small bits
Six 6-ounce fresh salmon fillets

In a small saucepan, stir together the vermouth and ¾ cup of the wine and bring to a boil. Reduce over high heat to between ½ and ¼ cup, stirring frequently. Add the mustard and whisk thoroughly. Bring to a boil, whisk, and remove from heat. Whisk in the butter, a bit at a time, until the sauce has thickened and turned glossy. Set aside and keep warm.

Preheat oven to 475° F. Place the fillets in a large shallow baking pan and bake with the remaining wine for 10 – 12 minutes, or until the fillets flake easily with a fork.

Pool ¼ cup of the mustard sauce on each serving plate and place the fillets on top of the sauce. Serve immediately.

Cranberry-Blueberry Mustard

1 ½ cups fresh cranberries
1 ½ cups fresh blueberries
⅔ cup raspberry vinegar
⅔ cup granulated sugar
¼ cup port wine
⅔ cup Coleman's dry mustard
1 cup water
6 egg yolks

In a large saucepan, mix together the cranberries, blueberries, vinegar, sugar, and wine and cook until the cranberries begin to pop, about 15 minutes. Set aside to cool.

In a blender or food processor, puree the cooled cranberry mixture and strain through a medium-mesh sieve. Set aside.

In the top of a double boiler, combine the dry mustard and water and beat until smooth. Add the egg yolks, one at a time, whisking constantly until the mixture thickens.

Remove from heat and stir in the reserved cranberry puree. Makes 4 cups. (The mustard can be stored in the refrigerator for two weeks.)

Yield: 6 servings

SHELBURNE INN/THE SHOALWATER RESTAURANT
Seaview, Washington

Poached Salmon in Cabbage Leaves

1 head green cabbage
Salt
One 3 – 3 ½-pound fresh Norwegian salmon fillet
1 recipe *Court Bouillon* (see recipe below)
1 recipe *Saffron Sauce* (see recipe below)

Steam the whole head of cabbage, removing the outer leaves
while cooking. Remove the head and drain. Cut out the core
and lightly pound the leaves with a meat cleaver, making them
larger and more tender.

Lightly salt the fillet and wrap with the cabbage leaves. Place the
fillet in a poacher and poach in the boullion for about 15 minutes.

Remove the fillet from the poacher and slice into 5-inch pieces.
Place each piece on a serving plate and cover with the saffron
sauce. Serve immediately.

Court Bouillon
2 quarts water
1 bay leaf
1 small onion, peeled
½ cup coarsely chopped celery
¼ cup chopped carrots
1 cup dry white wine
½ teaspoon salt
2 tablespoons dried parsley

In a poacher, bring the water to a boil, then add the remaining
ingredients. When the water returns to a boil, place the fillet on the
poaching tray and immerse in the water. Immediately reduce heat
to simmer and poach, uncovered, for required amount of time.

Saffron Sauce

1 cup fish stock
1 cup chicken stock
1 cup white wine
1 bay leaf
2 shallots
1 small clove garlic
4 tablespoons (½ stick) butter
2 tablespoons all-purpose flour

½ cup heavy cream
4 pieces orange zest
Salt and pepper to taste
¼ teaspoon saffron threads
½ cup diced fresh plum tomatoes
1 tablespoon chopped fresh dill

In a large saucepan, combine the first six ingredients. Bring to a boil and reduce by half.

In a small saucepan, melt the butter and stir in the flour to make a roux. Add the roux to the sauce and stir until lightly thickened. Add the cream, orange zest, salt, pepper, and saffron and simmer for 3 – 5 minutes. Strain and return the sauce to the saucepan.

Before serving, add the tomatoes and dill, stirring to just combine. Makes 1 ½ cups.

Yield: 4 servings

INN AT SAWMILL FARM
West Dover, Vermont

Baked Whitefish with Apples & Mustard Sauce

4 tablespoons (½ stick) butter
6 tablespoons all-purpose flour
1 ½ cups seafood stock or chicken stock
1 cup white wine
¾ cup apple cider
14 teaspoons stone-ground mustard
4 teaspoons Dijon mustard
Salt and pepper to taste
¼ cup heavy cream
Four 8-ounce fresh whitefish fillets
2 large red tart apples, unpeeled and very thinly sliced

In a small saucepan, melt the butter and stir in the flour to make a roux, cooking until light and foamy. Set aside to cool.

In a large saucepan, blend together the stock, wine, and ½ cup of the cider and bring to a boil. Gradually add the reserved roux, whisking constantly until the mixture heavily coats a spoon. Stir in 10 teaspoons of the stone-ground mustard, the Dijon mustard, salt, and pepper. Whisk in the cream and blend well. Set aside and keep warm.

Preheat oven to 350° F. Place the fillets in a large shallow baking dish and spread the remaining stone-ground mustard on the fillets. Top with the apple slices and remaining cider and bake until the fillets flake easily with a fork, about 5 – 7 minutes for a Lake Michigan whitefish fillet.

Place each fillet on a serving plate and pour the reserved mustard sauce over the top. Serve immediately.

Yield: 4 servings

THE WHITE GULL INN
Fish Creek, Wisconsin

Boneless Trout Supreme

Four 8-ounce fresh trout fillets
Salt and pepper
Poultry seasoning
Flour
3 tablespoons clarified butter*
1 lemon, halved
1 cup dry white wine
8 medium fresh mushrooms, sliced
½ cup heavy cream
4 teaspoons chopped fresh parsley
4 – 6 lemon slice twists

Rinse the trout in cold water and pat dry with paper towels. Lightly season the insides with the salt, pepper, and poultry seasoning. Close the trout and dredge in the flour, shaking off excess.

In a large skillet, melt the butter and sauté the fillets until lightly browned. Turn to brown the other side and squeeze the lemon juice over all. When cooked through, place the fillets on serving plates and keep warm.

Deglaze the hot skillet with the wine and add the mushrooms. Reduce the wine by half, stirring frequently. Stir in the cream and parsley and continue cooking until slightly thickened.

Pour the sauce over the warmed fillets and garnish with the lemon twists. Serve immediately.

THE WHITE GULL INN

The White Gull Inn is located in the picturesque village of Fish Creek in the heart of Wisconsin's Door Peninsula, known for its miles of rugged shoreline and natural beauty. The prestigious Peninsula Players Summer Theatre and the Peninsula Music Festival are located here, and the Door County fish boil is a long-standing tradition in Fish Creek.

Since 1896, the inn has been in continuous operation—first, across the frozen waters of Green Bay and now in its present location, after having been painstakingly relocated, building by building.

Andy and Jan Coulson offer three meals a day to their guests in their beautiful dining room. Breakfast features White Gull Granola, freshly brewed coffee, and pure Door County maple syrup. The inn uses only fresh produce, and the desserts change seasonally to reflect the best locally available fresh fruits.

Yield: 4 servings

THE HERMITAGE
Wilmington, Vermont

To make clarified butter: Melt butter over low heat. When completely melted, remove from heat and let stand until the milk solids settle to the bottom. Skim off the butterfat from the top and store the clarified butter in a sealed container in the refrigerator for no more than 24 hours. Clarified butter can be frozen for 3 – 4 weeks.

Baked Catfish

Six 8-ounce fresh catfish fillets
One 12-ounce can evaporated milk
1 ¼ cups all-purpose flour
⅔ cup grated Parmesan cheese
½ teaspoon baking powder
1 teaspoon onion powder
¼ teaspoon garlic powder
1 tablespoon ground paprika
½ teaspoon Greek Cavender's or Italian seasoning
½ teaspoon salt
1 teaspoon pepper
½ cup (1 stick) butter
½ cup margarine
Toasted almonds or pecans

Place the fillets in a shallow glass baking pan large enough to lay the fillets flat. Pour the milk over the fillets and marinate overnight in the refrigerator.

Preheat oven to 400° F. In a medium-sized bowl, mix together the next nine ingredients and dredge the fillets in this mixture.

In a small saucepan, melt together the butter and margarine. Place the marinated fillets on a greased, rimmed baking sheet and drizzle the butter mixture over the fillets. Bake for 20 minutes. Do not turn.

Place the fillets on warmed serving plates and top with the almonds. Serve immediately.

Yield: 6 servings

THE BURN
Natchez, Mississippi

CHAPTER 6

Side Dishes

Mushroom Strudel with Potato-Leek Sauce❖

4 tablespoons (½ stick) sweet butter
6 cups minced fresh mushrooms
1 teaspoon salt
¼ teaspoon curry powder
½ cup sherry
4 tablespoons chopped shallots
1 cup sour cream
½ cup dried bread crumbs
1 package frozen phyllo dough, thawed
½ cup (1 stick) sweet butter, melted
1 cup dried bread crumbs
1 recipe *Potato-Leek Sauce* (see recipe below)
Fresh parsley

In a large skillet, melt the butter and sauté the mushrooms with the salt, curry, sherry, and shallots over medium-low heat until the mushrooms are tender and the liquid is evaporated, about 20 minutes. Cool. Stir in the sour cream and the ½ cup bread crumbs and mix together well. Set aside.

Carefully unwrap the dough and place one sheet of the dough on a large working surface. Brush with ⅛ cup of the melted butter and sprinkle with ¼ cup of the 1 cup bread crumbs. Repeat the procedure for a total of four layers.

Spoon one-quarter of the reserved mushroom mixture onto the narrow end of the dough. Turn the long sides of the dough in about one inch to seal the filling. Roll the dough in jelly-roll fashion. Brush the roll with the butter and sprinkle with a few more crumbs.

Preheat oven to 375° F. Place the roll on a lightly greased baking sheet and mark with a sharp knife four equal slices. Repeat the procedure using the remaining mushroom filling to make three more strudels. Bake the strudels for 25 minutes.

Spoon the sauce on each serving plate and place two slices of the strudel on top of the sauce. Garnish with the parsley and serve immediately.

Potato-Leek Sauce

3 medium baking potatoes, peeled and quartered

2 leeks, sliced (white part only)
2 cups chicken stock
Salt to taste
Freshly ground white pepper to taste
½ cup heavy cream

In a large saucepan, combine the potatoes, leeks, and stock and cook over medium heat until the potatoes are tender, about 15 minutes.

In a food processor, combine the potato mixture, salt, and white pepper and puree, while slowly adding the cream. Keep warm until ready to use.

Yield: 8 servings

INTERLAKEN INN
Lake Placid, New York

Glazed Carrots, Turnips & Chestnuts❖

½ pound carrots, sliced into ⅛-inch rounds
½ pound turnips, sliced into ⅛-inch rounds
¾ cup (1 ½ sticks) butter
2 tablespoons brown sugar
One 8-ounce can whole water chestnuts, drained and well rinsed
Fresh whole nutmeg

In a medium-sized saucepan, cook the carrots and turnips in boiling salted water until crisp-tender, about 4 – 6 minutes. Drain under cold water and set aside.

In a medium-sized skillet, melt the butter and add the sugar and the reserved carrots and turnips. Toss to cover all surfaces and cook until the sugar has dissolved and made a glaze for the vegetables.

Cut the water chestnuts into matchstick pieces and add ¼ cup of the pieces to the skillet and heat through. Grate the nutmeg over the top of the vegetables and mix together. Serve immediately.

Yield: 6 servings

THE FEARRINGTON HOUSE
Pittsboro, North Carolina

Honey-Mustard Carrots❖

2 tablespoons butter
2 tablespoons minced shallots
1 pound carrots, diagonally sliced
¼ cup dry white wine
2 tablespoons honey
1 tablespoon Dijon mustard
1 tablespoon chopped fresh chives

In a medium-sized noncorrosive saucepan, melt the butter and sauté the shallots and carrots for 5 minutes.

Add the wine and cook for 10 minutes more, or until the carrots are crisp-tender and the liquid is nearly evaporated.

Add the honey and mustard and cook for 5 minutes more. Toss in the chives and serve immediately.

Yield: 4 servings

STEAMBOAT INN
Steamboat, Oregon

Broccoli with Two Sauces❖

1 large head fresh broccoli, trimmed and cut into florets
2 cups mayonnaise
4 large hard-cooked eggs, chopped
1 small onion, grated
1 teaspoon Worchestershire sauce
2 tablespoons vegetable oil
1 ½ cups grated sharp cheddar cheese

In a medium-sized saucepan, steam or blanch the broccoli until crisp-tender, about 5 – 7 minutes. Drain quickly and rinse under cold water. Set aside.

Preheat oven to 325° F. In a medium-sized bowl, combine the mayonnaise, eggs, onion, Worchestershire sauce, and oil.

Place the reserved broccoli in a shallow baking dish and spread the mayonnaise mixture over the broccoli. Top with the cheese and bake for 10 minutes, or until heated through and the cheese has melted. Serve immediately.

GLEN-ELLA SPRINGS INN

Yield: 6 servings

GLEN-ELLA SPRINGS INN
Clarksville, Georgia

Cauliflower with Sun-Dried Tomatoes❖

1 pound cauliflower, separated into bite-sized florets
8 slices sun-dried tomatoes packed in garlic-basil olive oil
1 tablespoon seasoned oil from the tomatoes
2 cloves garlic, minced
⅓ cup chicken stock
2 tablespoons thickly sliced green onion tops
¼ teaspoon salt (if using unsalted stock)
Dash cayenne pepper

In a medium-sized saucepan, blanch the cauliflower in lightly salted water for 10 minutes. Drain and immerse in ice water to stop the cooking process. Drain again and set aside.

Cut the sun-dried tomatoes into ¼-inch dice. Set aside.

In a medium-sized skillet, heat the oil and sauté the garlic for 3 – 5 minutes or until soft. Add the reserved tomatoes and the chicken stock and bring to a boil. Reduce heat and simmer for 2 minutes. Add the reserved cauliflower and toss to combine. Cook for 5 minutes more. Add the green onions, salt if needed, and cayenne. Serve immediately.

Yield: 4 servings

STEAMBOAT INN
Steamboat, Oregon

Fried Green Tomatoes❖

6 medium green tomatoes, cut into ¼-inch slices
1 ½ cups buttermilk
1 cup cornmeal
½ cup unbleached all-purpose flour
1 tablespoon salt
Freshly ground pepper to taste

1 ½ teaspoons cayenne pepper
2 teaspoons dried thyme
¼ cup peanut oil
¼ cup vegetable oil

In a large bowl, soak the tomato slices in the buttermilk. In a small bowl, mix together the cornmeal, flour, salt, black pepper, cayenne, and thyme.

In a large skillet, heat both oils and dredge the tomato slices in the cornmeal mixture. Add the coated tomato slices and sauté over medium heat for 2 minutes per side or until golden.

Drain on paper towels and serve immediately.

Yield: 6 servings

THE FEARRINGTON HOUSE
Pittsboro, North Carolina

Jenelle's Tomatoes Rockefeller❖

4 – 6 medium to large tomatoes
4 tablespoons butter
1 small onion, diced
2 cloves garlic, pressed
½ cup fresh whole-wheat bread crumbs
1 teaspoon dried oregano
½ teaspoon dried basil
⅛ teaspoon dried rosemary
Salt and pepper to taste
One 10-ounce package frozen chopped spinach, well thawed
   and drained*
1 egg, well beaten
¼ cup grated Parmesan cheese

Cut off the blossom end of the tomatoes and scoop out the pulp with a serrated spoon. (Reserve the pulp for other uses.) Turn the tomatoes upside down to drain on paper towels.

In a medium-sized skillet, melt the butter and sauté the onion and garlic for 3 – 5 minutes, or until the onion is soft. Stir in the next six ingredients and remove from heat. Add the egg and cheese and mix together well. Cool.

THE FEARRINGTON HOUSE

This highly regarded country inn consisting of fourteen guest rooms, nine suites, and a sophisticated award-winning restaurant is the crown jewel of Pittsboro's village center—a delightful European-style village of craft shops, bookstores, food emporiums, tennis courts, and elegant, private residences.

Jenny and R. B. Fitch have developed an oasis of country life and style that respects the history of the original 1786 farm purchased by Jesse Fearrington's great-great-great grandfather. Located only eight miles south of Chapel Hill, the 640-acre farm was purchased by the Fitch's in 1974 and has evolved into what can only be described as a magnificent obsession.

Although the dairy barn and silo still dominate the landscape of the village and "designer cattle," known as Belted Galloways, still graze peacefully in the meadow, the spirit of the inn today is captured in Fearrington's Main House and its restaurant, which has received the AAA Four-Diamond award for culinary excellence. You must go to Fearrington!

Preheat oven to 400° F. Stuff the reserved tomato shells with the cooled spinach mixture and place on a baking sheet. Bake for 20 minutes, or until the tops are slightly browned and crunchy. Serve immediately.

*Fresh spinach can be used in this recipe, but there is no appreciable difference, so use fresh or frozen, whichever is convenient.

Yield: 4 to 6 servings

DAIRY HOLLOW HOUSE
Eureka Springs, Arkansas

THE REDBUD INN

Innkeeper Jan Drammer's Redbud Inn is located in historic Murphys, California, a town in the heart of California's gold country and known as the "Queen of the Sierra."

The Redbud Inn is a classic American country inn with eleven tastefully appointed guest rooms and suites with fireplaces, whirlpool tubs, and private balconies, where you can enjoy your morning coffee beneath the sycamore trees. The inn is also the first newly constructed inn to be built in this thoroughly charming town in the past 136 years.

As you savor the local chardonnay and the inn's innovative and elegant appetizers, take time to gaze through the large, beautiful bay window in the Redbud dining room: with a little imagination, it is almost possible to see the dusty, sunbaked faces of the California dreamers who came to Murphys in search of the mother lode a century ago.

Grilled Eggplant

2 – 3 Japanese eggplant (about 12 inches long, 2 inches diameter)
¼ cup good-quality olive oil
2 – 3 cloves garlic, chopped
Salt and pepper to taste

Cut the eggplant into ½-inch slices (do not peel). In a small bowl, combine the oil, garlic, salt, and pepper. Set aside.

In a large shallow glass baking pan, place the eggplant slices and pour the reserved marinade over all. Marinate for 1 – 2 hours, stirring occasionally to evenly coat the eggplant.

Skewer as many slices as possible (about 4 – 6) through the skin on bamboo skewers and grill 3 – 4 inches from the heat over medium-hot coals until lightly browned. Serve hot on the skewers.

Yield: 6 to 8 servings, 2 skewers per person

THE REDBUD INN
Murphys, California

Braised Leeks❖

6 medium leeks
1 tablespoon sweet butter
1 tablespoon olive oil
½ cup good-quality white wine
Pinch granulated sugar

Salt to taste
Fresh whole nutmeg

Cut off the green tops and roots of the leeks and wash thoroughly. Cut into thick slices and soak in water to remove any remaining dirt. Keep rinsing if necessary.

In a large heavy skillet, melt the butter with the oil and sauté the leeks until they begin to look milky, but not browned, about 3 – 5 minutes.

Add the wine, sugar, and salt and grate a generous amount of nutmeg over the top. Cover and simmer until tender, about 10 – 15 minutes. Add more wine (or water) if all the liquid evaporates before the leeks are done. Serve immediately.

Yield: 4 servings

BLUEBERRY HILL
Goshen, Vermont

Sautéed Vegetables❖

4 medium carrots, cut into ⅛-inch diagonal slices
Pinch salt
6 tablespoons (¾ stick) unsalted butter
1 medium onion, chopped
1 clove garlic, minced
1 large shallot, minced
4 small zucchini, cut into ⅛-inch diagonal slices
½ pound fresh shiitake mushrooms, sliced ¼-inch thick
1 medium red bell pepper, julienned
½ pound snow peas, strings removed
1 teaspoon raspberry vinegar
Salt to taste
Freshly ground pepper to taste

In a small saucepan of boiling water, blanch the carrots with the pinch of salt for 4 minutes. Remove from heat and drain. Immediately immerse the carrots in ice water for 2 minutes to stop the cooking. Drain well and set aside.

In a large skillet, melt the butter and sauté the onion, garlic, and shallot for 3 minutes. Add the reserved carrots and sauté for 5 minutes more. Add the zucchini and mushrooms and continue to sauté for another 5 minutes.

Add the bell pepper, snow peas, and vinegar and sauté for 3 minutes more. Season with the salt and pepper and serve immediately.

Yield: 6 servings

THE NEWCASTLE INN
Newcastle, Maine

Spinach & Artichoke Soufflé❖

1 pound fresh spinach, washed, stemmed, and chopped
4 tablespoons sweet butter
½ cup chopped onions
½ cup chopped green bell pepper
½ cup grated Parmesan cheese
2 cups sour cream
One 16-ounce can artichoke hearts in water, drained and finely diced
Salt to taste
Freshly ground black pepper to taste

Preheat oven to 350° F. Lightly butter a medium-sized soufflé dish.

Steam the spinach and drain well. Squeeze out as much liquid as possible and set aside.

In a medium-sized skillet, melt the butter and sauté the onions and bell pepper over medium heat for 5 minutes, or until the onions are translucent. Combine the onion mixture with the reserved spinach, then stir in all of the remaining ingredients.

Pour the mixture into the prepared dish and sprinkle with some more grated cheese. Bake for 30 minutes or until hot and bubbly. Serve immediately.

Yield: 6 servings

BLUEBERRY HILL
Goshen, Vermont

Chèvre Mashed Purple Potatoes

2 pounds purple potatoes, peeled and cut into large cubes
3 tablespoons unsalted butter
½ cup half-and-half
7 ounces soft creamy chèvre cheese
2 teaspoons salt
¾ teaspoon white pepper

Place the potato cubes in a large saucepan and cover with water.
Bring to a boil and cook until fork tender, about 12 minutes.

While the potatoes are cooking, combine the butter, half-and-
half, and cheese and heat until the cheese melts, stirring constantly. Set aside.

Drain the potatoes and return to the saucepan. Cover with a
towel and shake over medium heat for 30 seconds, or until the
potatoes are dry. Add the reserved cheese mixture and mash
with a hand masher until smooth, adding the salt and white
pepper as you mash. Serve immediately.

Yield: 6 servings

CARTER HOUSE/HOTEL CARTER
Eureka, California

Mashed Potatoes
North Coast Style

6 pounds Yukon Gold potatoes or other local variety, peeled
6 tablespoons (¾ stick) sweet butter
2 tablespoons olive oil
3 large Walla Walla onions or other sweet onions, sliced
1 tablespoon brown sugar
Splash balsamic vinegar
2 large cloves garlic, minced
1 ½ cups half-and-half
Kosher salt to taste
Freshly ground pepper to taste
½ cup grated Parmesan cheese
1 cup minced fresh basil
1 ⅛ cups grated Gruyère cheese

HARBOR HOUSE INN BY THE SEA

Three unimaginably beautiful hours of coastline driving north from San Francisco puts you in the tiny cliff-top village of Elk, California. Dean and Helen Turner's splendid Harbor House Inn stands watch over the village from its breathtaking perch at the north end of the settlement.

Built in 1916 by the Goodyear Redwood Lumber Company as an executive guest house, the inn is constructed entirely of virgin redwood with the interior beautifully preserved by hot-polished beeswax. In spite of the warmth and coziness generated by the lovely antiques, mammoth open-hearth fireplace, and the plush Persian rug in the parlor, it's the glass-walled dining room, which dominates the entire west wall, that will stop your heart.

The views from the Harbor House Inn dining room are among the finest on the entire North Coast. Nevertheless, the outstanding meals of organically grown vegetables and herbs, naturally raised meats, and homemade desserts served at the inn might distract your attention from the ever-changing Pacific just long enough for a dining experience you will never forget.

Place the potatoes in a large pot and boil in salted water until tender, about 20 – 25 minutes.

In a large skillet, melt 2 tablespoons of the butter with the oil and sauté the onions over low heat for 20 minutes. Add the sugar, vinegar, and garlic and continue to sauté for 10 minutes more. (Onions should be slightly carmelized.) Set aside.

Drain the potatoes and pass through a food mill. Add the remaining butter and the half-and-half and mix together well. Season with the salt and pepper. (The potatoes should be quite runny.)

Preheat oven to 400° F. Butter a 9 x 13-inch glass baking dish. Layer half of the potato mixture, then the reserved onion mixture, the Parmesan cheese, the basil, and the remaining potato mixture. Sprinkle the Gruyère cheese over the entire top. Place the dish on a baking sheet and bake for 30 minutes, or until the potatoes are very hot and well browned. Serve immediately.

Yield: 8 servings

HARBOR HOUSE INN BY THE SEA
Elk, California

Stafford's Herb Duchess Potatoes

6 pounds white Idaho potatoes, peeled and cooked
8 eggs, beaten
½ cup (1 stick) butter, melted
2 teaspoons minced fresh basil
2 teaspoons minced fresh rosemary
2 green onions, minced
Salt and pepper to taste

Preheat oven to 375° F. In a large mixing bowl, whip all of the ingredients together and place, in batches, in a large pastry bag.

Pipe the mixture into large rosettes on a nonstick baking sheet and bake until golden brown, about 25 – 30 minutes. Serve immediately.

Yield: 6 to 8 servings

STAFFORD'S BAY VIEW INN
Petoskey, Michigan

Hawaiian Sweet Potatoes❖

2 ¼ cups cooked and mashed sweet potatoes
¼ cup (½ stick) butter, melted
1 ¼ cups crushed pineapple in juice
⅓ cup packed light brown sugar
⅓ cup evaporated milk
¼ cup raisins
1 egg, beaten
⅛ cup apricot brandy
⅛ cup orange liqueur
1 tablespoon grated orange rind
¼ cup chopped pecans

Preheat oven to 350° F. In a food processor, puree the potatoes and butter. Remove the potato mixture and combine with the pineapple and juice, sugar, milk, raisins, and eggs in a medium-sized bowl.

Stir in the brandy, liqueur, and orange zest and pour into a buttered baking dish. Sprinkle the pecans on top and bake for 20 minutes. Serve immediately.

Yield: 4 to 6 servings

THE HIDDEN INN
Orange, Virginia

Praline Sweet Potatoes❖

4 cups cooked and mashed sweet potatoes
2 cups packed brown sugar, divided
3 eggs, beaten
¼ cup (½ stick) butter
1 teaspoon pure vanilla extract
1 cup chopped pecans
1 cup grated coconut
⅓ cup butter
⅓ cup all-purpose flour

Preheat oven to 350° F. In a large bowl, mix together the potatoes, 1 cup of the sugar, the eggs, ¼ cup butter, and vanilla.

In a small bowl, combine the remaining sugar, the pecans, coconut, ⅓ cup butter, and flour and mix well.

THE HIDDEN INN

Surrounded by seven lushly wooded acres and nestled in historic Orange, Virginia, The Hidden Inn beckons her guests to relax and enjoy true southern hospitality. Ray and Barbara Lonick are as proud of the meticulous attention to detail shown in the restoration of their inn, as they are to the thoughtful touches of candlelight at tea time.

In the morning, you awake to the aroma of home cooking, as the innkeepers prepare your full country breakfast to be served in the large, sunny inn's dining room. Or, if you prefer a lighter morning meal, muffins and morning coffee will be served on the wraparound veranda overlooking the inn's tranquil gardens.

Located just seventy-seven miles west of Washington, D.C., The Hidden Inn is the perfect stepping-off place for exploring Virginia's best wineries and the many famous Civil War sites nearby.

MAST FARM INN

The Mast Farm Inn is located in a beautiful mountain valley between Boone and Banner Elk, North Carolina. This secluded, historic homestead combines country accommodations and family-style dining to create a memorable visit to the North Carolina mountains.

Built in 1885, the Mast Farm Inn was first operated as an inn in the early 1900s and was widely known for its hospitality and good food. In 1972, the Mast Farm was placed in the National Register of Historic Places as one of the best examples of a self-contained mountain homestead in the North Carolina high country. The eighteen-room house has been restored along with the two-room log cabin, springhouse, washhouse, icehouse, large barn, blacksmith shop, and gazebo. Each room is tastefully decorated with mountain crafts and flowers. Guests get the feeling of stepping back into time, but without a loss of modern conveniences.

Inn guests are treated to a hearty breakfast, always including homemade breads, jams, and fresh fruit. The food at Mast Farm Inn has been described as "country cooking with a gourmet touch," and "honest food." Guests enjoy generous portions of fresh vegetables and salads—straight from the garden. There are always hot breads and a choice of two or three freshly baked desserts. Everything is served family style—so help yourself!

Pour the potato mixture into a buttered baking dish and top with the coconut mixture. Bake for 30 – 40 minutes or until golden. Serve immediately.

Yield: 8 servings

INTERLAKEN INN
Lake Placid, New York

Mast Farm Inn Sweet Potato & Apple Casserole❖

3 medium sweet potatoes, peeled and sliced
¼ cup packed brown sugar
¼ cup pecan pieces
¼ cup (½ stick) butter
2 large apples, sliced

Preheat oven to 375° F. Lightly butter a 9 x 13-inch baking pan.

Layer half of the potato slices in the pan. Sprinkle the sugar and pecans over the potatoes and dot with the butter. Arrange the apples in a layer over the butter and top with the remaining potato slices.

Cover tightly with aluminum foil and bake for 1 hour, or until the potatoes are tender. Lightly stir and serve immediately.

Yield: 4 to 6 servings

MAST FARM INN
Valle Crucis, North Carolina

Roasted Polenta with Balsamic Sauce

4 cups chicken stock
2 cups heavy cream
Pinch ground nutmeg
1 teaspoon salt
¼ teaspoon pepper
2 cups coarse cornmeal
¼ cup grated fontina cheese

1 cup grated Parmesan cheese
1 recipe *Balsamic Sauce* (see recipe below)

In a large heavy saucepan, combine the stock, cream, nutmeg, salt, and pepper and bring to a boil. Gradually add the cornmeal, stirring constantly, until the polenta pulls away from the sides of the saucepan, about 10 minutes. Remove from heat and stir in the fontina cheese and ¾ cup of the Parmesan cheese.

Evenly spread the polenta in an oiled tray or rectangular baking pan to a thickness of ¾ inch. Cool to room temperature. Cover and refrigerate.

Preheat oven to 500° F. Cut the cooled polenta into squares or triangles and place on a buttered baking sheet. Sprinkle with the remaining Parmesan cheese and bake until golden brown, about 15 – 20 minutes. Serve immediately with the sauce.

Balsamic Sauce

1 pint balsamic vinegar
1 shallot, chopped
2 quarts chicken or veal stock
6 black peppercorns
2 bay leaves
8 tablespoons (1 stick) unsalted butter
Salt and pepper to taste

In a large heavy saucepan, combine the vinegar and shallot and bring to a boil. Reduce over high heat, stirring frequently, to a syrup consistency. Add the stock, peppercorns, and bay leaves and reduce over high heat, stirring frequently, to a sauce consistency. Strain.

Bring the mixture to a boil again. Reduce heat to low and whisk in the butter, 1 tablespoon at a time. Season with the salt and pepper. Keep warm until ready to serve.

Yield: 6 servings

HARBOR HOUSE INN BY THE SEA
Elk, California

Poppy Seed-Wild Rice Patties❖

¼ cup uncooked wild rice
1 cup water

2 teaspoons salt
2 small baking potatoes, peeled and cooked
2 egg yolks, slightly beaten
1 tablespoon sour cream
4 slices bacon, diced
4 scallions, thinly sliced
1 tablespoon minced fresh parsley
Pinch ground marjoram
Salt and pepper to taste
1 tablespoon poppy seeds
Pinch ground nutmeg
2/3 cup fresh bread crumbs
1 tablespoon butter

In a small saucepan, bring the rice, water, and salt to a boil. Reduce heat and simmer, covered, for 50 minutes. Drain, rinse, and set aside. In a medium-sized bowl, mash the potatoes with the egg yolks and sour cream and set aside.

In medium-sized sauté pan, cook the bacon until crisp. Add the scallions, parsley, and marjoram and sauté for 3 minutes. Cool.

Mix together the reserved potato, rice, and bacon mixtures and season with the salt and pepper. Stir in the poppy seeds, nutmeg, and bread crumbs and chill until firm.

Form the chilled mixture into patties. In the sauté pan, melt the butter and sauté the patties over medium heat until golden brown, about 4 minutes on each side, turning once. Serve immediately.

Yield: 4 servings

GRANT CORNER INN
Santa Fe, New Mexico

Hoppin' John

Rice:
1 tablespoon vegetable oil
2 tablespoons diced bacon
1/3 cup diced onions
1 teaspoon chopped garlic
1 cup converted white rice
2 cups chicken stock
1/2 teaspoon salt
1 tablespoon butter

⅓ cup chopped scallions
⅓ cup diced red bell pepper
⅓ cup diced celery
⅓ cup diced country ham

Black-eyed peas:
1 tablespoon butter
½ cup diced onions
¼ cup diced celery
1 teaspoon minced garlic
1 cup black-eyed peas (soaked in cold water overnight)
¼ teaspoon red pepper flakes
1 bay leaf
½ teaspoon pickling spice
1 tablespoon chopped fresh thyme
1 ham hock

For the rice: In a large saucepan, heat the oil and cook the bacon in the oil until crispy. Add the onions and sauté for 3 – 5 minutes, or until the onions are translucent. Add the garlic and sauté for 30 seconds more. Add the rice, stock, and salt and simmer for 15 minutes.

In a medium-sized skillet, melt the butter and briefly sauté the scallions, bell pepper, celery, and ham, about 2 – 3 minutes. Stir the ham mixture into the rice mixture. Set aside and keep warm.

For the black-eyed peas: In a large saucepan, melt the butter and sauté the onions and celery for 3 – 5 minutes, or until the onions are translucent. Add the garlic and sauté for 30 seconds more. Add the black-eyed peas, pepper flakes, bay leaf, pickling spice, thyme, and ham hock. Cover with water and simmer until the beans are tender, about 1 hour.

Spoon the reserved warm rice on each serving plate, making a well in the center. Spoon the black-eyed peas over the rice and serve immediately.

Yield: 6 servings

THE INN AT BLACKBERRY FARM
Walland, Tennessee

Durham House Texas Pecan Rice

3 cups chicken stock
½ cup (1 stick) butter, divided

DURHAM HOUSE
BED & BREAKFAST INN

Listed in the National Register of Historic Places, this lovely Queen Anne-style, six-room inn has become a popular choice for murder mystery fans all over the southwest. Original mysteries, written exclusively for the inn, are offered for the entertainment of house guests, who become stars in their own mysteries and who help solve the mystery as the plot unfolds.

Whether you select this cozy little inn for its unusual entertainment or its terrific location, just five minutes from downtown Houston, you are in for a nostalgic visit to the Victorian era. The rare 1860 walnut bed in the Rose Room is a particular favorite of innkeeper Marguerite Swanson's regular guests.

¼ teaspoon liquid red pepper seasoning
2 small bay leaves
¼ teaspoon salt
1 ½ cups uncooked long grain white rice
½ cup coarsely chopped pecans

Preheat oven to 350° F. In a medium-sized saucepan, bring the stock, ¼ cup of the butter, pepper seasoning, bay leaves, and salt to a boil. Place the rice in a 10 x 14-inch glass baking dish and pour the hot broth mixture over the rice. Tightly cover with aluminum foil and bake for 30 minutes.

During the last 5 minutes of baking, melt the remaining butter in a small saucepan and sauté the pecans until golden brown.

Remove the rice from the oven and fluff with a fork. Pour the pecans evenly over the rice and serve immediately.

Yield: 6 servings

DURHAM HOUSE BED & BREAKFAST INN
Houston, Texas

Lemon Rice with Almonds❖

1 tablespoon butter
⅓ cup minced onions
1 cup uncooked long grain white rice
1 ¾ cups chicken stock
¼ cup fresh lemon juice
Grated rind of 1 lemon
¼ cup lightly toasted slivered almonds

In a medium-sized saucepan, melt the butter and sauté the onions over medium heat for 5 minutes or until translucent, but not browned.

Blend in the rice and stir until all of the grains are coated. Add the stock, lemon juice, and lemon zest and bring to a a boil. Reduce heat and simmer, covered, for 20 minutes, or until all of the liquid is absorbed. Stir in the almonds and serve immediately.

Yield: 6 servings

THE FEARRINGTON HOUSE
Pittsboro, North Carolina

CHAPTER 7

Breads and Muffins

Wild Rice Bread❖

2 tablespoons active dry yeast
½ cup hot buttermilk (110° – 115°)
2 tablespoons hot honey (110°)
1 tablespoon salt
2 cups well-cooked wild rice, well drained
3 cups all-purpose flour
½ cup melted butter
½ cup warm honey
2 eggs, at room temperature
½ cup warm buttermilk
1 ½ cups all-purpose flour

In a small bowl, dissolve the yeast in the hot buttermilk and hot honey. Set aside.

In a food processor, blend together the salt, rice, and the 3 cups flour until the rice is finely processed.

In a large mixing bowl, combine the rice mixture and reserved yeast mixture. Add the butter, warm honey, eggs, and warm buttermilk. Add enough of the 1 ½ cups flour to form a dough.

Turn out the dough onto a floured surface and knead for 5 – 10 minutes, or until the dough is no longer sticky. Place the dough in a large buttered bowl. Lightly butter the top and cover with a small towel. Let rise until double in bulk. Punch down and knead briefly. Cover and let rise again for 30 minutes.

Place the dough on a floured surface and divide in half. Form into two large balls and let stand for 15 minutes.

Preheat oven to 350° F. Shape the dough into two loaves and place in two buttered 8 ½ x 4 ½-inch loaf pans. Cover and let rise until double in bulk. Bake for 45 minutes, or until the loaves sound hollow when tapped. Cool on a wire rack.

Yield: 2 loaves

OLD RITTENHOUSE INN
Bayfield, Wisconsin

OLD RITTENHOUSE INN

Located on its own emerald green hill in the quiet vacation village of Bayfield, Wisconsin, the Queen Anne-styled Old Rittenhouse Inn has instant appeal. Built during the Civil War, the inn weathered many changes before the current innkeepers, Mary and Jerry Phillips, acquired it.

Built originally as a summer cottage for the Fuller family, the inn now has twenty guest rooms, all furnished with private baths and filled with antique furniture, original lamps, and woodburning fireplaces. The entire inn includes three turn-of-the-century homes, all within a four-block radius in Bayfield's historic district. For the hopelessly romantic, some rooms even have double whirlpool baths.

Evenings are topped off by a six-course gourmet dinner everyday from May to October, but only on weekends from November to April. *The Milwaukee Journal Magazine* featured the inn among their "25 Best Restaurants in Wisconsin." In the midst of history and beauty, the innkeepers not only maintain their award-winning dinners, but they enliven the evening with their own impromptu music performances. Great fun!

Chocolate Bread with Vanilla Butter❖

1 cup milk
2 tablespoons butter
½ cup granulated sugar
1 teaspoon pure vanilla extract
1 package active dry yeast
¼ cup lukewarm water
1 tablespoon granulated sugar
2 eggs, beaten
3 ½ cups all-purpose flour
⅔ cup sifted cocoa
1 cup chopped walnuts
Granulated sugar
1 recipe *Vanilla Butter* (see recipe below)

In a large saucepan, scald the milk. Remove from heat and add the butter, stirring until the butter melts. Add the ½ cup sugar and the vanilla and set aside to cool. In a small bowl, dissolve the yeast in the lukewarm water with the 1 tablespoon sugar and set aside.

When the milk mixture is cool, add the reserved yeast mixture, which should be very frothy. Add the eggs and stir well. Set aside.

Measure the flour and cocoa into a large bowl. Stir in the nuts. Add the reserved milk and yeast mixture and stir vigorously. Turn out the dough onto a floured surface and knead for 5 minutes, adding flour if necessary to yield a smooth dough. Place the dough in a large greased bowl, cover with a small towel, and let rise for 1 hour 30 minutes.

Punch down the dough and let rise again. Knead ten times. Shape and place in a 9 x 5-inch loaf pan. Let rise again for 30 minutes.

Preheat oven to 350° F. Sprinkle sugar on top of the loaf and bake for 30 minutes, or until the loaf sounds hollow when tapped. Cool for 10 minutes in the pan on a wire rack. Serve with the vanilla butter.

Vanilla Butter

¾ cup (1 ½ sticks) butter
2 tablespoons pure vanilla extract
¾ cup confectioners' sugar

HEARTHSTONE INN

In a small bowl, beat all of the ingredients together until smooth and fluffy.

Yield: 1 loaf

HEARTHSTONE INN
Colorado Springs, Colorado

Oatmeal-Molasses Bread

2 cups water
1 cup quick-cooking rolled oats
1 ½ tablespoons butter
1 package active dry yeast
½ cup lukewarm water
½ cup molasses
2 teaspoons salt
4 ⅔ cups all-purpose flour

In a medium-sized saucepan, bring the 2 cups water to a boil. Remove from heat and stir in the oats and butter. Let stand for 1 hour.

In a large mixing bowl, dissolve the yeast in the ½ cup lukewarm water for 5 minutes, stirring until completely dissolved. Add the molasses, salt, and reserved oatmeal mixture, stirring well. Mix in the flour. Turn out the dough onto a floured surface and knead for 8 minutes. Place in a large greased bowl and cover with a small towel. Let rise in a warm place until double in bulk.

Divide into two pieces and shape into two loaves. Place on a non-stick baking sheet, cover, and let rise again until double in bulk.

Preheat oven to 375° F. Bake for 35 minutes, or until the loaves sound hollow when tapped. Cool on a wire rack.

Yield: 2 loaves

RABBIT HILL INN
Lower Waterford, Vermont

THE BABBLING BROOK

Helen King's Babbling Brook inn is at the northern end of Monterey Bay, 90 miles south of San Francisco. Cascading waterfalls, a meandering creek, and a romantic garden gazebo grace one acre of gardens, pines, and redwoods, which surrounds this secluded inn built in 1909 on the foundations of an 1870s tannery, a 1790s gristmill, and 2,000-year-old Indian fishing village.

A large country breakfast and an afternoon wine and cheese buffet complement the inn's twelve Country French guest rooms, all named and themed around artists and flowers. The Monet Room is an outstanding example, done in the artist's favorite delft blue and white hues with an open beam ceiling and private deck with a special view of the restored 1925 cascading waterfall and covered footbridge. This special guest room also has a lovely corner fireplace of imported tiles and a blue moiré-canopied queen-sized bed, complete with down comforter and pristine white embroidered linens. Such elegance!

Persimmon Bread

2 eggs
2 cups packed brown sugar
3 tablespoons butter
2 cups fresh persimmon pulp
2 cups chopped walnuts
1 cup raisins
1 cup chopped dates
1 tablespoon grated orange rind
4 cups all-purpose flour
4 teaspoons baking soda
3 teaspoons baking powder
2 teaspoons ground cinnamon
½ teaspoon ground cloves
½ teaspoon ground allspice
½ teaspoon ground nutmeg
1 cup buttermilk
2 teaspoons pure vanilla extract

Preheat oven to 325° F. In a large mixing bowl, beat together the eggs, sugar, butter, and persimmon. Stir in the walnuts, raisins, dates, and orange zest and set aside.

In a medium-sized bowl, sift together the flour, baking soda, and all of the spices. Add the flour mixture to the reserved egg and fruit mixture alternately with the buttermilk and vanilla.

Pour the batter into two well-greased 9 x 5 x 3-inch loaf pans and bake for 1 hour 15 minutes, or until a tester inserted in the center comes out clean. Cool on a wire rack.

Yield: 2 loaves

THE BABBLING BROOK
Santa Cruz, California

Kiwi-Banana Bread

2 ½ cups all-purpose flour
1 teaspoon baking soda
1 ½ teaspoons baking powder
½ cup margarine
½ cup granulated sugar
2 eggs

2 teaspoons pure vanilla extract
1 ripe banana
3 kiwis, sliced crosswise; reserve 3 slices
½ cup buttermilk
½ cup chopped pecans

Glaze:
½ cup granulated sugar
4 teaspoons fresh lemon juice

Preheat oven to 350° F. In a medium-sized mixing bowl, combine the flour, baking soda, and baking powder and set aside.

In a large mixing bowl, beat the margarine and sugar at medium speed with an electric mixer for 3 minutes. Add the eggs, vanilla, banana, and kiwi slices and mix until well blended. Stir in the buttermilk. Add the reserved flour mixture and mix to moisten.

Pour the batter into a 9 x 5 x 3-inch loaf pan and bake for 1 hour 15 minutes, or until a tester inserted in the center comes out clean. Cool on a wire rack.

In a small saucepan, melt the sugar with the lemon juice over low heat until the sugar has completely dissolved. Spread the glaze over the cooled bread and garnish with the reserved kiwi slices.

Yield: 1 loaf

RANCHO SAN GREGORIO
San Gregorio, California

Old Thyme Inn Best Ever Banana-Walnut Bread

1 ¾ cups all-purpose flour
1 cup granulated sugar
1 teaspoon baking soda
½ teaspoon salt
2 large eggs
2 ripe medium bananas, mashed (1 cup)
½ cup vegetable oil
¼ cup plus 1 tablespoon buttermilk
1 teaspoon pure vanilla extract
1 cup chopped walnuts

RANCHO SAN GREGORIO

Framed by the surrounding oaks and pine-covered hills, Rancho San Gregorio overlooks historic San Gregorio Valley. Here in the days of the Spanish land grants, our early California settlers enjoyed a peaceful, happy, and unhurried lifestyle.

When you enter the iron-trimmed doors of this Spanish mission-style home, you step into a more serene and contemplative time. The heavy redwood beams, bright terra-cotta tile floors, colorful cactus courtyard, and carved oak antiques lend a casual elegance to this delightful country retreat only forty-five minutes from the San Francisco airport.

For morning breakfast, partake of a congenial and hearty selection of fresh fruits, freshly ground coffee, and such featured surprises as home-baked Kiwi-Banana Bread, Chard-Sausage Eggs, Rancho Soufflé, or Swedish Egg Cake with wild blackberry sauce. Bud and Lee Raynor built the inn as their private dream home in 1971 and now share it and their warm hospitality with the first four lucky folks who make reservations each evening.

OLD THYME INN

There are many romantic, Victorian-style inns in America, but there aren't many such inns serving guests today that were built in 1899 and live on in renewed splendor, nestled in a genuine English herb garden with over fifty pampered varieties of herbs and flowers.

Flowers and herbs reign supreme in this exquisite seven-guest room inn. With guest rooms and suites named Rosemary, Thyme, Mint, Lavender, and Chamomile, it's not surprising to find fresh-cut flowers everywhere and to come across a spirited kitchen, which prides itself in fresh homegrown and homemade delights.

Like a lot of people, innkeepers George and Marcia Dempsey clearly enjoy gardening, innkeeping, cooking, and entertaining. Unlike a lot of people, they have managed to turn an avocation into a delightful vocation. George, a former attorney-turned-banker-turned innkeeper is the chef and his creativity abounds. Lemon-Thyme Pound Cake, Banana-Walnut Bread, Orange-Pecan Popovers, and frittatas are regular favorites of returning guests.

Preheat oven to 350° F. In a medium-sized mixing bowl, stir together the flour, sugar, baking soda, and salt and set aside.

In another mixing bowl, combine the eggs, bananas, oil, buttermilk, and vanilla. Add the egg mixture to the reserved flour mixture, stirring just until combined. Fold in the walnuts.

Pour the batter into a greased 9 x 5 x 3-inch loaf pan and bake for 50 – 60 minutes, or until a tester inserted in the center comes out clean. Cool on a wire rack.

Yield: 1 loaf

OLD THYME INN
Half Moon Bay, California

Durham House Pear Bread

3 cups all-purpose flour
1 teaspoon baking soda
1 teaspoon baking powder
1 teaspoon salt
1 tablespoon ground cinnamon
1 cup chopped pecans
¾ cup vegetable oil
3 eggs, slightly beaten
2 cups granulated sugar
2 cups peeled and diced very ripe pears
1 tablespoon pure vanilla extract

Preheat oven to 350° F. In a large mixing bowl, combine the first six ingredients and make a well in the center of the mixture. Set aside.

In a medium-sized bowl, mix together the remaining ingredients and add to the reserved flour mixture, stirring just until moistened.

Spoon into two well-greased and floured 8 ½ x 4 ½ x 3-inch loaf pans and bake for 1 hour, or until a tester inserted in the center comes out clean. Cool for 10 minutes on a wire rack before removing from pans.

Yield: 2 loaves

DURHAM HOUSE BED & BREAKFAST INN
Houston, Texas

Bob's Sour Cream, Orange & Pecan Bread❖

½ cup (1 stick) butter, softened
¾ cup granulated sugar
2 eggs
⅓ cup sour cream
¼ cup fresh orange juice
Grated rind of 2 oranges
1 ¾ cups all-purpose flour
1 ½ teaspoons baking powder
1 ½ cups chopped pecans

Preheat oven to 325° F. In a large mixing bowl, beat together the first five ingredients.

In medium-sized mixing bowl, combine the remaining ingredients and add to the egg mixture. Do not overmix.

Pour the batter into a greased 9 x 5 x 3-inch loaf pan and bake for 45 – 50 minutes, or until a tester inserted in the center comes out clean. Cool on a wire rack.

Yield: 1 loaf

SHELBURNE INN
Seaview, Washington

Very Lemony Lemon Bread

½ cup vegetable shortening
1 ¼ cups granulated sugar
2 eggs, slightly beaten
1 ¼ cups sifted all-purpose flour
1 teaspoon baking powder
½ teaspoon salt
½ cup milk
½ cup finely chopped nuts
Grated rind and juice of 1 lemon

Gingerbread Mansion Inn

Preheat oven to 350° F. In a medium-sized mixing bowl, cream together the shortening and 1 cup of the sugar. Mix in the eggs and set aside.

In a small mixing bowl, sift the flour again with the baking powder and salt. Alternately add the flour mixture and milk to the reserved shortening mixture, stirring constantly. Mix in the nuts and lemon zest.

Pour the batter in a greased 9 x 5 x 3-inch loaf pan and bake for 50 minutes, or until a tester inserted in the center comes out clean.

In a small bowl, mix together the remaining sugar and the lemon juice. Remove the baked bread from the oven. Poke holes in the top with a fork and pour the sugar mixture over the top of the bread. Cool on a wire rack.

Yield: 1 loaf

THE GINGERBREAD MANSION
Ferndale, California

Zucchini Bread❖

2 ½ cups granulated sugar
1 ¼ cups corn oil
4 eggs
1 tablespoon plus ½ teaspoon pure vanilla extract
4 cups all-purpose flour
1 ½ teaspoons salt
2 teaspoons baking soda
1 teaspoon baking powder
4 cups grated zucchini (use medium-sized zucchini)
1 cup raisins or toasted chopped nuts

Preheat oven to 350° F. In a large mixing bowl, mix together the sugar and oil. Beat in the eggs and vanilla.

In another large bowl, sift together the flour, salt, baking soda, and baking powder. Add the flour mixture to the sugar mixture and mix just until blended. Stir in the zucchini and raisins.

Pour the batter into two greased 9 x 5 x 3-inch loaf pans and bake for 45 – 60 minutes, or until a tester inserted in the center comes out clean. Cool on a wire rack.

Yield: 2 loaves

THE SETTLERS INN
Hawley, Pennsylvania

THE SETTLERS INN

The Settlers Inn reflects the architecture of an old English manor house and is located in Hawley, a small Pennsylvania town alive with history and embracing many cultural points of interest in the beautiful Lake Wallenpaupack region of the Poconos.

The building that is now The Settlers Inn is the result of the ups and downs that preceded the emergence of the recreation industry in the Lake Wallenpaupack area. Construction began in 1927, but the inn did not open until shortly after World War II.

Jeanne Genzlinger, the innkeeper, is proud to serve a seasonal menu, featuring locally grown organic fruits and vegetables that complement each dinner choice and that also showcases Pennsylvania wines and beers, matched perfectly to each entrée. According to *Philadelphia Magazine*, "The food at The Settlers Inn is surely the best in the Poconos." Fresh cream, Amish farm cheeses, fresh mushrooms, trout, fresh blueberries, and pure maple syrup all find their way onto the menu at The Settlers Inn.

Peanut Butter Bread❖

4 cups all-purpose flour
2 cups granulated sugar
2 teaspoons salt
4 teaspoons baking powder
2 cups chunky peanut butter
2 eggs
2 cups milk

Preheat oven to 325° F. In a large mixing bowl, mix together the flour, sugar, salt, and baking powder. Add the peanut butter and blend well. Set aside.

In a small bowl, mix together the eggs and milk and add to the reserved peanut butter mixture. Do not beat.

Pour the batter into two greased 9 x 5 x 3-inch loaf pans and bake for 1 hour, or until a tester inserted in the center comes out clean. Cool on a wire rack.

Yield: 2 loaves

HEARTHSTONE INN
Colorado Springs, Colorado

The Governor's Gram's Graham Bread❖

1 ½ cups graham flour
2 cups all-purpose flour
½ cup packed brown sugar
½ cup molasses
2 cups soured whole milk*
2 teaspoons baking powder
1 teaspoon salt

Preheat oven to 350° F. In a large mixing bowl, mix together all of the ingredients until just blended. Spray four small loaf pans with cooking spray.

Pour the batter into the loaf pans and bake for 35 minutes, or until a tester inserted in the center comes out clean. Cool on wire racks for 5 minutes. Remove from pans and continue to cool or serve warm.

Yield: 4 small loaves

THE GOVERNOR'S INN
Ludlow, Vermont

To sour milk: Place 2 tablespoons of cider vinegar in a 2-cup measure. Fill the cup with milk and allow to stand for 5 minutes.

HAWTHORNE INN

The main section of the Hawthorne Inn was built around 1870 on the same road trod by the founding fathers of the nation, the famed "Battle Road" of 1775.   Seven guest rooms, all with private baths are handsomely appointed with antique furnishings, beautifully designed handmade quilts, original art, antique Japanese Ukiyoye prints, and sculpture by innkeeper Gregory Burch.

The Hawthorne Inn is situated on land that once belonged to Ralph Waldo Emerson, the Alcotts, and Nathaniel Hawthorne. It was here, through Emerson's largess, that Bronson Alcott planted his fruit trees and made pathways to the Mill Brook and erected his Bath House.

Directly across the road from the inn, Gregory's innkeeping partner, Marilyn Mudry, is pleased to point out Hawthorne's house, Wayside, and next door to the Wayside is the Alcott's Orchard House. On the other side is Grapevine Cottage, where the Concord grape was developed. History and serenity converge at the Old North Bridge where the "shot heard round the world" was fired, and nearby is Sleepy Hollow Cemetery where Daniel Chester French, Emerson, the Alcotts, the Thoreaus, and Hawthorne himself were all laid to rest. History abounds.

Brown Breakfast Bread

¾ **cup honey**
¾ **cup molasses**
3 ½ **cups whole-wheat flour**
2 **teaspoons baking soda**
2 **teaspoons ground ginger**
2 **teaspoons ground cinnamon**
2 **teaspoons ground allspice**
Dash salt
2 **cups milk**
1 **cup raisins**
2 **tablespoons orange marmalade**

Preheat oven to 350° F. In a large mixing bowl, beat together the honey and molasses. Add the next eight ingredients and mix well. Stir in the marmalade.

Pour the batter into a large buttered baking dish and bake for 1 hour 15 minutes, or until a tester inserted in the center comes out clean. Cool before serving.

Yield: 6 to 8 servings

HAWTHORNE INN
Concord, Massachusetts

Irish Soda Bread

4 **cups all-purpose flour**
1 **teaspoon baking soda**
2 **teaspoons baking powder**
1 **teaspoon salt**
½ **cup (1 stick) butter, softened**

1 cup granulated sugar
2 eggs
1 ¼ cups buttermilk
1 tablespoon caraway seeds
1 cup raisins
2 teaspoons granulated sugar

Preheat oven to 350° F. In a large mixing bowl, combine all of the ingredients, except the 2 teaspoons sugar, and mix until blended. Batter will be stiff.

Turn into a well-greased and floured, 4-quart cast-iron Dutch oven. With a knife, cut a cross on the top of the batter about ¼ inch deep by 4 inches long. (This will help the bread to cook through.)

Sprinkle the remaining sugar over the top and bake for 1 hour. Cool for 15 minutes in the pan. Remove and continue cooling on a wire rack.

Yield: 6 to 8 servings

THE WEATHERVANE INN
South Egremont, Massachusetts

Cheesy Jalapeño Corn Bread❖

1 ½ cups yellow cornmeal
½ cup vegetable oil
2 eggs
1 cup sour cream
1 cup cream-style corn
1 cup grated cheddar cheese
3 teaspoons baking powder
1 teaspoon salt
3 jalapeño peppers, chopped

Preheat oven to 350° F. In a large mixing bowl, combine all of the ingredients and mix just until moistened.

Pour the batter into a greased 9 x 9-inch baking dish and bake for 45 minutes, or until a tester inserted in the center comes out clean. Cool before serving.

Yield: 6 to 8 servings

THE HEARTSTONE INN
Eureka Springs, Arkansas

THE HEARTSTONE INN

Iris and Bill Simantel have created what many people describe as a perfect inn. Surrounded by the proverbial white picket fence, The Heartstone is located on a quiet tree-shaded street in the heart of the Ozarks. Bill and Iris heartily invite you to enjoy what the *New York Times* has described as the "Best Breakfast in the Ozarks."

Stone-Ground Corn Bread

6 tablespoons peanut oil
2 cups good-quality stone-ground cornmeal
1 teaspoon salt
1 teaspoon granulated sugar
1 teaspoon baking powder
1 teaspoon baking soda
2 cups buttermilk

Adjust oven rack to center position. Preheat oven to 400° F.
Add the oil to a well-seasoned, 9-inch cast-iron skillet and heat
to the smoking point in the oven.

Meanwhile, combine all of the dry ingredients in a medium-sized
mixing bowl and blend thoroughly. Set aside.

When the oil is hot, add the buttermilk to the dry ingredients
and mix with a stiff whip. Carefully remove the skillet from the
oven and pour the hot oil into the batter, mixing with the whip
while pouring. Pour the batter into the skillet and bake for 30
minutes or until golden brown and set.

Cool for 10 – 15 minutes in the skillet. Carefully loosen the bread
from the edges with a spatula. Slide the spatula under the bread
and invert onto a flat surface. Place on a serving dish and serve.

Yield: 6 servings

McNINCH HOUSE
Charlotte, North Carolina

Cottage Cheese & Pepper Bread or Rolls❖

1 pound small curd cottage cheese
1 tablespoon melted butter
2 eggs
2 teaspoons freshly ground pepper
2 tablespoons chopped fresh chives or scallion tops
½ cup water
2 teaspoons salt
¼ cup granulated sugar
½ teaspoon baking soda

1 package active dry yeast
¼ cup lukewarm water
4 cups bread flour
Bread flour

In a large mixing bowl, mix together the cottage cheese, butter, eggs, pepper, chives, ½ cup water, salt, sugar, and baking soda. Dissolve the yeast in the ¼ cup lukewarm water.

Add the dissolved yeast and flour to the cottage cheese mixture. Mix and knead the dough until elastic. (This dough tends to be a bit sticky.) Let stand for about 5 minutes and knead again, adding only enough additional flour so the dough can be handled.

Place the dough in a large greased bowl and cover with a small towel. Let rise until double in bulk. Punch down and divide into two loaves or make twenty-four rolls.

Place the loaves in two greased 9 x 5 x 3-inch loaf pans or the rolls in greased muffin cups. Let rise again until double in bulk. Bake the loaves for 50 minutes, or until the loaves sound hollow when tapped, or bake the rolls for about 25 minutes. Remove from pans and cool on a wire rack. (Rolls not served can be frozen.)

Yield: 2 loaves or 24 rolls

THE SETTLERS INN
Hawley, Pennsylvania

Savory Almond-Buttermilk Biscuits❖

3 tablespoons butter, divided
1 small onion, finely chopped
2 cloves garlic, minced
2 cups all-purpose flour
1 tablespoon baking powder
1 teaspoon salt
½ teaspoon baking soda
⅓ cup vegetable shortening
1 cup buttermilk
½ cup toasted and coarsely chopped slivered almonds
2 tablespoons chopped fresh parsley
2 tablespoons chopped fresh herbs (combination sage, rosemary, and thyme)

Preheat oven to 450° F. In a small skillet, melt 1 tablespoon of the butter over medium heat and sauté the onion and garlic for 5 minutes, stirring occasionally. Remove from heat and cool completely.

In a medium-sized bowl, mix together the flour, baking powder, salt, and baking soda. Cut in the shortening with a pastry blender. (Particles of the shortening should remain.) Stir in the buttermilk, almonds, parsley, and herbs to make a soft dough.

Turn out the dough onto a lightly floured surface and knead just until the dough comes together. Pat or roll out the dough to ½-inch thickness and cut out the biscuits with a round biscuit cutter. Place on an ungreased baking sheet, 1 inch apart, and bake for 10 – 15 minutes or until golden brown.

In a small saucepan, melt the remaining butter. Remove the biscuits from the oven and brush the tops with the butter. Serve hot or warm.

Yield: 12 biscuits

DAIRY HOLLOW HOUSE
Eureka Springs, Arkansas

Durham House Sour Cream Heart Scones

½ cup currants
1 cup hot water
2 cups all-purpose flour
3 tablespoons granulated sugar
2 tablespoons baking powder
1 teaspoon baking soda
¾ teaspoon salt
5 tablespoons butter
1 egg, separated
1 cup sour cream

Preheat oven to 425° F. Place the currants in a small bowl and stir in the water. Set aside to cool.

In a medium-sized mixing bowl, combine the flour, sugar, baking powder, baking soda, and salt and mix well. Cut in the butter with a pastry blender until the mixture resembles coarse bread crumbs. Drained the reserved, cooled currants and add to the flour mixture. Stir together well.

In a small bowl, mix together the egg yolk and sour cream, then add to the flour mixture. The mixture will now form a sticky dough. Mix just until it holds together.

Turn out the dough onto a floured surface and knead 6 – 10 times just to form a ball. Pat out the dough to about ¾ inch thick and cut out the scones with a deep heart-shaped cookie cutter. Place the scones on an ungreased baking sheet and bake for 11 minutes. (Do not overbake; bottoms should be tan, sides will still be light.) Cool on a wire rack.

Yield: 10 to 12 scones

DURHAM HOUSE BED & BREAKFAST INN
Houston, Texas

Buttermilk Scones

2 cups all-purpose flour
⅓ cup granulated sugar
1 ½ teaspoons baking powder
½ teaspoon baking soda
¼ teaspoon salt
6 tablespoons (¾ stick) chilled unsalted butter, cubed
1 large egg
½ cup buttermilk
1 ½ teaspoons pure vanilla extract
⅔ cup raisins
Homemade jam
Butter
Clotted cream

Preheat oven to 400° F. In a medium-sized mixing bowl, mix together the flour, sugar, baking powder, baking soda, and salt. Cut in the butter with two knives in a scissorlike motion.

In a small bowl, mix together the egg, buttermilk, and vanilla and pour over the flour mixture. Add the raisins and mix until just combined. (Do not overmix.)

Pat the dough into an 8-inch circle on an ungreased baking sheet and bake for 18 – 20 minutes. Cool on a wire rack. Cut into wedges and serve with the jam, butter, and cream.
(Text continues on page 151, following photographs.)

SEA CREST BY THE SEA

It's not every day that you have an opportunity to sleep on luxurious, Egyptian cotton linen sheets trimmed with Belgian lace. That is unless your name is John or Carol Kirby, and you have decided to leave the "fast lane" and become country innkeepers.

Sea Crest By The Sea is a thirty-five-room mansion with twelve exquisite, private bath guest rooms just a half block from the Atlantic Ocean in charming Spring Lake, New Jersey. Surrounded by opulent summer homes, this century-old inn offers a unique combination of entertaining alternatives for its special guests. There's a croquet court in the side yard, of course, and a rack filled with bicycles in waiting.

Carol's homemade scones and muffins and afternoon teas with "live" music from John's cherished antique player piano await you after your ride along the beach. An extensive collection of fine French and English antiques is combined pleasingly with family heirlooms to provide an environment somewhat like relaxing in a comfortable museum.

Warm Salad of Baked Chèvre & Fresh Baby Greens with Fruit Vinaigrette.
Carter House/Hotel Carter, Eureka, California.

New England Clam Chowder. The Red Lion Inn, Stockbridge, Massachusetts.

Tournedos of Beef with Port Wine Sauce.
Prospect Hill Plantation Inn, Trevilians, Virginia.

Rack of Lamb with Red Currant Sauce.
Interlaken Inn, Lake Placid, New York.

Fresh Pacific Salmon with Olive Oil & Herbs; Chèvre Mashed Purple Potatoes.
Carter House/Hotel Carter, Eureka, California.

PATRICIA BRABANT

Scampi Mediterranean. Rose Inn, Ithaca, New York.

Spectrum of Summer Salad with Herbed
Croquettes of Oklahoma Goat Cheese
& Beet Vinaigrette.
Dairy Hollow House, Eureka Springs, Arkansas.

JOHN McDERMOTT

Loin of Venison with Bourbon & Mango
Chutney Sauce.
L'Auberge Provençale, White Post, Virginia.

CELESTE BOREL

Rose Inn Honey-Almond Duck. Rose Inn, Ithaca, New York.

Buttermilk Scones. Sea Crest By The Sea. Spring Lake, New Jersey.

Morning Baked Bluefish.
The 1661 Inn/Hotel Manisses,
Block Island, Rhode Island.

Mushroom Strudel with Potato-Leek Sauce.
Interlaken Inn, Lake Placid, New York.

Savory Almond-Buttermilk Biscuits. Dairy Hollow House, Eureka Springs, Arkansas.

Wild Berry Cobbler with Lemon Curd Sauce. Carter House/Hotel Carter, Eureka, California.

Lemon Berry Mille-Feuille. Prospect Hill Plantation Inn, Trevilians, Virginia

Three Berry Oat Mousse. The Oaks Bed and Breakfast Inn, Christiansburg, Virginia.

Hazelnut Cheesecake (lower left). Oliver Loud's Inn/Richardson's Canal House, Pittsford, New York.

Indian Pudding. The Red Lion Inn, Stockbridge, Massachusetts.

Wines of the Inn at Sawmill Farm, West Dover, Vermont.

(Recipe begins on page 150, preceding photographs.)

Yield: 6 servings

SEA CREST BY THE SEA
Spring Lake, New Jersey

Chocolate Macaroon Muffins❖

2 cups all-purpose flour
½ cup granulated sugar
3 ½ tablespoons unsweetened Dutch-processed cocoa
1 tablespoon baking powder
½ teaspoon salt
1 egg
1 cup milk
⅓ cup vegetable oil

Filling:
1 ¼ cups sweetened flaked coconut
½ cup sweetened condensed milk
½ teaspoon pure almond extract

Preheat oven to 400° F. In medium-sized mixing bowl, combine the flour, sugar, cocoa, baking powder, and salt and set aside.

In a small bowl, mix together the egg, milk, and oil. Make a well in the reserved flour mixture and pour in the egg mixture, stirring until moistened (mixture will be lumpy).

In another small bowl, mix together all of the filling ingredients and set aside.

Fill greased muffin cups ½ full and spoon about 2 teaspoons of the reserved filling on top of each muffin. Top with the remaining batter and bake for 20 – 22 minutes or until lightly browned. Cool on a wire rack.

Yield: 12 muffins

GRANT CORNER INN
Santa Fe, New Mexico

good!

Cranberry Muffins❖

1 cup fresh cranberries
⅓ cup confectioners' sugar
2 cups unbleached all-purpose flour
2 teaspoons baking powder
½ teaspoon salt
⅓ cup granulated sugar
1 egg, lightly beaten
1 cup milk
3 tablespoons unsalted butter, melted

Preheat oven to 400° F. Grease muffin cups. Pick over, wash, and drain the cranberries. Sprinkle with the confectioners' sugar and set aside.

In a small mixing bowl, sift together the flour, baking powder, salt, and granulated sugar. Sift a second time into a large bowl and set aside.

In a small bowl, stir together the egg and milk, then stir in the butter. Add the milk mixture to the reserved flour mixture, stirring as little as possible, just enough to moisten the dry ingredients. Fold in the reserved cranberries.

Fill prepared muffin cups ⅔ full and bake for 20 – 25 minutes. Cool briefly on a wire rack.

Yield: 12 muffins

THE RHETT HOUSE INN
Beaufort, South Carolina

Bonnie's Lemon-Blueberry Muffins

½ cup milk
Grated rind of 1 lemon
1 tablespoon chopped fresh lemon balm
6 tablespoons (¾ stick) butter, at room temperature
1 cup granulated sugar
2 eggs, slightly beaten
2 cups all-purpose flour
2 teaspoons baking powder

THE RHETT HOUSE INN

The Rhett House Inn is an antebellum house filled with antique furniture and beautifully patterned fabrics. Nestled in historic Beaufort, South Carolina, this authentic bed and breakfast beautifully recreates the feeling of the true Old South. The inn is within convenient walking distance of fine shops and restaurants and one block from the recently restored waterfront, which is a great place to stroll and watch the boats going up and down the Intracoastal Waterway.

The house originally belonged to a southern aristocrat, Thomas Rhett, and his wife, Caroline Barnwell, in the years before the Civil War. Now it is the home of former fashion design and marketing executives, Marianne and Steve Harrison. Their creative flair is evident throughout the inn.

Movie buffs will be interested to know that Barbra Streisand called The Rhett House Inn home during her filming of *The Prince of Tides*, based on the book by local author Pat Conroy. Three-course dinners, including homemade breads, prepared by the owners and served by candlelight are everyday occurrences. Off to the beach? Picnics are one of the specialties of the house at The Rhett!

WHITE LACE INN

As featured in *Country Inns and Back Roads*, the White Lace Inn is nestled in a friendly old neighborhood and is bordered by a white picket fence and surrounded by gardens, lawns, and brick-lined pathways. On a quiet tree-lined residential street, the White Lace Inn is just a two-block walk from historic downtown Sturgeon Bay with its hometown atmosphere.

Innkeepers Dennis and Bonnie Statz offer enchanting guest rooms in three historic homes. The Main House was originally built in 1903 as a grand private residence. Other buildings include a Garden House built in the 1880s and the old-fashioned Washburn House.

A complimentary, homemade continental breakfast is served to guests of the inn in the oak-paneled dining room. Breakfast choices include freshly brewed morning coffee, fresh-baked muffins, breads, or coffee cake along with fresh fruit and juice.

Pinch salt
3 tablespoons fresh lemon juice
2 cups fresh blueberries
Confectioners' sugar

Preheat oven to 400° F. In a small saucepan, heat the milk. Remove from heat and add the lemon zest and lemon balm. Set aside to cool.

In a large mixing bowl, cream the butter and gradually add the granulated sugar, beating until creamy. Slowly add the eggs and beat well. Set aside. In a separate bowl, combine the flour, baking powder, and salt and set aside.

Add the reserved milk mixture to the reserved butter mixture and stir in 2 tablespoons of the lemon juice. Mix together well. Add the reserved flour mixture and blend well. Gently stir in the blueberries until just mixed.

Fill greased muffin cups ¾ full and bake for 20 – 22 minutes. (Do not overbake, muffins will be very light in color, not brown.) Cool on a wire rack.

Whisk together the remaining lemon juice and enough confectioners' sugar to make a thick paste. While muffins are still slightly warm, drizzle the glaze over each muffin.

Yield: 14 to 16 muffins

WHITE LACE INN
Sturgeon Bay, Wisconsin

Apple Strudel Muffins

2 cups sifted all-purpose flour
½ cup packed brown sugar
3 teaspoons baking powder
1 teaspoon salt
½ cup (1 stick) butter
1 – 2 medium apples, peeled and diced
1 egg
⅔ cup milk
¼ cup chopped nuts
1 tablespoon granulated sugar

Preheat oven to 425° F. In a medium-sized mixing bowl, mix together the flour, brown sugar, baking powder, and salt. Cut in the butter with a pastry blender until the mixture resembles cornmeal. Remove ½ cup of the flour mixture and set aside.

Add the apples, egg, and milk to the flour mixture and blend until just smooth. Fill greased muffin cups ⅔ full.

Add the nuts and granulated sugar to the reserved ½ cup flour mixture. Divide evenly on the muffins and bake for about 20 minutes. Cool on a wire rack.

Yield: 12 muffins

THE OAKS HISTORIC BED & BREAKFAST COUNTRY INN
Christiansburg, Virginia

This is a basic muffin recipe that we use to make many variations:
- *Mix flours—whole wheat, oat bran, and all-purpose.*
- *Substitute fruit juice for milk.*
- *Add raisins.*
- *Use chopped firm pears with 1 tablespoon fresh lemon juice.*
- *Soak dried apricots in boiling water, drain and chop.*
- *Substitute chopped fresh cranberries for apples.*

Pookie Muffins

3 eggs, beaten
½ cup vegetable oil
½ cup buttermilk
⅓ cup packed brown sugar
⅓ cup granulated sugar
1 teaspoon pure vanilla extract
1 cup all-purpose flour
1 cup whole-wheat flour
2 teaspoons baking soda
½ teaspoon salt
2 teaspoons ground cinnamon
1 ½ cups shredded apples
1 ½ cups shredded carrots
¾ cup shredded coconut
½ cup chopped dates
½ cup chopped nuts
½ tablespoon grated orange rind

THE BABBLING BROOK

Preheat oven to 375° F. In a large mixing bowl, combine the

eggs, oil, buttermilk, both sugars, and vanilla and set aside.

In a medium-sized mixing bowl, sift together both flours, baking soda, salt, and cinnamon. Slowly add the flour mixture to the reserved egg mixture. Stir in the apples, carrots, coconut, dates, nuts, and orange zest until just mixed.

Filled greased muffin cups ⅔ full and bake for 15 – 20 minutes. Cool on a wire rack.

Yield: 12 muffins

THE BABBLING BROOK
Santa Cruz, California

VICTORIAN TREASURE BED & BREAKFAST

It's 1897 and lumber is king in timber-rich Lodi, Wisconsin. It's not surprising that one of the finest residences built during the era was constructed for lumberyard owner and politician, Senator William G. Bissell.

The Victorian Treasure Bed & Breakfast inn is now located in the Senator's splendid Queen Anne Victorian home in Lodi, a quaint Victorian community with an historic main street and a spring-fed creek running through the center of the town.

Besides the usual, single guest bed & breakfast accommodation, the entire five-guest room inn is available in a unique hospitality package that innkeepers Todd and Kimberly Seidl call "Rent-A-Treasure." For a very reasonable price, your family and friends can privately enjoy every aspect of the inn, including the beveled glass mirrors, brass lighting fixtures, and the elegant furnishings and chandeliers. Plus, they can spend a leisurely time on the elegant wraparound porch, sleep comfortably for the night, and gather together in the morning for a lovely breakfast. Family reunions will never be the same!

Carrot-Apple Muffins

1 ¾ cups all-purpose flour
⅓ cup firmly packed dark brown sugar
½ teaspoon salt
1 ½ teaspoons ground cinnamon
Generous dash ground mace
1 teaspoon baking powder
½ teaspoon baking soda
1 egg, beaten
⅔ cup crushed pineapple in juice
½ cup vegetable oil
2 teaspoons pure vanilla extract
2 cups shredded carrots
½ cup peeled diced apples
½ cup softened raisins

Preheat oven to 350° F. In a medium-sized mixing bowl, mix together the first seven ingredients.

In another bowl, stir together the egg, pineapple, oil, and vanilla. Add the egg mixture to the flour mixture and stir to combine. Stir in the carrots, apples, and raisins.

Fill greased muffin cups ⅔ full and bake for 15 – 20 minutes. Cool on a wire rack.

Yield: 20 muffins

VICTORIAN TREASURE BED & BREAKFAST
Lodi, Wisconsin

Maple Spice Muffins*

¾ cup whole-wheat flour
⅔ cup all-purpose flour
¼ cup quick-cooking rolled oats
1 teaspoon baking powder
1 teaspoon ground cinnamon
½ teaspoon baking soda
¼ teaspoon ground cloves
1 egg, beaten
½ cup plain yogurt
½ cup pure maple syrup
¼ cup packed brown sugar
¼ cup vegetable oil
½ cup chopped walnuts
⅓ chopped banana
Pure maple syrup

Preheat oven to 400° F. In a small mixing bowl, stir together the
flours, oats, baking powder, cinnamon, baking soda, and cloves.
Set aside.

In a medium-sized mixing bowl, combine the egg, yogurt, and
the ½ cup syrup. Beat in the sugar and oil. Add the reserved
flour mixture, the walnuts, and banana and stir just until mixed.

Fill greased muffin cups ⅔ full and bake for 15 – 20 minutes.
Cool on a wire rack. While warm, drizzle with additional maple
syrup and serve warm.

Yield: 15 muffins

GRANT CORNER INN
Santa Fe, New Mexico

Poppy Seed Muffins*

2 cups all-purpose flour
¼ cup poppy seeds
½ teaspoon salt
¼ teaspoon baking soda
½ cup (1 stick) butter, at room temperature
¾ cup granulated sugar
2 eggs
¾ cup sour cream

½ teaspoon pure vanilla extract

Preheat oven to 375° F. In a medium-sized mixing bowl, combine the flour, poppy seeds, salt, and baking soda and set aside.

In another small bowl, cream the butter and sugar with an electric mixer until thick and light. Beat in the eggs, one at a time, and blend in the sour cream and vanilla. Gradually beat in the reserved flour mixture.

Fill greased 2-inch diameter muffin cup ⅔ full and bake for about 20 minutes.

Yield: 12 small muffins

THE RHETT HOUSE INN
Beaufort, South Carolina

Pineapple Corn Breakfast Muffins

1 ¼ cups all-purpose flour
1 cup cornmeal
1 tablespoon baking powder
1 teaspoon salt
½ cup granulated sugar
1 cup milk
¼ cup vegetable oil
2 eggs, lightly beaten
2 cups crushed pineapple

Preheat oven to 400° F. In a medium-sized mixing bowl, sift together all of the dry ingredients. Stir in the milk, oil, and eggs until just moist. Stir in the pineapple.

Fill greased muffin cups to the top and bake for 25 minutes or until lightly brown. Cool for 10 minutes on a wire rack.

Yield: 12 muffins

THE INN AT BUCKEYSTOWN
Buckeystown, Maryland

THE INN AT BUCKEYSTOWN

The Inn at Buckeystown is an elegantly restored 1897 eighteen-room mansion opened in 1981 by innkeeper Dan Pelz to provide bed, board, and luxury to his guests. The inn is in the heart of Buckeystown, a Nationally Registered Historic Village with prerevolutionary roots and a strong Civil War influence.

The grounds on which the inn is situated are carefully manicured and aesthetically in keeping with the entire village on the banks of the Monocacy River. Breakfast and dinner at the inn are a study in pampered and stylish dining. The food is superb, running the creative gamut of a variety of cuisines, fresh ingredients, and artful presentations. Service is on Victorian china and period silver and glassware. After dinner, perhaps a cup of freshly brewed coffee in the parlor or a quiet symphony of night sounds from the wraparound side porch might provide the perfect end to a splendid day at The Inn at Buckeystown.

CHAPTER 8

Desserts

Bourbon Apple-Pecan Pie

⅓ cup vegetable shortening
2 tablespoons cold butter
2 cups all-purpose flour, divided
⅛ cup cold water
4 cups peeled and sliced apples
5 tablespoons plus 1 teaspoon cornstarch
1 cup packed brown sugar, divided
¼ cup bourbon whiskey
½ cup chopped pecans
¼ cup melted butter, divided
¼ teaspoon cinnamon
½ cup rolled oats

In a medium-sized mixing bowl, cut the shortening and butter into 1 cup of the flour with a pastry blender until crumbly. Add the water and mix together well. Shape into a ball and wrap with plastic wrap. Chill for 30 minutes.

In a large bowl, mix together the apples, cornstarch, ½ cup of the sugar, whiskey, pecans, and ⅛ cup of the butter. Roll out the chilled dough to fit a 9-inch pie pan and pour the filling into the pie shell.

Preheat oven to 350° F. In a small bowl, stir together the remaining flour, sugar, and butter, the cinnamon, and oats until crumbly. Sprinkle the flour mixture over the pie and bake for 2 hours. Serve.

Yield: 6 to 8 servings

ASA RANSOM HOUSE
Clarence, New York

Sour Cream-Apple Pie

1 cup all-purpose flour
¼ teaspoon baking powder
½ teaspoon salt
¼ cup lard
½ cup (1 stick) cold butter, divided
3 tablespoons cold water
2 tablespoons all-purpose flour
Pinch salt

²/₃ cup granulated sugar
1 egg
1 cup sour cream
1 teaspoon pure vanilla extract
¼ teaspoon ground nutmeg
2 cups peeled and diced apples
⅓ cup packed brown sugar
1 teaspoon ground cinnamon
⅓ cup all-purpose flour

In a medium-sized mixing bowl, mix together the 1 cup flour, baking powder, and salt. Cut in the lard and ¼ cup of the butter until the mixture resembles small peas. Add enough cold water to hold the mixture together. Turn onto a floured surface and knead gently for a few seconds. Roll out the dough to fit a 9-inch pie pan. Set aside.

Preheat oven to 400° F. In a medium-sized mixing bowl, mix together the 2 tablespoons flour, pinch salt, and granulated sugar. Add the egg, sour cream, vanilla, and nutmeg and beat to a smooth thin batter. Stir in the apples. Pour the batter into the reserved pie shell and bake for 15 minutes. Reduce temperature to 350° and continue baking for 30 minutes more.

In a small bowl, combine the brown sugar, cinnamon, ⅓ cup flour, and remaining butter and mix until crumbly. Set aside.

After baking for 30 minutes, remove the pie from the oven and sprinkle the reserved brown sugar mixture over the pie. Increase temperature to 400° and bake for 10 minutes more. Serve.

Yield: 6 to 8 servings

THE INN AT STARLIGHT LAKE
Starlight, Pennsylvania

THE INN AT STARLIGHT LAKE

Peach Custard Pie❖

1 ½ cups all-purpose flour
½ cup granulated sugar
1 teaspoon baking powder
½ cup (1 stick) butter
1 large egg
1 tablespoon peach schnapps
6 tablespoons granulated sugar
1 tablespoon all-purpose flour

2 large eggs
¾ cup sour cream
¾ teaspoon pure vanilla extract
Pinch lemon zest
Generous dash freshly ground nutmeg
Pinch salt
1 tablespoon peach schnapps
6 large ripe freestone peaches, peeled and sliced
¾ cup apple jelly, melted

In a food processor, combine the first six ingredients and process using the pulse action until just combined. (Do not let the mixture form a ball.) Press the dough evenly into the bottom and up the sides of a greased 9 x 1 ½-inch deep pie pan. Set aside.

Preheat oven to 350° F. In a small mixing bowl, combine the remaining ingredients, except the peaches and jelly. Pour the filling evenly into the reserved pie shell. Arrange the peach slices over the filling in a circular pattern and bake for 20 minutes.

Remove the pie from the oven. Spoon the warm jelly over the top and bake for 30 minutes more. Serve slightly warm.

Yield: 6 to 8 servings

GLEN-ELLA SPRINGS INN
Clarksville, Georgia

Deep-Dish Buttermilk Pie

1 ½ cups graham cracker crumbs
3 ⅓ cups granulated sugar
¼ cup melted butter
8 large eggs, beaten
2 cups buttermilk
½ cup heavy cream
1 cup sour cream
1 tablespoon pure vanilla extract
1 pound cream cheese

In a small mixing bowl, combine the crumbs, ⅓ cup of the sugar, and the butter and press into the bottom and up the sides of a greased 9-inch springform pan. Set aside.

Preheat oven to 350° F. In a medium-sized mixing bowl, blend together the remaining sugar and all of the remaining ingredients

GLEN-ELLA SPRINGS INN

This century-old inn in the northeast Georgia mountains enjoys the distinction of being listed in the National Register of Historic Places. Innkeepers Bobby and Barrie Aycock thoroughly restored the inn in 1987 and have lovingly furnished each pine-paneled guest room with antiques and interesting, locally crafted original pieces.

Gourmet dining, featuring such regional specialties as Vidalia Onions Baked in Sherry Sauce, Trout Pecan (a mountain trout sautéed in butter with lime juice, fresh herbs, and pecans), or a special summer treat of Peach Custard Pie are frequent additions to their sophisticated, constantly changing menu.

THE GREYSTONE INN

Innkeepers Tim and Boo Boo Lovelace love telling The Greystone Inn story: "In the beginning, there was a famous inn in the Blue Ridge Mountains that hosted the likes of Henry Ford, Thomas Edison, John D. Rockefeller, and Harvey Firestone. . . ."

The story goes on to captivate the imagination and stir the spirit. The six-level 1915 Swiss mansion home of Savannah native and highly regarded socialite Lucy Armstrong Moltz literally echoed the finesse and substance of Europe at its best. And then disaster struck. Less than eighteen months after the completion of Lake Toxaway's most famous residence, it was destroyed by a tragic fire. Sixty-nine years after the fire, The Greystone Inn was reopened by Tim and Boo Boo Lovelace. After a meticulous and costly restoration process, the elegance and luxury of Lucy Moltz's original mansion lives once again.

Just as the house itself has been restored, so too has its richly textured style and old world hospitality. Which translates, of course, to afternoon tea and cakes served on the wicker-filled sun porch and gourmet award-winning dining. No wonder every guest can't help but feel all is truly right with the world.

with an electric mixer until smooth. Slowly pour the batter into the prepared crust and bake for 1 hour 15 minutes, or until the pie is set. Serve.

Yield: 6 to 8 servings

THE GREYSTONE INN
Lake Toxaway, North Carolina

Peanut Butter Pie❖

1 cup graham cracker crumbs
¼ cup firmly packed brown sugar
¼ cup (½ stick) unsalted butter, melted
2 cups creamy peanut butter
2 cups granulated sugar
Two 8-ounce packages cream cheese, at room temperature
2 tablespoons unsalted butter
2 teaspoons pure vanilla extract
1 ½ cups heavy cream
4 ounces semisweet chocolate
3 tablespoons plus 3 teaspoons coffee

In a small bowl, combine the crumbs, brown sugar, and the ¼ cup melted butter. Press into the bottom (not the sides) of a greased 9-inch springform pan. Set aside.

In a large mixing bowl, beat together the peanut butter, granulated sugar, cream cheese, the 2 tablespoons butter, and the vanilla until smooth and creamy. In a small bowl, beat the cream until thick. Fold the cream into the peanut butter mixture and spoon into the prepared crust. Chill for at least 6 hours.

In the top of a double boiler, melt the chocolate with the coffee over gently simmering water. Spread the chocolate mixture over the pie and chill until ready to serve.

Yield: 8 servings

WINDHAM HILL INN
West Townshend, Vermont

Brandy Alexander Pie

1 ½ cups very finely crushed chocolate wafer crumbs
6 tablespoons melted butter
1 envelope unflavored gelatin
½ cup cold water
⅔ cup granulated sugar
Pinch salt
2 eggs, separated
¼ cup cognac
¼ cup crème de cacao
2 cups heavy cream, whipped

Preheat oven to 300° F. In a small mixing bowl, mix together the crumbs and butter and pat firmly into the bottom and up the sides of a 9-inch springform pan and bake for 15 minutes.

In a large saucepan, sprinkle the gelatin over the water. Stir in ⅓ cup of the sugar, the salt, and egg yolks and blend well. Heat over low heat, stirring constantly, until the gelatin dissolves and the mixture thickens. Remove from the heat and stir in the cognac and crèam de cacao. Chill until the mixture starts to mound slightly.

In a medium-sized bowl, beat the egg whites until stiff peaks form. Gradually beat in the remaining sugar and fold the egg white mixture into the chilled gelatin mixture. Fold in 1 cup of the whipped cream. Turn the mixture into the prepared crust and chill for at least 2 hours or until set.

Top with the remaining whipped cream and serve.

Yield: 6 to 8 servings

THE LYME INN
Lyme, New Hampshire

Wild Berry Cobbler with Lemon Curd Sauce

½ cup (1 stick) unsalted butter
1 cup all-purpose flour
2 cups granulated sugar
1 teaspoon baking powder

½ cup heavy cream
2 cups mixed fresh wild berries (any combination)
1 recipe *Lemon Curd Sauce* (see recipe below)

In a 10-inch baking dish, melt the butter. In a medium-sized mixing bowl, mix together the flour, 1 cup of the sugar, and baking powder. Stir in the cream. Spoon the mixture over the melted butter in the baking dish.

Preheat oven to 350° F. In a medium-sized saucepan, heat together the remaining sugar and the berries until just warm. Pour the berry mixture over the crust mixture and bake until the crust rises to the surface and turns golden brown, about 45 – 50 minutes. Spoon the lemon sauce onto each dessert plate and top with a slice of the warm cobbler. Serve immediately.

Lemon Curd Sauce

6 egg yolks, beaten
1 cup granulated sugar
1 cup fresh lemon juice
¾ – 1 cup (1 ½ – 2 sticks) unsalted butter, cut into small
   pieces
1 tablespoon grated lemon rind

Strain the egg yolks through a sieve into a medium-sized saucepan. Add the sugar and lemon juice and stir together well. Cook over low heat until the mixture thickens and coats the back of a wooden spoon.

Stir in the butter, 1 piece at a time, until fully blended and continue to cook until the sauce reaches the desired consistency. Fold in the lemon zest. Keep warm until ready to serve.

Yield: 8 servings

CARTER HOUSE/HOTEL CARTER
Eureka, California

Fresh Nectarine Toasted Walnut Tart

1 ¼ cups all-purpose flour
½ cup ground toasted walnuts
¾ cup granulated sugar

¾ cup (1 ½ sticks) cold sweet butter
1 egg yolk
2 – 3 drops pure vanilla extract
6 ripe sweet nectarines, peeled and thinly sliced
1 tablespoon fresh lemon juice
1 teaspoon arrowroot
Pinch freshly ground nutmeg
2 tablespoons sweet butter
1 cup peach preserves
2 tablespoons peach schnapps
¼ cup quartered toasted walnuts
Confectioners' sugar
Fresh mint leaves, chopped
Fresh whipped cream, unsweetened

In a medium-sized mixing bowl, mix together the flour, ground walnuts, and ½ cup of the granulated sugar. Cut in the ¾ cup butter with a pastry blender until the mixture is crumbly.

In a small bowl, blend together the egg yolk and vanilla and lightly stir the egg yolk mixture into the flour mixture with a fork. Work the dough with hands into a smooth, evenly blended ball. Press the dough into an 11-inch round tart pan with removable bottom until the dough conforms to and reaches up the sides of the pan.

Preheat oven to 400° F. Arrange the nectarine slices in the bottom of the prepared crust. In a small bowl, mix together the remaining granulated sugar, the lemon juice, arrowroot, and nutmeg and sprinkle over the nectarines. Dot the fruit with the 2 tablespoons butter and bake for 10 minutes. Reduce the temperature to 350° and continue baking until the nectarines are tender and the crust is lightly browned, about 30 minutes. Cool in the pan on a wire rack.

In a small saucepan, heat the preserves until melted and bubbling. Strain out the solids. Add the schnapps and mix well. Spoon the glaze over the tart and arrange the quartered walnuts around the outside edge to create a border.

Dust the edges of the tart with the confectioners' sugar and garnish with the mint leaves. Remove the pan sides and serve at room temperature with the whipped cream.

Yield: 6 to 8 servings

CARTER HOUSE/HOTEL CARTER
Eureka, California

Strawberry Napoleans

1 recipe *Puff Pastry* (see recipe below)
4 ¼ cups fresh strawberries
2 tablespoons granulated sugar
1 teaspoon Framboise liqueur
1 recipe *Grand Marnier Sabayon* (see recipe below)
2 cups *Raspberry Sauce* (see recipe below)
3 tablespoons confectioners' sugar

On a lightly floured surface, roll the pastry ⅟₁₆ inch thick. Dock the pastry. (To dock the pastry, pierce holes with the tines of a fork all over the surface of the pastry.) Cut into 12 pieces, each 4 x 5 inches. Freeze the pastry for at least 1 hour.

Preheat oven to 375° F. Line two baking sheets with parchment paper and place the frozen pastry on the sheets. Cover with inverted wire mesh cooling racks and bake for 15 – 20 minutes or until golden brown.

In a medium-sized bowl, toss together the strawberries, sugar, and liqueur. Put one piece of pastry on each of six plates. Spoon on some of the berry mixture and then some of the sabayon. Drizzle on the raspberry sauce. Sprinkle the remaining six pieces of pastry with the confectioners' sugar and place on top. Serve.

Puff Pastry

(If time is not available, puff pastry in squares and sheets is available in specialty gourmet food shops.)

2 ½ cups all-purpose flour
½ teaspoon salt
1 pound cold sweet butter
½ cup ice-cold water

Combine 2 cups of the flour and the salt on the work surface. Cut the butter into ¼ inch-cubes. Toss the butter with the flour mixture so that all of the cubes are coated well. Shape the mixture into a mound and make a well in the center.

Pour the water into the well and with fingertips work in the water so that a rough dough begins to form. (It will look like torn and knotted rags.) Gently press the dough together so that all of the dry flour is absorbed. Form this dough into a rectangle about 6 x 8 x 1 ¼ inches thick. Carefully wrap the dough in plastic wrap and chill for 1 hour.

Roll out the chilled dough on a lightly floured surface into a rectangle about 7 x 16 x ½ inch thick. (If the butter is breaking through the flour, let the dough sit out for 5 minutes at room temperature before attempting to roll it.) With the short end of the dough closest to you, bring the top down two-thirds of the way and fold the bottom over the top. This is a single turn.

Give the dough a quarter turn so that the open seam is on your right and the closed seam on your left. Repeat the rolling and folding process, giving the dough another single turn. Carefully wrap the dough in plastic wrap and chill for 1 hour.

Give the chilled dough two more single turns, rolling and folding, and making sure to give it a quarter turn between single turns. Rewrap the dough and chill for 1 hour more.

Again give the chilled dough two single turns, rolling and folding. Rewrap again and chill for 1 hour to overnight before rolling to desired thickness. Makes ten 5 x 5 x ⅛-inch thick pieces or twenty 4 x 5 x ¹⁄₁₆-inch thick pieces. (The pastry can be frozen for later use.)

Tips for rolling puff pastry

1. *Place the pastry on a floured surface. Sprinkle flour on top and roll to the thickness specified in the recipe. Keep the edges of the puff pastry straight and even as you roll. Occasionally sprinkle flour underneath and on top to prevent the pastry from sticking.*

2. *Brush off excess flour. Cut the pastry by pressing a knife down with a rocking motion to make a clean cut. Do not drag the knife through the pastry. Freeze pastry pieces until ready to use.*

3. *To create the traditional mille-feuille (1,000 layers) for napoleans, pierce holes with the tines of a fork all over the pastry. (This is called docking and prevents the dough from rising.) Place an inverted wire mesh cooling rack over the pastry when baking to further prevent it from rising.*

Grand Marnier Sabayon

8 large egg yolks
½ cup granulated sugar
Pinch salt
½ cup Grand Marnier liqueur
½ cup fresh orange juice

1 cup heavy whipping cream

In a large stainless steel bowl, combine the egg yolks, sugar, and salt. Whisk in the liqueur and orange juice and set aside.

Fill a large bowl one quarter full of ice water and set aside.

Place the reserved stainless steel bowl over a pot of boiling water and whisk the egg mixture vigorously for 5 minutes or until thick and tripled in volume. (The sabayon should mound slightly when dropped from the whisk.) Immediately put the stainless steel bowl over the reserved bowl of ice and whisk until cold.

Pour the whipping cream into another large bowl and with an electric mixer at high speed, whip until soft peaks form. Fold the whipped cream into the sabayon and chill until ready to serve. Makes 5 cups.

Raspberry Sauce

1 pint fresh raspberries
2 tablespoons granulated sugar
½ teaspoon fresh lemon juice
Pinch salt

In a food processor, puree the raspberries. Strain the puree through a medium-mesh sieve to eliminate any remaining seeds.

Stir in the sugar, lemon juice, and salt. Taste and adjust for sweetness. Chill until ready to use. Makes 1 cup.

Yield: 6 servings

RICHMOND HILL INN
Asheville, North Carolina

RICHMOND HILL INN

Lemon Berry Mille-Feuille

1 puff pastry sheet
1 egg, slightly beaten
1 recipe *Chantilly Cream* (see recipe below)
1 recipe *Raspberry Sauce* (see recipe below)
1 recipe *Lemon Sauce* (see recipe below)
1 ½ – 2 cups poached fresh peach slices
1 cup fresh blueberries
1 cup fresh raspberries

6 fresh mint leaves
6 fresh whole strawberries, washed with stems

Preheat oven to 400° F. Cut the pastry into 3 x 5-inch rectangles and place on a flat baking sheet. Lightly brush the pastry with the egg until covered. (Try not to get too much egg on the baking sheet.) Bake for 10 – 15 minutes or until golden brown and nicely puffed. Cool.

When cool, cut the rectangles in half lengthwise with a serrated knife and fill with the chantilly cream. Gently replace the top half and set aside.

Pour enough raspberry sauce in the bottom of six dessert plates to cover. Place a filled pastry shell in the center of the sauce and drizzle about 3 tablespoons lemon sauce over the center of the pastry. Top with the peach slices, blueberries, and raspberries and garnish each with a mint leaf and a strawberry. Serve immediately.

Chantilly Cream

2 cups heavy cream
1 teaspoon pure vanilla extract
¼ – ½ cup confectioners' sugar, or to taste

In a medium-sized bowl, whip the cream with an electric mixer on medium speed until slightly thickened. Add the vanilla and sugar and beat on medium speed until stiff peaks form. (Do not overbeat.) Chill until ready to serve.

Raspberry Sauce

1 ½ cups fresh raspberries
2 tablespoons Chambord liqueur
1 teaspoon pure vanilla extract
Granulated sugar to taste
1 ½ tablespoons cornstarch
1 tablespoon cold water

Place the raspberries in a medium-sized saucepan and fill with tap water just until the berries are almost covered. Bring to a boil, stirring frequently. When the pulp and seeds have separated, about 4 – 5 minutes, strain and discard seeds. Return the sauce to a boil and reduce by one-third and add the sugar.

In a small bowl, mix together the cornstarch and water and add to the sauce, stirring constantly to thicken. Reduce to a low boil for 1 minute, then strain sauce into a small bowl. Cool before serving.

Lemon Sauce

2 eggs
⅓ cup plus 2 tablespoons granulated sugar
½ cup fresh lemon juice
Grated rind of 1 large lemon
2 ½ tablespoons butter

In a medium-sized saucepan, beat together the eggs and sugar. Add the lemon juice, lemon zest, and butter and mix together well. Bring to a low boil and cook for 30 seconds, stirring constantly until the sauce thickens.

Pour into a small bowl and cover to prevent skin from forming on top. Cool before serving.

Yield: 6 servings

PROSPECT HILL PLANTATION INN
Trevilians, Virginia

Fresh Coconut Cake

1 fresh coconut
Milk
3 cups sifted cake flour
1 tablespoon baking powder
1 cup (2 sticks) butter
2 cups granulated sugar
1 teaspoon pure vanilla extract
4 egg yolks
4 egg whites
1 ¼ cups heavy cream
1 recipe *No Cook Frosting* (see recipe below)

Use an ice pick to punch out the eyes of the coconut shell. Drain out the coconut milk and strain into a measuring cup. Add enough of the milk to equal 1 cup liquid. Set aside.

Grease and lightly flour three 8 x 1 ½ or 9 x 1 ½-inch round baking pans. In a medium-sized bowl, stir together the flour and baking powder. In a large mixing bowl, beat the butter with an electric mixer at medium speed for about 30 seconds. Add the sugar and vanilla and beat until well combined. Add the egg yolks, one at a time, beating for 1 minute after each addition. Add the flour mixture alternately with the reserved coconut milk to the egg yolk mixture and beat at low speed until combined.

Preheat oven to 350° F. Thoroughly wash the beaters. In a medium-sized bowl, beat the egg whites at medium speed for 1 minute 30 seconds, or until stiff peaks form. Gently fold into the cake batter. Turn into the prepared pans and bake for 30 – 35 minutes, or until a tester inserted in the center comes out clean. Cool for 10 minutes on wire racks. Remove from pans and cool completely on wire racks.

Remove the coconut meat from the shell. Cut off the brown skin and discard. Shred the whole coconut and set aside.

In a small mixing bowl, whip the cream until stiff peaks form. Place one cake layer on a cake plate and spread with half the whipped cream. Add the second layer and spread with the remaining whipped cream. Add the third layer, top side up. Spread the frosting over the top and sides of the cake and sprinkle with the reserved shredded coconut. Cover and chill until ready to serve.

No Cook Frosting

2 egg whites
1 teaspoon pure vanilla extract
Dash salt
¼ cup granulated sugar
½ cup corn syrup

In small mixing bowl, beat the egg whites, vanilla, and salt with an electric mixer at medium speed for 1 minute, or until soft peaks form.

Gradually beat in the sugar until stiff peaks form, about 1 ½ minutes. Gradually add the corn syrup and beat at high speed until stiff peaks form, about 2 – 3 minutes more. Spread the frosting on the cooled cake.

Yield: 8 to 10 servings

INN AT SAWMILL FARM
West Dover, Vermont

INN AT SAWMILL FARM

What happens when a successful architect and his wife, the equally successful interior designer, decide to bid the big city adieu and combine their love of inns and skiing with their skills at design and decor? Rod and Ione Williams fell in love with the 1770 farmhouse, which was to become the Inn at Sawmill Farm, during their frequent family vacations to Mount Snow.

The Williams now have the distinction of owning and operating one of the nation's most successful country inns. Their sophisticated, twenty-one room hideaway is clustered around an old dairy barn, which has been remarkably transformed with floral fabrics, wallpapers, and antiques. The huge fireplace in the parlor is surrounded by nineteenth-century brass and copper household implements and serves as the favorite gathering place for inn guests before and after dinner.

Under the creative direction of Chef Brill Williams, Rod and Ione's son, the dining room at Sawmill has earned an international reputation for excellence. An award-winning wine cellar containing 24,000 bottles complements the chef's creations. Entrées range from Maine lobster to delicately braised veal piccata. A nearby game farm provides the inn with succulent geese, turkey, pheasant, and quail. The Inn at Sawmill's Fresh Coconut Cake draws rave reviews.

THE BAILIWICK INN

Anne and Ray Smith love their home, and they love sharing it with their guests. This nineteenth-century inn in the heart of historic Fairfax, Virginia, is located on one of the nation's oldest toll roads, the old "Ox Road."

The Bailiwick is a completely refurbished, wonderfully cozy, and hopelessly romantic inn with four-teen guest rooms patterned after those of Virginia's fabulous "hunt country" mansions. Choose a lovely guest room with its own working fireplace, a Jacuzzi, or queen- or king-sized bed, or if you prefer, you may select the bridal suite for a very special occasion.

Historians with an eye for elegant architectural detail have described The Bailiwick as a small "treasure." From the polished balustrade and fresh-cut flowers in the foyer to the cheery fires crackling in the book-lined parlors to streams of sunlight dancing on gleaming sil-ver and crystal in the breakfast room, you'll find this inn delights the eye and refreshes the spirit.

Blueberry Tea Cake❖

2 cups sifted all-purpose flour
2 teaspoons baking powder
½ teaspoon salt
¼ cup (½ stick) butter
¾ cup granulated sugar
1 egg
½ cup milk
1 pint fresh blueberries

Topping:
½ cup granulated sugar
¼ cup all-purpose flour
½ teaspoon ground cinnamon
¼ cup (½ stick) butter

Preheat oven to 375° F. In a small mixing bowl, sift together the flour, baking powder, and salt and set aside.

In a medium-sized mixing bowl, cream the butter and gradually beat in the sugar. Add the egg and milk and beat until smooth. Add the reserved flour mixture and blend until smooth. Gently fold in the blueberries.

In a small bowl, combine all of the topping ingredients and mix to form coarse crumbs. Spread the batter in a greased and floured 8- or 9-inch square baking pan and sprinkle the crumb mixture over the top. Bake for 1 hour, or until a tester inserted in the center comes out clean. Cool on a wire rack. Serve.

Yield: 6 servings

THE BAILIWICK INN
Fairfax, Virginia

Sour Cream Pound Cake with Cream Cheese-Butter Cream Icing❖

1 ½ cups (3 sticks) butter
3 cups granulated sugar
6 eggs
2 teaspoons pure vanilla extract
3 cups unbleached all-purpose flour

¼ teaspoon salt
¼ teaspoon baking soda
1 cup sour cream
1 recipe *Cream Cheese-Butter Cream Icing* (see recipe below)

All of the ingredients should be at room temperature. Preheat oven to 300° F.

In a medium-sized mixing bowl, cream the butter until fluffy. Gradually add the sugar, ½ cup at a time, and beat until very light and fluffy. Add the eggs, one at a time, and beat until well blended. Stir in the vanilla. Set aside.

In a separate bowl, sift together the flour, salt, and baking soda. Add the flour mixture to the reserved egg mixture, alternately with the sour cream. Pour the batter into two greased, medium-sized loaf pans and bake for 1 hour and 15 – 30 minutes, or until the cake is deeply golden, cracked on top, and a tester inserted in the center comes out clean. Cool in the pans for 30 minutes before turning out on wire racks.

Frost the cake with the icing and serve.

Cream Cheese-Butter Cream Icing

6 tablespoons (¾ stick) softened butter
One 8-ounce package cream cheese, softened
One 16-ounce package confectioners' sugar
1 teaspoon pure vanilla extract
Dash salt
1 – 4 tablespoons heavy cream

In a medium-sized bowl, cream together the butter and cream cheese until fluffy. While beating, sift in the confectioners' sugar, a little at a time, and beat until fluffy.

Add the vanilla, salt, and cream and blend well. (May need to add extra confectioners' sugar or cream to get just the right consistency for piping. In hot weather, the icing will not hold well at room temperature if piped.) Makes enough icing to frost and fill one 2-layer 9-inch cake.

Variations for the icing:

Orange: Add the zest of 1 orange and use orange juice or an orange liqueur instead of the cream.

*Lemon: Add the zest of 1 lemon and use lemon juice instead of the
cream.*

*Chocolate: Add 2 – 3 squares unsweetened chocolate, coarsely
chopped and melted, to the butter-cream cheese mixture.*

*Mocha: Follow the chocolate variation, but use coffee as the liquid
instead of the cream.*

Yield: 2 large loaves

DAIRY HOLLOW HOUSE
Eureka Springs, Arkansas

Chocolate Mousse Cake

1 pound semisweet chocolate
6 eggs
¾ cup granulated sugar
⅛ cup warm brewed coffee
½ ounce rum
½ ounce brandy
1 cup heavy cream
Fresh whipped cream
Chocolate curls

All of the ingredients should be at room temperature, except the
whipped cream and chocolate curls. Melt the 1 pound chocolate
in the top of a double boiler over medium heat. Keep warm.

Place the uncracked eggs in a large stainless steel bowl and cover
with tap water (warmed to 180°) for 10 minutes. Pour out the
water and crack the eggs into the warm bowl. Whip until ribbon
consistency, while slowly adding the sugar. Add the coffee, rum,
and brandy. Slowly fold in the warm chocolate.

Preheat oven to 350° F. In a medium-sized bowl, whip the cream
to a light peak and fold into the chocolate mixture. Pour into a
buttered 10-inch round, nonstick cake pan. Place the pan in a
larger pan filled with water half way up the cake pan sides and
bake for 1 hour, or until the top is firm. Turn off the oven and
let the cake remain in the oven for 15 – 20 minutes. Remove the
cake and cool on a wire rack.

To serve, heat the cake in the pan over low heat, then turn out
onto a flat serving dish. Slice and top each slice with the

whipped cream and chocolate curls. Serve immediately.

Yield: 8 servings

THE WHITE INN
Fredonia, New York

White Chocolate Cheesecake

2 pounds cream cheese, at room temperature
1 cup granulated sugar
1 teaspoon pure vanilla extract
4 eggs
8 ounces white chocolate, melted
2 cups sweetened and pureed fresh raspberries

Preheat oven 450° F. In a medium-sized mixing bowl, cream
together the sugar and cream cheese. Add the vanilla and beat in
the eggs, one at a time. Blend in the chocolate.

Pour into a 9-inch springform pan and bake in a water bath for
10 minutes. Reduce the temperature to 250° and bake for 1 hour
more. Cool overnight before removing from the pan.

Drizzle the raspberry puree over the top of each serving and serve.

Yield: 8 servings

SEA CREST BY THE SEA
Spring Lake, New Jersey

SEA CREST BY THE SEA

Hazelnut Cheesecake

1 ½ cups graham cracker crumbs
¼ cup granulated sugar
¼ cup (½ stick) butter, melted

Filling:
Nine 3-ounce packages cream cheese, at room temperature
1 cup granulated sugar
1 cup ground toasted hazelnuts
4 eggs, at room temperature
1 egg yolk, at room temperature
½ teaspoon fresh lemon juice

OLIVER LOUD'S INN

Built in 1812 and 1818, respectively, Oliver Loud's Inn and Richardson's Canal House restaurant are two solid gold bookends of hospitality excellence on the Erie Canal. Innkeeper Vivienne Tellier has maintained an unparalleled reputation for pampering her guests since acquiring the property in the late 1970s and meticulously restoring it—right down to the historically accurate butter yellow paint and gas lanterns.

VIP welcome trays and personally hand-delivered, generous breakfast hampers are standard fare at Oliver Loud's, and the seasonal savory offerings in Richardson's Tavern are served in a choice of cobblestone informality or candlelit elegance. Located only twelve miles from Rochester, New York, this early nineteenth-century inn and tavern will transport you at the leisurely drawn pace of the canal to an elegance you will always treasure.

½ teaspoon pure vanilla extract
¼ teaspoon pure almond extract
Pinch salt
2 tablespoons plus 1 teaspoon cornstarch
1 cup half-and-half
Boiling water

Preheat oven to 350° F. Grease a 10-inch round cake pan.

In a medium-sized bowl, mix together the crumbs, the ¼ cup sugar, and butter. Press the mixture into the bottom and sides of the prepared pan and bake until golden brown, about 10 – 12 minutes. Cool to room temperature on a wire rack.

Preheat oven again to 350°. In a large bowl, beat the cream cheese and the 1 cup sugar with an electric mixer until smooth and light. Mix in the hazelnuts, eggs, egg yolk, lemon juice, both extracts, and salt. In a small bowl, dissolve the cornstarch in the half-and-half, then blend into the cream cheese mixture.

Pour the filling into the cooled crust and place the cake pan in a large roasting pan. Add enough boiling water to the roasting pan to come halfway up the sides of the cake pan. Bake until the cheesecake is light brown and pulls away from the sides of pan, about 1 hour. Cool completely on a wire rack.

Cover and chill for at least 4 hours or overnight. Let stand at room temperature for 20 minutes before serving. Serve.

Yield: 8 to 10 servings

OLIVER LOUD'S INN/RICHARDSON'S CANAL HOUSE
Pittsford, New York

Miniature Cheesecakes

1 pound cream cheese, softened
¾ cup granulated sugar
2 eggs
1 tablespoon fresh lemon juice
1 teaspoon pure vanilla extract
Vanilla wafers
1 cup sour cream
2 tablespoons granulated sugar
½ teaspoon pure vanilla extract
1 pint homemade strawberry preserves

Preheat oven to 350° F. In a small mixing bowl, combine the first five ingredients and beat with an electric mixer at medium speed until well mixed. Place tiny paper liners in gem-sized muffin cups and place one wafer in each liner. Spoon the cream cheese mixture over each wafer and bake for 15 minutes.

In a small bowl, combine the sour cream, 2 tablespoons sugar, and ½ teaspoon vanilla and spoon on the baked cheesecakes. Return the cheesecakes to the oven and bake for 5 minutes more. Cool to room temperature. Spoon the preserves over the cooled cheesecakes and chill. Serve.

Yield: 6 to 8 servings

GRANDVIEW LODGE
Waynesville, North Carolina

Boysenberry Swirl

Bottom Layer:
½ cup (1 stick) butter
1 cup granulated sugar
2 eggs, beaten
1 teaspoon pure vanilla extract
1 cup sour cream
2 cups all-purpose flour
1 teaspoon baking soda
1 teaspoon baking powder
2 – 4 heaping tablespoons boysenberry jam or preserves

Middle Layer:
One 8-ounce package cream cheese, softened
6 tablespoons sour cream
3 drops fresh lemon juice

Top Layer:
⅓ cup melted butter
¾ cup granulated sugar
¼ cup all-purpose flour

To make the bottom layer: In a large bowl, cream together the butter and sugar. Add the eggs, vanilla, and sour cream and mix well. In a small bowl, combine the flour, baking soda, and baking powder and add to the sour cream mixture. Mix together well.

Spray the bottom and sides of a 9-inch springform pan with

GRANDVIEW LODGE

You've heard the story before or dreamed it yourself. Bright, young successful couple fed up with life in the "fast lane" decides to take the next exit ramp and buy a little inn someplace.

In 1986 that's exactly what happened to Stan and Linda Arnold when they bought the Grandview Lodge. Their inn/lodge is located in the beautiful Blue Ridge Mountains of western North Carolina. With four distinct seasons of recreation activity, there is no wonder the property has been welcoming overnight guests for more than fifty years. Situated on two and a half acres of gently rolling land, the lodge has its own apple orchards, grape arbors, and rhubarb patch.

Linda uses only the freshest possible ingredients in her kitchen. A neighbor furnishes the inn with fresh "pot-ready" homegrown vegetables, and whole-grain flours are always used for baking. Barbecued beef ribs, corn pudding, and homemade ice cream are always hits with the guests.

cooking spray and pour the batter into the pan. Swirl the jam into the batter with a knife. Set aside.

To make the middle layer: In a medium-sized bowl, beat together the cream cheese, sour cream, and lemon juice with an electric mixer at medium speed until smooth. Spread evenly over the reserved bottom layer. Set aside.

To make the top layer: Preheat oven to 350° F. In a small bowl, mix together the butter, sugar, and flour with a fork (the mixture should be lumpy). Sprinkle evenly over the reserved middle layer and bake for 45 – 55 minutes, or until a tester inserted in the center comes out clean. Cool on a wire rack. Serve.

Yield: 6 to 8 servings

CHANEL ROAD INN
Santa Monica, California

Rich Chocolate Torte❖

6 ounces semisweet chocolate chips
1 cup all-purpose flour
6 tablespoons unsweetened nonalkalized cocoa powder
1 tablespoon baking powder
½ teaspoon baking soda
Pinch salt
½ cup (1 stick) softened unsalted butter
1 ½ cups granulated sugar
¾ cup almond paste
3 large eggs, at room temperature
2 teaspoons pure vanilla extract
1 ½ cups sour cream, at room temperature
1 recipe *Chocolate Frosting* (see recipe below)
Fresh raspberries
Fresh mint leaves
Sliced almonds

Position a rack in the center of the oven and preheat to 350° F. Lightly butter the bottom and sides of two 9-inch round cake pans. Line the bottom of each pan with a circle of baking parchment or wax paper. Dust the sides of the pans with flour and tap out the excess.

In the top of a double boiler over hot (not simmering) water, melt the chocolate chips, stirring frequently until smooth.

Remove the top part of the double boiler and cool the chocolate for 5 – 10 minutes or until lukewarm.

In a medium-sized bowl, sift together the flour, cocoa, baking powder, baking soda, and salt. Set aside.

In a large bowl, cream together the butter and sugar with an electric mixer at medium speed for 1 ½ – 2 minutes until light. Beat in the almond paste and mix for 1 ½ – 2 minutes or until well blended. Beat in the eggs, one at a time, blending well after each addition. Beat in the vanilla and blend in the cooled chocolate. At low speed, blend in the reserved flour mixture alternately with the sour cream.

Divide the batter evenly between the prepared pans and bake for 30 – 40 minutes, or until a tester inserted in the center of each layer comes out clean. Cool in the pans on wire racks for 10 minutes.

Run a knife around the edges of the layers to loosen and invert the layers onto the racks. Peel off the paper and place loosely on the bottom of the layers. Holding the papers in place, reinvert the layers so the layers are right-side up on other wire racks. Cool completely before frosting.

Using a long, serrated knife, trim the tops of each cake layer on an inverted cake pan or a cake decorating stand. Using a metal cake spatula, spread about ¾ cup of the frosting on top of the cake layer. Place the second cake layer on top of the frosted layer and gently press into place.

Using the metal spatula, frost the top and then the sides of the cake with two layers of the frosting. The first layer (a crumb coating) should be very thin to seal the cake. The second layer should be a bit thicker and applied smoothly and evenly.

Finish the top of the cake by holding the spatula at a slight angle and, with several strokes, smooth the raised lip of the frosting around the edge towards the center of the cake until the top of the cake is completely smooth. Garnish with the raspberries, mint leaves, and almonds and serve.

Chocolate Frosting

1 pound 2 ounces semisweet chocolate chips
1 ½ cups (3 sticks) softened unsalted butter
2 teaspoons pure vanilla extract

STEAMBOAT INN

The Steamboat Inn is a cozy country inn located on the banks of the North Umpqua River in southern Oregon. In addition to the main building, there are eight cabins that share a common veranda. This inn is located just forty miles from many beautiful lakes and the wineries of Douglas County.

The "steamboat" name comes from the days before the turn of the century when gold was mined in the area. Some people contend the word describes a particular mining activity. It is more likely that the term comes from the practice of overestimating the value of a claim and the seller's catching the steamboat immediately upon completion of the sale.

The owners, Jim and Sharon Van Loan, along with the help of manager, Pat Lee, however, are here for the long haul, offering the nightly "Fisherman's Dinner." The dinner is served just after dark all summer long and on winter weekends. This is a festive affair, served creatively family style on massive slab tables.

In the top of a double boiler over hot (not simmering) water, melt the chocolate, stirring frequently until smooth. Remove the top part of the double boiler and cool the chocolate for 5 – 10 minutes or until lukewarm.

In a medium-sized bowl, beat the butter with an electric mixer at medium speed for 2 – 3 minutes or until creamy. At low speed, add the cooled chocolate and the vanilla and continue beating until smooth. Chill the frosting for 10 – 20 minutes or until thickened to a spreadable consistency. Makes enough frosting for one 2-layer 9-inch cake.

Yield: 6 to 8 servings

STEAMBOAT INN
Steamboat, Oregon

Chalet Suzanne's Gâteau Christina

4 egg whites
1 ½ cups granulated sugar
⅓ cup blanched ground almonds
2 egg whites
½ cup granulated sugar
2 tablespoons sweetened cocoa
1 cup (2 sticks) softened butter
4 ounces semisweet chocolate, melted

Preheat oven to 250° F. Cut aluminum foil into four 8-inch circles and grease each lightly. In a medium-sized bowl, whip the 4 egg whites until stiff peaks form, gradually adding the 1 ½ cups sugar and the almonds as the eggs begin to stiffen.

Place the foil rounds on a large baking sheet. Spread each evenly with the meringue and bake for 15 minutes, or until the meringue is dry. Carefully turn the meringue over and bake for 5 minutes more. Cool.

In the top of a double boiler over hot (not boiling) water, beat the 2 egg whites until foamy. Gradually add the ½ cup sugar, the cocoa, butter, and chocolate and beat until thick and creamy. Cool.

Place the best meringue layer on the bottom and spread with the filling. Top with another meringue, pressing down lightly to make the layers fit together. Spread with the filling. Repeat until all of the meringues are used and the top is liberally coated with the filling. Cover and chill for at least 24 hours. Serve.

Yield: 6 to 8 servings

CHALET SUZANNE
Lake Wales, Florida

Strawberry-Rhubarb Crisp❖

4 cups diced fresh rhubarb
5 cups hulled and diced fresh strawberries
1 cup granulated sugar
1 tablespoon grated orange rind
2 tablespoons cornstarch
⅓ cup Grand Marnier liqueur
¾ cup (1 ½ sticks) sweet butter, cut into small pieces
2 cups unbleached all-purpose flour
1 cup old-fashioned rolled oats
¾ cup packed brown sugar
1 tablespoon ground cinnamon
¾ cup slivered almonds
Pinch salt
1 egg, lightly beaten
2 cups heavy whipping cream
1 – 2 tablespoons confectioners' sugar
1 – 2 teaspoons pure almond extract

Preheat oven to 350° F. Lightly butter the bottom of a 4-quart baking dish.

In a large bowl, toss the rhubarb and strawberries with the granulated sugar and orange zest. In a small bowl, dissolve the cornstarch in the liqueur and toss with the rhubarb mixture until well coated. Spoon the mixture into the prepared dish and set aside.

In a medium-sized mixing bowl, combine the butter, flour, oats, brown sugar, and cinnamon with a pastry blender until crumbly. Stir in the almonds and salt, then stir in the egg with a fork to bind the mixture. Spread the mixture evenly over the rhubarb mixture and bake for 45 minutes or until browned and bubbly. Remove from the oven and keep warm.

In a medium-sized bowl, whip the cream with the confectioners' sugar until soft peaks form. Whip in the almond extract. Cut the warm crisps into squares and serve topped with generous dollops of the whipped cream.

Yield: 8 servings

BLUEBERRY HILL
Goshen, Vermont

JORDAN HOLLOW FARM INN

Jordan Hollow Farm Inn is a full-service country inn in Virginia's beautiful Shenandoah Valley. This restored colonial horse farm has a restaurant, pub, recreation room, fully equipped meeting rooms, and a riding stable. Jordan Hollow Farm Inn is the only country inn in Virginia with a full training program for carriage driving. Some of Virginia's most prized purebred horses graze in surrounding pastures and are in full view from every window of the inn.

Southern Living's "Travel South" says to have your cameras ready when you come up the drive because the pictures will surely be an enduring treasure. Innkeepers Jetze and Marley Beers offer a continental/country selection of entrées in four charming dining rooms in the farmhouse. The Beers offer delicious desserts, a fine selection of wines, and an pleasantly unexpected, but superb touch of African cuisine.

Mother's Apple Crisp

6 cups peeled and sliced McIntosh or Granny Smith apples
⅓ cup fresh orange juice
½ teaspoon pure vanilla extract
2 tablespoons rum or apple schnapps
¾ cup packed brown sugar
½ cup granulated sugar
¾ cup all-purpose flour
1 teaspoon ground cinnamon
½ cup rolled oats
¼ cup chopped pecans
¾ cup (1 ½ sticks) butter, melted
Fresh whipped cream

Preheat oven to 325° F. Butter a 7 ½ x 11 ½-inch glass baking dish.

Place half of the sliced apples in the prepared dish. In a small bowl, mix together the orange juice, vanilla, and rum and pour half of the mixture over the apples. In a medium-sized bowl, mix together both sugars, flour, cinnamon, oats, and pecans and sprinkle half of the mixture over the apples.

Place the remaining apple slices over the sugar mixture. Pour the remaining orange juice mixture over the apples and sprinkle the remaining sugar mixture over the apples. Drizzle the butter over the top and bake for 1 hour 30 minutes. Serve with the whipped cream.

Yield: 8 servings

JORDAN HOLLOW FARM INN
Stanley, Virginia

Indian Pudding❖

3 cups milk
¼ cup (½ stick) butter
¼ cup plus 1 tablespoon cornmeal
1 egg
1 ⅓ cups molasses
1 ½ tablespoons ground cinnamon
½ tablespoon ground ginger
½ cup peeled and thinly sliced apples
¼ cup raisins

Butter a 2-quart shallow, ovenproof baking dish.

In a large saucepan, combine 2 cups of the milk and the butter
and bring just to a boil. In a small bowl, stir together the remaining milk and the cornmeal. Add the cornmeal mixture to
the scalded milk and cook over low heat for 20 minutes, stirring
frequently. (Do not burn.)

Preheat oven to 300° F. In a small bowl, mix together egg,
molasses, and spices and add to the thickened cornmeal mixture,
whisking thoroughly. Pour the mixture into the prepared dish
and bake for 1 hour.

In another small bowl, combine the apples and raisins. Remove
the pudding from the oven. Stir the apple mixture into the
pudding and bake for 1 hour more, or until a tester inserted in
the center comes out clean. Cool slightly. Serve warm.

Yield: 4 to 6 servings

THE RED LION INN
Stockbridge, Massachusetts

Magnolia's Corn Pudding

¼ cup (½ stick) butter
¼ cup all-purpose flour
2 teaspoons salt
1 ½ tablespoons granulated sugar
1 ¾ cups milk
3 cups fresh-cut corn
3 eggs, well beaten

HISTORIC 1842 INN

It would be difficult to imagine an inn in a setting more typically "old south" than Macon's Four-Diamond 1842 Inn, owned by Dr. Richard Meils and Phillip Jenkins. The twenty-two guest rooms and public areas of this exquisite Greek Revival, antebellum mansion will captivate you.

Crystal and brass chandeliers sparkle above antiques artfully displayed on oriental carpeting. A friendly staff stands ready to serve you day or night with fresh coffee or fragrant tea in the parlor or an aperitif in the Taft Stateroom.

When the housekeeper turns down your eyelet-edged bed linens, she leaves you a bedtime treat of imported chocolate mints. And while you sleep, the staff shines your shoes and prepares your breakfast tray, complete with fresh-cut flowers and your morning paper, of course. It's enough to make Rhett reconsider his ambivalence!

Preheat oven to 350° F. In a medium-sized saucepan, melt the butter and stir in the flour, salt, and sugar and cook until bubbly. Add the milk and cook until thickened. Stir in the corn and eggs and mix together well.

Pour into a well-buttered baking dish and bake in a hot water bath for 45 minutes, or until a knife inserted in the center comes out clean. Serve.

Yield: 8 servings

HISTORIC 1842 INN
Macon, Georgia

Louisiana Bread Pudding with Whiskey Sauce❖

½ loaf stale French or Italian bread, crust removed and cut into ½-inch slices
1 cup whipping cream
¾ cup milk
4 egg yolks
1 cup granulated sugar
½ cup raisins
2 teaspoons pure vanilla extract
3 egg whites
3 tablespoons granulated sugar
1 recipe *Whiskey Sauce* (see recipe below)

Preheat oven to 350° F. Place the bread slices in a large bowl and pour the cream and milk over the bread. Set aside.

In a medium-sized bowl, beat together the eggs yolks and the 1 cup sugar until light. Stir in the raisins and vanilla. Gently stir the egg yolk mixture into the reserved bread mixture. Let stand for 10 minutes.

In a small mixing bowl, beat the egg whites with an electric mixer at medium speed until foamy. Gradually beat in the 3 tablespoons sugar. Beat the egg white mixture until stiff, but not dry. Gently fold the egg white mixture into the bread mixture and pour into a buttered 2-quart soufflé dish.

Place the dish in a large, deep baking pan and pour boiling water into the pan until the water comes one-third up the side of the dish. Bake for 1 hour, or until the top is puffed and golden and a knife inserted in the center comes out clean. Cool on a wire rack.

Spoon the pudding into small bowls and serve warm or at room temperature with the sauce.

Whiskey Sauce

3 egg yolks
½ cup granulated sugar
1 cup hot whipping cream
⅓ cup hot milk
1 teaspoon pure vanilla extract
1 tablespoon bourbon whiskey

In a medium-sized saucepan, beat the egg yolks and sugar until light. Stir in the cream and milk and cook over low heat, stirring constantly, until the mixture thickens and coats the back of a spoon, about 15 minutes.

Stir in the vanilla and cook, stirring constantly, for 10 minutes. Stir in the whiskey and cook, stirring constantly, for 5 minutes more. Cool.

Yield: 6 to 8 servings

THE BAILIWICK INN
Fairfax, Virginia

Banana Bread Pudding

½ loaf thin-sliced Pepperidge Farm Bread, crusts removed
4 ounces cream cheese, divided
4 bananas, sliced into rounds
¼ cup chopped walnuts
1 ½ cups milk
3 eggs, beaten
⅓ cup pure maple syrup
⅛ cup rum
Fresh whipped cream

Lay the bread slices on the bottom of a baking dish. Dot half of the cream cheese on top of the bread. Spread half of the banana slices over the cream cheese and sprinkle half of the walnuts over the bananas. Repeat the procedure for the second layer.

ADAMS EDGEWORTH INN

This century-old, three-story, restored Victorian inn on the grounds of the Monteagle Assembly (often referred to as the "Chautauqua of the South") is a splendid example of a very good inn going through metamorphosis and emerging as a great inn.

Innkeepers Wendy and David Adams have succeeded in placing their own family imprint on the inn by furnishing it with their own eclectic collection of museum-quality art, as well as antiques and interesting mementos they and their grown children have accumulated in their world travels. In addition, they have some spectacular treasures from the years Wendy's father spent as a U.S. ambassador, including the gold-edged ambassadorial china upon which Wendy serves dinner. Handmade quilts made by Wendy's mother and grandmother adorn several of the guest rooms. It is not possible to spend even a moment in this warm historic place and not feel surrounded by a sense of family and an uncompromising dedication to hospitality.

Classical music surrounds you as you rock on the front porch in deep contemplation of the evening's entrée selections. Shall it be Baked Salmon in Lemon Chive Sauce, or perhaps Garlic and Herb-Boned and Rolled Chicken Breast, or maybe the Filet Mignon with Mustard and Thyme Marinade, accompanied by New Potatoes in Pesto and Gingered Baby Carrots? Decisions, Decisions, Decisions.

In a small bowl, mix together the milk and eggs and pour evenly over the pudding. Pour the syrup over the top. Let stand for about 1 hour.

Preheat oven to 350° F. Bake for 30 minutes, or until a knife inserted in the center comes out clean. Cool for 5 – 10 minutes on a wire rack.

Pour the rum over the top and flambé. Serve immediately with the whipped cream on the side.

Yield: 8 servings

ADAMS EDGEWORTH INN
Monteagle, Tennessee

CHANEL ROAD INN

Originally constructed in 1910 for the Thomas McCall family, the Chanel Road Inn is a rare West Coast example of Shingle-Clad Colonial Revival architecture. In 1962, the home was moved intact to its present location — one block from the Pacific Ocean in Santa Monica Canyon.

Innkeepers Susan Zolla and Kathy Jensen have given each of the inn's fourteen rooms and suites its own individual "signature" by having each of fourteen talented friends decorate a room. The results are a pleasant, eclectic blend of the old and the new. In the center of the oak-floored living room, where tea is served each afternoon, pastel silk upholstered pieces complement the beautiful, lavender Chinese rug in the center of the room.

A bountiful breakfast of fresh fruits and baked goods begins each day in this inn described by the *Los Angeles Times* as, "One of the most romantic places in Los Angeles."

French Bread Custard

½ cup (1 stick) butter, melted
1 loaf French bread, sliced, or 6 – 8 large croissants, sliced and cut in half
Ground cinnamon
10 eggs
1 cup granulated sugar
4 cups milk
4 cups half-and-half
2 tablespoons pure vanilla extract
1 teaspoon ground nutmeg

Preheat oven to 350° F. Brush a 9 x 13-inch baking dish with 1 tablespoon of the melted butter and arrange the bread to fit snugly in the dish. Drizzle the remaining butter over the bread and dust lightly with the cinnamon.

In a large bowl, beat together the eggs and the remaining ingredients and pour over the bread. Bake for 40 – 45 minutes, or until brown and puffy and a knife inserted in the center comes out clean. Serve warm.

Yield: 8 servings

CHANEL ROAD INN
Santa Monica, California

Blueberry Cottage Pudding

6 cups fresh blueberries
½ cup honey
1 egg, well beaten
1 tablespoon cornstarch
1 ½ cups all-purpose flour
½ cup granulated sugar
2 teaspoons baking powder
Pinch salt
½ cup milk
½ cup (1 stick) unsalted butter, melted
1 egg, well beaten
Blueberry ice cream

Preheat oven to 375° F. Butter an 8 x 2-inch square baking dish.

In a large bowl, mix together the first four ingredients and place the mixture in the prepared dish. In a medium-sized bowl, sift together the flour, sugar, baking powder, and salt and set aside.

In a small bowl, combine the milk, butter, and remaining egg and add to the reserved flour mixture, mixing until just combined. Spoon the mixture over the blueberries, spreading to the edges and bake for 45 minutes, or until a knife inserted in the center comes out clean. Serve warm with the ice cream.

Yield: 4 to 6 servings

OLIVER LOUD'S INN/RICHARDSON'S CANAL HOUSE
Pittsford, New York

Pumpkin Caramel Flan

2 cups heavy cream
1 cup granulated sugar
1 cup pumpkin puree
1 teaspoon pure vanilla extract
¼ teaspoon ground nutmeg
½ teaspoon ground cinnamon
Dash ground cloves
7 large eggs
1 recipe *Caramel* (see recipe below)

Spray eight 4 ½-ounce ramekins with cooking spray.

In a large saucepan, stir together the cream, ½ cup of the sugar, pumpkin, vanilla, and spices and bring to a boil. Remove from heat and set aside to cool.

In a medium-sized bowl, whip the eggs with the remaining sugar until frothy. Add the cooled cream mixture to the egg mixture and strain. Set aside.

Preheat oven to 350° F. When the caramel is prepared, immediately pour into each prepared ramekin ¼ inch thick. When the caramel begins to set, top with the reserved flan and bake the ramekins in a water bath for 35 – 45 minutes, or until the flan is firm to the touch. Cover and cool overnight.

Invert the ramekins over serving dishes and serve immediately.

Caramel

½ cup granulated sugar
¼ cup water
¼ teaspoon cream of tartar
½ teaspoon white wine vinegar

In a small saucepan, combine all of the ingredients and cook over medium-heat, stirring constantly, until the sugar is melted. Reduce heat to medium and cook, stirring frequently, until golden brown, about 8 – 10 minutes more.

Yield: 8 servings

L'AUBERGE PROVENÇALE
White Post, Virginia

Raspberry Crème Brulée❖

12 ounces fresh frozen raspberries, thawed and drained
¾ cup granulated sugar
2 teaspoons raspberry liqueur
5 egg yolks
2 cups whipping cream
½ teaspoon pure vanilla extract
5 tablespoons butter
⅓ cup packed brown sugar

In a medium-sized bowl, gently toss together the raspberries, ¼ cup of the granulated sugar, and the liqueur. Divide the berry mixture among six custard cups.

In a heavy saucepan, whisk together the egg yolks and remaining granulated sugar until pale and thick, about 3 minutes. Add the cream and vanilla. Set the saucepan over medium heat and stir until the custard thickens and leaves a path on the back of a spoon. (Do not boil!) Add the butter and stir until melted. Carefully spoon the hot mixture over the berries and chill for at least 3 hours.

Preheat the broiler. Press the brown sugar through a sieve over the custards and broil until the brown sugar begins to melt and caramelize, about 2 minutes. Chill for 3 hours. Serve.

Yield: 6 servings

THE INTERLAKEN INN
Lake Placid, New York

Three Berry Oat Mousse

1 recipe *Raspberry Sauce* (see recipe below)
3 tablespoons rolled oats
1 ¼ cups milk
1 tablespoon granulated sugar
1 tablespoon B & B liqueur
1 tablespoon unflavored gelatin
2 tablespoons water
½ cup vanilla yogurt
1 ½ cups whipping cream
Fresh strawberries, washed and hulled
Fresh raspberries, rinsed
Fresh blueberries, rinsed

Prepare the raspberry sauce. Chill a medium-sixed bowl and beaters in the freezer.

In a large saucepan, combine the oats and milk and simmer over medium heat for 4 – 6 minutes, stirring constantly. Stir in the sugar and remove from heat. Cool. Add the liqueur and set aside.

In a small saucepan, sprinkle the gelatin over the water and heat over medium-high heat until the gelatin is dissolved. Cool.

Add the cooled gelatin and yogurt to the reserved oat mixture and whisk together well. In the chilled bowl, whip the cream until stiff and fold into the oat mixture. Gently pour the mixture into a ring mold and chill for several hours or overnight.

Unmold onto a serving dish and carefully pour the chilled raspberry sauce around the edge. Fill the center with the fresh berries and surround the outside edge with additional berries. Pour additional sauce over the berries in the center. Serve immediately.

Raspberry Sauce

10 ounces fresh frozen raspberries, thawed
1 tablespoon red currant jelly
1 teaspoon orange zest
2 tablespoons B & B liqueur

In a medium-sized saucepan, bring the raspberries to a boil, stirring frequently. Remove from heat and strain through a fine-mesh sieve, pressing as much pulp as possible through the sieve with a wooden spoon. Combine the pulp with the berry juice and return to the saucepan. Add the jelly and orange zest. Bring to a low boil and cook for 2 – 3 minutes. Cool slightly, then add the liqueur.

When completely cool, chill until ready to serve.

Yield: 8 servings

THE OAKS HISTORIC BED & BREAKFAST COUNTRY INN
Christiansburg, Virginia

Maple Mousse

1 tablespoon unflavored gelatin
½ cup water
4 egg yolks
1 cup pure maple syrup
½ cup packed light brown sugar
4 egg whites
2 cups heavy cream, whipped

In the top of a double boiler, whisk together the gelatin, water, egg yolks, and syrup over medium heat until smooth. Add the sugar and continue to whip until the sugar is dissolved. Remove from heat and cool slightly.

In a medium-sized bowl, beat the egg whites until stiff, but not dry. Fold the egg whites and the whipped cream into the gelatin mixture and pour into champagne glasses. Chill until firm and serve.

Yield: 4 servings

THE LYME INN
Lyme, New Hampshire

Lyme Soufflé

4 ½ teaspoons unflavored gelatin
½ cup hot water
1 ¼ cups milk
8 egg yolks
1 cup granulated sugar
1 cup fresh lime juice
2 cups heavy cream
6 drops green food coloring
14 egg whites

In a small bowl, dissolve the gelatin in the water. In the top of a double boiler, bring the milk to a simmer and blend in the dissolved gelatin. Set aside.

In a medium-sized bowl, beat together the egg yolks and sugar until light and airy. Add the egg yolk mixture to the reserved milk mixture and return the pan to the boiler. Whip the mixture over heat until thickened. Remove from heat and add the lime juice. Chill until the mixture starts to set.

In a medium-sized bowl, whip the cream with the food coloring until almost stiff and fold into the chilled mixture. Chill again.

In a large bowl, beat the egg whites until stiff, but not dry and fold into the chilled mixture. Spoon into stemmed glasses and chill until set. Serve.

Yield: 6 to 8 servings

THE LYME INN
Lyme, New Hampshire

THE LYME INN

Ten miles north of Dartmouth lies the historic town of Lyme, situated in the shadows of New Hampshire's White Mountains. In the midst of this refreshing atmosphere presides The Lyme Inn, a four-story, shuttered building with an authentic sense of its past and with new owners, Mickey and Tammy Doud.

Built in 1809 and originally owned by a descendant of John Alden, the inn has built a two-century-old reputation for fine food and comfortable accommodations. Stenciled wallpaper, wing chairs, wicker furniture on a huge screened porch, and ten fireplaces distinguish The Lyme Inn as a place for a visit, not just a place to spend the night.

The Lyme Inn offers superb, unhurried dining in one of the most charming parts of New England. The dining room offers a continually changing menu, featuring entrées from many countries, as well as traditional New England fare. Although fresh seafood is the specialty, veal, lamb, beef, and pork are prepared to perfection and served in an informal country setting.

THE WEATHERVANE INN

The Murphy family has placed its own unique imprint on this elegant nineteenth-century farm and coach house. There is a continuity of hospitality at this inn, where with each visit, even if it is your first, you feel as if you're coming back home.

This AAA Three-Star Inn has been welcoming travel weary guests to the little village of South Egremont, Massachusetts, for thirteen years.

Gingersnaps

½ cup (1 stick) butter
½ cup packed light brown sugar
⅓ cup molasses
2 cups unsifted all-purpose flour
2 teaspoons baking soda
¼ teaspoon salt
½ teaspoon ground cloves
1 teaspoon ground cinnamon
1 ½ teaspoons ground ginger
1 large egg, beaten
¼ cup granulated sugar

In a small saucepan, melt the butter and stir in the brown sugar and molasses. Set aside to cool to room temperature.

Preheat oven to 350° F. Lightly spray two baking sheets with cooking spray.

Into a large bowl, measure the flour, soda, salt, cloves, cinnamon, and ginger. Stir the egg into the cooled molasses mixture, then stir the molasses mixture into the flour mixture until well mixed. (If the dough is too soft to handle, place in the freezer for 5 – 7 minutes.)

Divide the dough into 36 pieces on waxed paper. Roll each piece in hands to make a 1-inch ball. Roll the balls in the granulated sugar and place two inches apart on the prepared baking sheets. Do not flatten. Bake for 10 – 12 minutes or just until set. Cool. Serve.

Yield: 3 dozen

THE WEATHERVANE INN
South Egremont, Massachusetts

Mrs. King's Cookies

1 cup (2 sticks) butter
1 cup packed brown sugar
1 cup granulated sugar
2 eggs
1 teaspoon pure vanilla extract
2 cups all-purpose flour

1 teaspoon baking powder
1 teaspoon salt
1 teaspoon baking soda
1 cup white chocolate chips
1 cup chocolate chips
1 ½ cups raisins
1 ½ cups chopped nuts
1 cup old-fashioned rolled oats
1 ½ cups orange-almond granola

Preheat oven to 375° F. In a large mixing bowl, cream together the butter and both sugars until smooth and creamy. Add the eggs and vanilla and beat until well mixed.

In a small bowl, sift together the flour, baking powder, salt, and baking soda. Add the flour mixture to the egg mixture and beat until well blended. Stir in the remaining ingredients and mix together well.

Shape the dough into golf-ball sized balls and bake on ungreased baking sheets for 8 – 10 minutes or until barely golden. Serve warm.

Yield: About 3 dozen

THE BABBLING BROOK
Santa Cruz, California

Cream Cheese & Nut Crescents❖

1 cup (2 sticks) softened butter
8 ounces whipped cream cheese
2 ¼ cups all-purpose flour
1 cup granulated sugar
1 tablespoon ground cinnamon
½ cup chopped walnuts
Confectioners' sugar

In a medium-sized bowl, blend together the butter, cream cheese, and flour. Chill.

Preheat oven to 350° F. In a small bowl, mix together the granulated sugar, cinnamon, and walnuts and set aside.

Dust a work surface with the confectioners' sugar and roll out the chilled dough ¼ inch thick. Cut into small triangles (1 – 1½-inch base). Spread the reserved sugar mixture on the triangles and roll up from the wide end to the point. Turn the ends inward to form crescents and bake on an ungreased baking sheets for 20 minutes. Serve.

Yield: 3 dozen

MANOR HOUSE
Cape May, New Jersey

Barrows House Brown's Better Brownies

4 squares unsweetened chocolate
⅔ cup vegetable oil
4 eggs
2 cups granulated sugar
1 ⅓ cups all-purpose flour
1 teaspoon baking powder
½ teaspoon salt
2 teaspoons pure vanilla extract
Chopped nuts

In the top of a double boiler, melt the chocolate with the oil over heat. Remove from heat and cool.

Preheat oven to 350° F. In a large bowl, beat the eggs well, then gradually beat in the sugar. Stir in the cooled chocolate.

In a small bowl, sift together the flour, baking powder, and salt. Add the flour mixture to the chocolate mixture and mix together well. Stir in the vanilla and nuts.

Pour into a well-greased and floured 9-inch square baking pan and bake for 25 minutes, or until a tester inserted in the center comes out slightly sticky. (Do not overcook. The brownies should be fudgelike in the middle.) Cool. Cut into bars and serve.

Yield: 8 servings

BARROWS HOUSE
Dorset, Vermont

Chocolate Streusel Bars ❖

1 ¾ cups unsifted all-purpose flour
1 ½ cups confectioners' sugar
½ cup unsweetened cocoa
1 cup (2 sticks) cold butter
One 8-ounce package cream cheese, softened
One 14-ounce can sweetened condensed milk
1 egg
2 teaspoons pure vanilla extract
½ cup chopped walnuts

Preheat oven to 350° F. In a large bowl, combine the flour, sugar, and cocoa and cut in the butter with a pastry blender until crumbly and dry. Set aside 2 cups of the crumb mixture. Press the remaining crumb mixture in the bottom of a 9 x 13-inch baking pan and bake for 15 minutes.

In a another large bowl, beat the cream cheese until fluffy. Gradually beat in the milk until smooth. Add the egg and vanilla and mix well. Pour the batter over the baked crust.

Combine the nuts with the reserved crumb mixture and sprinkle evenly over the batter. Bake for 20 minutes or until bubbly. Cool. Cover and chill. Cut into bars and serve.

Yield: 8 servings

MAINSTAY INN & COTTAGE
Cape May, New Jersey

Lemon Bars

2 cups all-purpose flour
½ cup confectioners' sugar
1 cup (2 sticks) softened butter
1 ½ cups granulated sugar
1 teaspoon baking powder
3 eggs
¼ cup fresh lemon juice
1 tablespoon grated lemon rind
Confectioners' sugar

Preheat oven to 350° F. In a medium-sized bowl, mix together the flour, confectioners' sugar, and butter. Press the mixture into

MAINSTAY INN & COTTAGE

A pair of wealthy gamblers pooled their resources in 1872 and built an elegant, exclusive clubhouse where their friends could devote themselves to gambling and similar nineteenth-century debauchery. They spared no expense in the design of their grand villa, which included stately fourteen-foot ceilings, ornate plaster crown molding, elegant crystal chandeliers, and a sweeping veranda. Because luxury was paramount, they selected only the finest, richly ornamented walnut furnishings, twelve-foot beveled mirrors, marble-topped sideboards, and graceful love seats.

This beautiful nineteenth-century "casino" is now The Mainstay Inn in the heart of historic Cape May, New Jersey. Today the original coal stove in the front parlor warms guests—not gamblers. And the dining room's ornate brass chandelier is lit by electricity—not gas. But the Victorian atmosphere is preserved with many of the original furnishings still in place, revealing as grand an establishment as could be found anywhere in America in the last quarter of the nineteenth century.

Innkeepers Tom and Sue Carroll serve their overnight guests in the flamboyant Victorian splendor of antique beds with lofty headboards and matching ornate wardrobes. Croquet on the lawn? Of course. But remember "breakfast at nine . . . tea at four."

a well-oiled, rimmed baking sheet and bake for 20 minutes.

In another medium-sized bowl, combine the remaining ingredients and whip thoroughly. Spread the batter over the baked crust and bake for 25 minutes. Dust the top with more confectioners' sugar and cool until set. Cut into bars and serve.

Yield: 16 bars

STAFFORD'S BAY VIEW INN
Petoskey, Michigan

Geri's Sopaipillas ❖

4 cups all-purpose flour
2 tablespoons baking powder
1 teaspoon salt
¼ cup lard
1 ⅓ cups warm water
Confectioners' sugar
Butter
Honey

In a large bowl, combine the flour, baking powder, and salt. Cut in the lard with a pastry blender until the mixture resembles cornmeal. Gradually add the water, stirring with a fork until well mixed. Gently knead the dough for 10 – 12 strokes. Cover and let stand for about 30 minutes.

Divide the dough in half and roll out each piece to ¼-inch thickness. Cut the dough into shapes with a 2 – 2 ½-inch cookie cutter and fry in deep hot fat (375°) for 1 minute per side, turning once. Drain on paper towels. Dust with the confectioners' sugar and serve hot with the butter and honey.

Yield: 2 dozen

GRANT CORNER INN
Santa Fe, New Mexico

Oreillettes

3 ½ cups sifted all-purpose flour
¼ cup granulated sugar
3 eggs, beaten
Grated rind of 1 lemon
Grated rind of 1 orange
¼ cup orange flower water
2 tablespoons softened butter
Pinch salt
1 cup light vegetable oil
Confectioners' sugar

In a large bowl, mix together the flour, sugar, eggs, lemon zest, orange zest, orange water, and butter. Add the salt. Knead the dough, adding a little water, if needed. Cover and let stand for 2 hours.

On a lightly floured surface, roll out the dough to ¼ inch thick. With a pastry wheel or sharp knife, cut the dough into 4-inch squares.

In a large, deep frying pan, heat the oil until very hot and fry the dough until golden. Remove and drain on paper towels. Sprinkle with the confectioners' sugar and serve.

Yield: About 3 dozen

L'AUBERGE PROVENÇALE
White Post, Virginia

Hazelnut-Stuffed Pears en Croûte❖

2 tablespoons dried bread crumbs
¼ cup finely chopped hazelnuts
¼ cup granulated sugar
2 ounces semisweet chocolate, finely chopped
2 tablespoons Frangelico liqueur
3 ripe Williams pears or other small pears, peeled, halved, and seeded, with a 1 tablespoon-sized hollow in the center
2 recipes *Pâte Brisée* (see recipe below)
1 egg yolk
1 recipe *Crème Anglaise* (see recipe below)

L'AUBERGE PROVENÇALE

Nestled in the Shenandoah Valley near the Blue Ridge Mountains, this is the perfect place for a weekend lovers' tryst or an unforgettable fiftieth anniversary—complete with moonlit walks and intimate dinners. This tranquil spot offers views of charming flower gardens and of racehorses cavorting in the paddock. The inn is decorated in old world charm, reflected in wine racks, antique sideboards, and large fireplaces.

The 1753 stone farmhouse is situated on eight acres surrounded by six hundred acres of cattle, corn, and soybean farms. Shake off the city by sipping a glass of wine on the front porch of this French country inn.

No romantic weekend is complete without fine food, and innkeeper and chef Alain Borel's is exceptional. A native of Avignon, France, Chef Alain is nationally acclaimed for his Four-Diamond-rated restaurant. Herbs and spices grow in abundance along with the seasonal vegetables in Chef Alain's garden. Fruit trees provide a bounty of fresh treats for the breakfast plate, as well as contribute to the fantastic desserts created by the pastry chef.

In a food processor, combine the bread crumbs, hazelnuts, sugar, and chocolate. Add the liqueur and pulse until the mixture is moistened. Stuff the mixture into the hollows in the pears and set the pears aside.

Roll out half of the two recipes for pâte brisée to ¼-inch thickness. Place one pear half, stuffing-side down, near one edge of the dough. Cut out another section of dough large enough to completely cover the pear. Moisten the dough around the pear with a fingertip dipped in water and then press the top layer onto the bottom. Using a fork or pastry wheel, press the layers together.

With a paring knife, cut around the pear close to the markings, lift gently, and place the pear on a greased baking sheet. Repeat the procedure for the remaining five pear halves, using the remaining pâte brisée for the last three pears. Cut leaves out of the remaining dough.

Preheat oven to 400° F. In a small bowl, mix together the egg yolk and water to make an egg wash and brush each pear and each leaf with the wash. With the tip of a knife, draw the lines on the leaf. Lay each leaf on a pear where it looks natural and bake for 20 – 25 minutes or until golden brown. Cool slightly and serve warm with the warm crème.

Pâte Brisée

(Note: Reader can double the recipe and divide in half or make two separate recipes.)

3 ⅓ cups all-purpose flour
¼ cup granulated sugar
1 cup (2 sticks) cold butter, cut into ½-inch cubes
2 egg yolks
2 tablespoons vegetable oil
½ cup cold water

In a medium-sized mixing bowl, mix together the flour, sugar, and butter with an electric mixer at medium speed until the mixture resembles small peas. Add the egg yolks, oil, and water all at once and beat just until the doughs begins to clump.

Empty the bowl onto a floured surface and gently push into a mound. Using the heel of your hand, smear the flour and butter together by pushing against the mound and away from yourself. Work quickly, smearing all of the dough to about ⅛-inch thickness. Shape the dough into a ball. Repeat the entire recipe procedure to make another recipe of dough. Wrap the dough in plastic wrap and set aside until ready to use.

Crème Anglaise

2 cups half-and-half
3 egg yolks
¼ cup granulated sugar
2 tablespoons Frangelico liqueur
¼ teaspoon pure vanilla extract

In a medium-sized saucepan, heat the half-and-half until just before boiling.

In a medium-sized bowl, beat together the egg yolks and sugar with an electric mixer at medium speed until become pale yellow and begin to thicken. At low speed, add the hot half-and-half in a slow stream. Return the mixture to the saucepan and cook over low heat, stirring constantly, for several minutes until the crème begins to thicken and coats the back of a spoon.

Remove from heat and stir in the liqueur and vanilla. Keep warm until ready to serve. Makes 2 cups.

Yield: 6 servings

SHELBURNE INN/THE SHOALWATER RESTAURANT
Seaview, Washington

Poached Pears with Raspberry Sauce❖

6 firm ripe pears, peeled with stems
4 cups cold water
¼ cup fresh lemon juice
1 recipe *Raspberry Sauce* (see recipe below)

Cut a thin slice off the bottom of each pear so it will stand upright. Place the pears in a large saucepan and add the water and lemon juice. Bring to boil. Reduce heat and simmer, covered, for 10 – 15 minutes. Drain.

Place the pears in a baking dish, cover, and chill for 3 hours or overnight. Serve with the sauce.

Raspberry Sauce

1 cup fresh raspberries
½ cup fresh orange juice
2 tablespoons fresh lime juice
⅓ cup sifted confectioners' sugar

In a blender, place all of the ingredients and blend on high speed for 1 minute. Strain to remove seeds. Makes 1 ½ – 2 cups.

Yield: 6 servings

GRANT CORNER INN
Santa Fe, New Mexico

Baked Apples Red Lion❖

½ cup water
3 tablespoons bourbon whiskey
½ cup dark raisins
½ cup golden raisins
6 tart apples, cored and peeled halfway down
3 tablespoons butter
2 tablespoons all-purpose flour
½ cup firmly packed light brown sugar
½ teaspoon pure vanilla extract
Rum-flavored fresh whipped cream

Preheat oven to 425° F. Butter a large ovenproof baking dish with sides at least 1 inch high.

In a small bowl, combine the water and whiskey and add both raisins. Soak the raisins for 2 – 3 hours until plump. Stuff the raisins into the apples and place the apples in the prepared dish.

In a small saucepan, melt the butter and stir in the flour. Cook gently, stirring constantly, for 2 minutes. Remove from heat and stir in the sugar and vanilla. Spread the sugar mixture over the apples and bake for 20 minutes or until the crust is set on top. Reduce the temperature to 350° and continue to bake until tender, about 30 minutes more. Serve warm with the whipped cream.

Yield: 6 servings

THE RED LION INN
Stockbridge, Massachusetts

Sautéed Bananas with Brandy Cream Sauce❖

4 tablespoons (½ stick) butter
½ cup packed brown sugar
4 ripe bananas, cut in half lengthwise and crosswise
1 recipe *Brandy Cream Sauce* (see recipe below)
Ground cinnamon

In a medium-sized skillet, melt the butter with the sugar. Add the bananas and sauté for 5 minutes or until tender, turning once.

Place the bananas in serving dishes and pour the cream sauce over the top. Sprinkle with the cinnamon and serve immediately.

Brandy Cream Sauce

1 cup heavy cream
3 tablespoons confectioners' sugar
1 tablespoon brandy

In a small bowl, mix together all of the ingredients and beat until thickened. Makes 1 cup.

Yield: 8 servings

MANOR HOUSE
Cape May, New Jersey

Bananas Foster

½ cup (1 stick) butter
½ cup packed light brown sugar
½ teaspoon each pure maple, rum, and banana extracts
6 firm bananas, sliced into rounds
Ground cinnamon
French vanilla ice cream

In a large heavy skillet, melt the butter and add the sugar and all of the extracts. Stir over medium-low heat until the sugar is dissolved. Stir in the banana slices and blend well. Sprinkle the cinnamon over the sauce.

Scoop the ice cream into glass dessert bowls and spoon the

GREY GABLES BED & BREAKFAST

Bill and Linda Brooks Jones have a splendidly unique sense of time and place. Located in historic Rugby, Tennessee, in the heart of the lush, picturesque Cumberland Mountains, Grey Gables is furnished throughout with authentic period furniture that is right at home in this newly constructed (opened in June, 1990) dream-come-true inn.

How could you not be enchanted with an innkeeper/poet like Linda, who sums up her innkeeping approach this way:

"We welcome you to our home,
 Grey Gables,
You may rest in our beds and eat
 at our table,
Leave your worries and cares as
 you step inside
For God's Love and Peace in our
 home abides,
Please enjoy your stay at our
 Country Inn
You came as a guest, May you
 leave as a friend."

bananas and sauce over the top. Lightly sprinkle with more cinnamon and serve immediately.

GREY GABLES BED & BREAKFAST
Rugby, Tennessee

Chocolate Cherries Fandango

4 ounces semisweet chocolate
½ cup heavy cream
1 cup pitted fresh sweet cherries; reserve juice
½ tablespoon fresh lemon juice
¼ cup granulated sugar
¼ cup kirsch brandy
½ cup chopped hazelnuts
Vanilla ice cream

In the top of a double boiler, melt the chocolate. In a small saucepan, warm the cream and add to the chocolate. Stir until blended and set aside.

In a medium-sized sauté pan, combine the cherries, lemon juice, sugar, and enough of the reserved cherry juice to moisten. Cook, stirring frequently, until the sugar completely dissolves, then flambé with the brandy. Add the reserved chocolate mixture and blend together well. Toss in half of the hazelnuts and remove from heat.

Serve over and around scoops of the ice cream. Sprinkle with the remaining hazelnuts and serve immediately.

Yield: 4 servings

THE WHITE INN
Fredonia, New York

Vermont Berries & Champagne with Orange Flower Ice❖

¾ cup superfine sugar
3 cups water
1 ½ cups champagne
2 tablespoons orange flower water*

1 quart fresh berries (any local type), picked over and rinsed
Edible fresh flower blossoms

In a large saucepan, mix together the sugar and water and cook over medium heat until the sugar is completely dissolved, about 4 minutes. Remove from heat and stir in the champagne and flower water. Pour into a stainless steel pan and freeze.

Place the berries in crystal compote servers. Scrape about ¾ cup of the frozen sugar mixture and place over the berries. Garnish with the flower blossoms and serve immediately.

*Orange flower water is available at speciality gourmet food shops.

Yield: 6 to 8 servings

THE GOVERNOR'S INN
Ludlow, Vermont

Fresh Fruit with Raspberry Crème Fraîche

1 ½ pints fresh raspberries
3 ounces vanilla yogurt
1 cup *Crème Fraîche* (see recipe below)
3 fresh kiwis, peeled and sliced
3 bananas, sliced into rounds
½ pint fresh blueberries, rinsed
½ pint fresh raspberries, rinsed
6 fresh whole strawberries, washed with stems
Edible fresh flower blossoms

THE MANSAKENNING
CARRIAGE HOUSE

In a food processor, puree the raspberries. Pour the puree into a medium-sized saucepan and bring to a boil. Reduce until thick, about 10 – 15 minutes.

In a large bowl, combine the thickened puree, yogurt, and crème fraîche and mix gently. Chill overnight.

Place the chilled fraîche in dessert bowls. Divide the fruit among the servings and surround the fraîche with the fruit. Garnish with the flower blossoms and serve immediately.

Crème Fraîche

1 cup heavy cream
4 tablespoons buttermilk

In a sterilized glass container, mix together the cream and buttermilk. Cover and let stand in a warm place overnight or until thick. Makes 1 cup.

Yield: 6 servings

THE MANSAKENNING CARRIAGE HOUSE
Rhinebeck, New York

Coeur à La Crème with Strawberry Sauce

8 ounces mascarpone cheese, softened
⅔ cup confectioners' sugar
1 ¼ cups heavy cream
1 teaspoon pure vanilla extract
1 teaspoon fresh lemon juice
1 teaspoon Framboise liqueur
1 recipe *Strawberry Sauce* (see recipe below)
Fresh whole strawberries, washed, hulled, and halved

In a medium-sized bowl, beat the cheese with an electric mixer at medium speed until smooth. Add the sugar and blend well. In a separate bowl, whip the cream. Gently fold the two mixtures together, adding the vanilla, lemon juice, and liqueur.

Line one large heart mold or individual heart molds with dampened cheesecloth. Spread the mixture evenly into the mold and chill overnight with a drip pan under the mold.

Unmold the chilled crème and surround with the sauce and strawberries. Serve immediately.

Strawberry Sauce

1 ½ cups sliced fresh strawberries
Confectioners' sugar to taste
Fresh lemon juice to taste
Framboise liqueur to taste

THE INN AT LITTLE WASHINGTON

Look down from your private balcony on the sleepy village of Washington, Virginia, (population 158) or beyond to the Blue Ridge Mountains on the horizon. The views are charming, as is everything at The Inn at Little Washington.

In this splendidly romantic setting, The Inn at Little Washington is personally overseen by its proprietors, Chef Patrick O'Connell and Host Reinhardt Lynch. O'Connell is a culinary artist whose imaginative and personal adaptation of French-inspired, regional cooking led Craig Claiborne, former food editor of the *New York Times* to declare, "I had the most fantastic meal in my life."

The Inn at Little Washington was the first establishment in the Mobil Travel Guide's history to receive Five Stars for both its restaurant and its accommodations. The inn was, also, the first to receive the AAA Five-Diamond Award for both its food and accommodations. The list of honors, distinctions, and noteworthy praise goes on. If you've not yet been, go. Enough said.

In a food processor, puree the strawberries with the sugar, lemon juice, and liqueur. Pour into a covered container and chill until ready to serve. Makes 1 cup.

Yield: 6 servings

THE INN AT LITTLE WASHINGTON
Washington, Virginia

Swedish Crème with Raspberry-Currant Sauce

1 package unflavored gelatin
1 cup granulated sugar
2 cups half-and-half
2 cups sour cream
Pure vanilla extract to taste
1 recipe *Raspberry-Currant Sauce* (see recipe below)
Fresh mint leaves

In a small saucepan, mix together the gelatin and sugar. Add the half-and-half and heat until the gelatin is completely dissolved. Cool.

Add the sour cream and vanilla to the cooled mixture and whisk until smooth. Chill until set.

Spoon a little sauce in the bottom of each parfait glass and fill with the crème. Drizzle a little more sauce over the top. Garnish with a mint leaf and serve immediately.

Raspberry-Currant Sauce

10 ounces fresh frozen raspberries, thawed and crushed
1 ½ teaspoons cornstarch
1 ½ cups red currant jelly

In a small saucepan, mix together the raspberries, cornstarch, and jelly and bring to boil. Reduce heat and cook until clear and slightly thickened. Strain. Chill until ready to serve. Makes 1 ⅓ cups.

Yield: 4 to 6 servings

SNOWBIRD MOUNTAIN LODGE
Robbinsville, North Carolina

SNOWBIRD MOUNTAIN LODGE

Snowbird Mountain Lodge is located in the heart of the Nantahala National Forest, high up in Santeetlah Gap at an elevation of 2,880 feet. From the flagstone terrace, a guest has a panoramic view of the Snowbird Mountain Range. In the valley below the lodge lies sparkling Lake Santeetlah and the homes of the native Snowbird Indians.

Beautiful mountain scenery and ideal climate enhance the gracious hospitality of the lodge. Two huge stone fireplaces and wood paneling throughout the inn add to the warm feeling of this mountaintop getaway. Scenic side trips from the lodge include The Great Smoky Mountains National Park, comfortable hiking trails, and the Fontana Dam.

The mountain air stimulates the appetites of guests, and owners Eleanor and Jim Burbank are ready to serve plentiful portions of fine food in their cherry wood dining room. The Snowbird Mountain Lodge, also called the "lodge on the mountain top," has been featured in the *Chicago Sunday Tribune* and *Southern Living* magazine.

Strawberry Fool⋇

1 quart fresh strawberries, washed and hulled
½ cup granulated sugar
2 tablespoons Grand Marnier liqueur
2 cups heavy cream
White or semisweet chocolate, finely chopped

Place the strawberries in a medium-sized bowl and sprinkle with the sugar and liqueur. Let stand for 1 hour.

Before serving, whip the cream in a large bowl. Spoon some of the strawberries in a large wine glass and top with some of the whipped cream. Repeat for two more layers. Sprinkle the chocolate on top. Repeat the procedure for the remaining servings and serve immediately.

Yield: 8 servings

INTERLAKEN INN
Lake Placid, New York

Kiwi Margarita Mousse

8 ounces nondairy whipped topping
6 fresh kiwis, peeled
¾ cup granulated sugar
¼ cup fresh lime juice
¼ cup tequila
⅛ cup orange liqueur
3 egg whites, at room temperature
⅛ cup granulated sugar
Fresh whipped cream
2 fresh kiwis, peeled and sliced
12 fresh whole strawberries, washed with stems

In a medium-sized bowl, whip the topping with an electric mixer at medium speed to full volume and set aside.

In a blender or food processor, puree the kiwis, the ¾ cup sugar, lime juice, tequila, and liqueur. Set aside one-fifth of the mixture.

In a separate bowl, beat the egg whites until foamy. Continue to beat, adding the ⅛ cup sugar, one teaspoon at a time, until soft peaks form. Fold the four-fifths kiwi mixture into the egg white mixture, then gently fold in the reserved whipped topping.

Place one tablespoon of the reserved one-fifth kiwi mixture into the bottom of each margarita glass rimmed with sugar. Spoon in the mousse and freeze.

Garnish the frozen mousse with the whipped cream, kiwi slices, and strawberries and serve immediately.

Yield: 12 servings

WESTWAYS RESORT INN
Phoenix, Arizona

Frozen Grasshopper Parfaits❖

2 tablespoons crème de menthe liqueur
2 tablespoons brandy
One 14-ounce can sweetened condensed milk
1 cup heavy cream, whipped
Milk chocolate, shaved
Fresh mint leaves

In a large bowl, mix together the liqueur, brandy, and milk. Fold in the whipped cream.

Spoon the mixture into champagne glasses and freeze for at least 3 hours. Garnish with the chocolate and mint leaves and serve immediately.

Yield: 4 servings

WINDHAM HILL INN
West Townshend, Vermont

CHAPTER 9

Breakfast and Brunch

Smoked Salmon & Chive Potato Pancakes

3 pounds potatoes, peeled
½ cup chopped fresh chives
½ small onion, finely chopped
3 large eggs, beaten
⅓ cup all-purpose flour
¾ teaspoon Old Bay Seasoning
1 teaspoon seafood seasoning
¼ teaspoon freshly ground pepper
6 – 8 ounces smoked salmon, coarsely chopped and bones
   removed
1 tablespoon butter
1 – 2 tablespoons olive oil
1 recipe *Mock Sour Cream* (see recipe below)
Fresh chives, chopped
Zest of ½ lemon

In a food processor, grate the potatoes. Place the potatoes in a colander and rinse under cold water, then squeeze out excess moisture. In a large bowl, combine the potatoes, chives, onion, eggs, flour, seasonings, and pepper and mix thoroughly. Add the salmon and stir together well.

Preheat oven to 300° F. Layer several paper towels on a large rimmed baking sheet.

In a nonstick heavy frying pan, melt the butter with the olive oil and place 3 tablespoons of the potato mixture in the pan. Flatten to about ½ inch with a spatula and brown on both sides over medium heat. When browned, place the pancake on the prepared baking sheet to absorb extra moisture, then place on a second baking sheet in warm oven. Repeat for remaining batter.

Place three pancakes on each serving plate and top with a heaping tablespoon of the mock sour cream. Sprinkle with the chives and a pinch of the lemon zest. Serve immediately.

Mock Sour Cream

1 cup cottage cheese
¼ cup ricotta cheese
1 – 2 teaspoons fresh lemon juice

In a food processor, blend together all of the ingredients until

INN AT SWIFTS BAY

If the words romantic and privacy ring a mellow bell with you, then you owe it to yourself and your significant other to travel to the San Juan Islands, approximately eighty miles north of Seattle.

The Inn at Swifts Bay is a superbly renovated Tudor home just two miles from the ferry landing on Lopez Island. Innkeepers Robert Hermann and Christopher Brandmeir have created the ultimate place to be on a cold winter night. Once you've introduced yourself to your hosts, it's time for a short stroll. Just up the garden path under the cedar trees, your hosts have a steaming outdoor whirlpool spa waiting for you. And, as you will quickly observe, these innkeepers have anticipated your every need. Fluffy terry robes and towels, slippers, mineral water, and a flashlight to safely guide you back to the inn come with your overnight accommodations.

Christopher's breakfasts have been described as a work of art. Freshly baked muffins, hazelnut waffles with strawberries, kiwi fruit, blueberries, and crème fraîche might be alternated on any given day with an inspired combination of Smoked Salmon & Chive Potato Pancakes, Crab Cakes with Poached Eggs & Tarragon Hollandaise, or apple, ham, and Brie omelets. This very special place has only five elegant guest rooms, so it's a good idea to plan ahead.

very smooth, about 1 – 2 minutes. Taste for tartness and add more lemon juice if needed. Let stand for at least 1 hour or overnight, if possible.

Yield: 6 to 8 servings

INN AT SWIFTS BAY
Lopez Island, Washington

Feather Light Pancakes

2 eggs, slightly beaten
2 cups milk
4 tablespoons vegetable oil
1 ¾ cups sifted cake flour
¼ cup fine cornmeal
2 tablespoons oat bran
1 teaspoon salt
4 teapoons baking powder
1 tablespoon granulated sugar
¼ cup lightly toasted chopped pecans
Fresh peach slices
Butter pecan ice cream
Hot winter syrup*
Lightly toasted coconut
16 slices bacon, cooked and drained

Preheat oven to 350° F. In a large bowl, combine the eggs, milk, and oil. Add the next six ingredients and whisk until smooth. Stir in the pecans.

Ladle the batter on a lightly greased hot griddle and turn when bubbles appear. As the pancakes are ready, place on a platter and hold in the warm oven until ready to serve.

Place pancakes on serving plates and surround with the peach slices. Add a small scoop of the ice cream and top with the syrup. Garnish with the coconut and two slices of the bacon. Serve.

Yield: 8 servings

THE OAKS HISTORIC BED & BREAKFAST COUNTRY INN
Christiansburg, Virginia

Winter syrup
Squeeze half of a lemon per cup of syrup into commercial pancake or

waffle syrup. Heat the syrup in a microwave oven before pouring on the pancakes.

Summer syrup
Puree fresh strawberries or peaches and add 1 tablespoon Grand Marnier liqueur and confectioners' sugar to taste. Add fresh raspberries, chill, and pour the mixture on hot pancakes when ready to serve.

Pecan & Rolled Oats Pancakes❖

¾ cup whole-wheat flour
½ cup all-purpose flour
½ cup old-fashioned rolled oats
¼ cup cornmeal
½ tablespoon baking powder
1 teaspoon baking soda
Generous dash freshly grated nutmeg
⅓ cup cold butter, cut into small pieces
2 eggs
2 cups buttermilk
¼ cup honey
½ cup chopped pecans
Melted butter

In a food processor, combine all of the dry ingredients, except the pecans, and process until well blended. Add the butter and process until the mixture resembles coarse meal.

In a separate bowl, beat together the eggs and buttermilk. Beat in the honey. Stir in the flour mixture and mix well. Fold in the pecans.

Ladle the batter onto a hot griddle brushed with the melted butter and cook until golden brown. Serve with choice of topping.

Yield: 4 to 6 servings

MANOR HOUSE
Cape May, New Jersey

MANOR HOUSE

It's difficult not to be captivated by a pair of innkeepers who light-heartedly title their specialty cookbook *Mary's Buns & Tom's Puns.* Mary and Tom Snyder's Manor House is an inn with personality— two personalities especially.

Mary's Pecan & Rolled Oats Pancakes are reason enough to travel to Cape May, a historic Victorian town at the southernmost tip of New Jersey. But Tom's incessant "punny business" makes this warm and inviting place really something to experience. Come and share the adventure!

Orange-Almond Pancakes❖

¼ cup milk
½ cup fresh orange juice

2 tablespoons melted sweet butter
1 egg yolk
2 tablespoons grated orange rind
1 cup unbleached all-purpose flour
2 teaspoons baking powder
2 tablespoons granulated sugar
½ teaspoon salt
½ cup lightly toasted slivered almonds
1 egg white
Butter
Pure Vermont maple syrup, heated

In a medium-sized bowl, combine the milk, orange juice, melted butter, egg yolk, and orange zest and set aside.

In a large bowl, mix together the flour, baking powder, sugar, and salt. Slowly add the milk mixture to the flour mixture, stirring gently with a fork until just combined. Stir in the almonds. Beat the egg white in a small bowl until stiff peaks form. Fold into the flour and milk mixture.

Ladle the batter onto a lightly greased hot skillet or griddle to form 3-inch circles. Cook until bubbles form, turn, and cook until golden brown, about 1 minute. Serve with the butter and syrup.

Yield: 4 to 6 servings

BLUEBERRY HILL
Goshen, Vermont

Plum-Cottage Cheese Pancakes❖

6 eggs
2 ½ cups cottage cheese
¼ cup vegetable oil
½ cup all-purpose flour
½ teaspoon salt
1 tablespoon granulated sugar
3 fresh purple plums, pitted and coarsely chopped
3 fresh purple plums, pitted and sliced
Pure maple syrup, heated

Preheat a well-oiled griddle or a large nonstick sauté pan.

In a large mixing bowl, beat together the eggs and cottage cheese. Add, in order, the oil, flour, salt, and sugar, beating well after each addition. Stir in the chopped plums.

Ladle the batter onto the prepared griddle by the half-cupful and cook until golden brown on both sides, carefully turning once. Garnish each serving with the sliced plums and serve with the syrup.

Yield: 6 servings

GRANT CORNER INN
Santa Fe, New Mexico

Sally's Baked Apple Pancake❖

2 Granny Smith apples, peeled, cored, and thinly sliced
2 teaspoons ground cinnamon
½ cup granulated sugar
½ cup packed light brown sugar
¾ cup all-purpose flour
1 teaspoon baking powder
Pinch salt
¾ cup buttermilk
3 eggs, lightly beaten
2 tablespoons vegetable oil
5 tablespoons unsalted butter

Preheat oven to 375° F. Very lightly oil a well-seasoned, oven-proof 10-inch skillet with sloped sides.

In a small bowl, mix together the apple slices, cinnamon, and both sugars and set aside. In a medium-sized bowl, combine the flour, baking powder, and salt. Stir in the buttermilk, eggs, and oil just until the dry ingredients are moistened. Set aside.

In the prepared skillet, melt the butter over medium heat and add the reserved apple mixture. Cook, stirring frequently, until the sugars have melted and the apples are coated.

Pour the reserved batter over the apple mixture and bake until puffed, the edges are golden, and the apples are tender, about 25 – 35 minutes. Turn the pancake onto a serving platter and cut into servings. Serve immediately.

Yield: 4 servings

THE HEARTSTONE INN
Eureka Springs, Arkansas

THE INN AT STARLIGHT LAKE

"One morning long ago in the quiet of the world when there was less noise and more green. . . ." Although the words are J.R.R. Tolkien's from *The Hobbit*, they describe equally well the 1909 beginning for Pennsylvania's beloved Inn at Starlight Lake.

Jack and Judy McMahon welcome their guests year-round to this veritable "mountain jewel" of a lake. Pristine virgin forests and farmland meadows surround the fern banks, moss-covered boulders, shady dells, and natural woodland scenes that accent the beauty of clear, spring-fed Starlight Lake.

Return from your cross-country ski adventure or pleasant midsummer trek to the indoor comfort of warming wood fires, good hearty food, and an entertaining old movie from the innkeepers' private collection of films.

Raised Dough Waffles

2 tablespoons active dry yeast
2 ½ cups lukewarm water (105° – 115° F)
½ cup nonfat dry milk
½ cup vegetable oil
1 teaspoon salt
1 teaspoon granulated sugar
1 ½ cups all-purpose flour
½ cup whole-wheat flour
¼ cup wheat germ
2 eggs, well beaten
Pinch baking soda
Butter, at room temperature
Flavored syrup

In a large mixing bowl, dissolve the yeast in ½ cup of the lukewarm water. (Bowl should be large enough to allow batter to triple in size.) Let stand for 5 minutes.

Stir in the remaining water, dry milk, oil, salt, and sugar. Add, in order, the all-purpose flour, whole-wheat flour, and wheat germ, beating after each addition and mixing together well. Cover the bowl with a small towel and let stand overnight in a warm place.

Add the eggs and baking soda and mix well. Pour about ⅓ cup of the batter into a heated waffle iron and bake for 5 – 7 minutes or until golden brown. Serve immediately with the butter and syrup.

Yield: 4 to 6 servings

INN AT STARLIGHT LAKE
Starlight, Pennsylvania

Baked French Toast with Orange-Apricot Grand Marnier Sauce

¼ cup sugar-cinnamon mixture (to taste)
4 eggs, well beaten
2 cups milk
Pinch salt

Dash ground nutmeg
1 tablespoon pure vanilla extract
1 loaf Italian bread, cut into 1 ½-inch thick slices, 4 slices
Confectioners' sugar
Fresh fruit, sliced
1 recipe *Orange-Apricot Grand Marnier Sauce* (see recipe below)

In a medium-sized bowl, mix together the sugar-cinnamon, eggs, milk, salt, nutmeg, and vanilla and blend well. Place the bread slices in an 8 x 12 x 2-inch glass baking dish and pour half of the egg mixture over the slices. Let stand for 10 minutes.

Carefully turn the slices over and pour over the remaining egg mixture. Cover with plastic wrap and chill overnight.

Preheat oven to 300° F. Spray a jelly-roll pan with cooking spray. Carefully place the chilled bread on the pan (keep pieces from touching, if possible) and bake for 1 hour.

Place one slice of baked toast on each serving plate and dust with the confectioners' sugar. Top with the sliced fruit and serve with the warm sauce.

Orange-Apricot Grand Marnier Sauce

½ cup orange marmalade
¼ cup fresh orange juice
¾ cup apricot puree
2 tablespoons Grand Marnier liqueur

In a small bowl, mix together all of the ingredients. Heat before serving. Makes about 1 ½ cups.

Yield: 4 servings

THE INN AT STOCKBRIDGE
Stockbridge, Massachusetts

THE INN AT STOCKBRIDGE

There is something very special about a white-columned mansion set discreetly back from the road among the trees. If you're not looking for the traditional hand-carved pineapple sign on Route 7 as you travel north from Stockbridge, you'll probably miss it. That's all right, because this is one inn experience worth turning around for. *New York* magazine glowingly describes Lee and Don Weitz's inn by observing, "Goodwill is rampant. The atmosphere unobtrusively homey. The obvious contentment of the guests is testament to the consummate hospitality of the hosts."

Only sixteen fortunate people at one time can enjoy the ambience of the Inn with its eight uniquely adorned guest rooms. Whether you're lounging in the parlor over complimentary wine and cheese or frolicking in the pool, you are able to relax much as you would in the home of a somewhat aristocratic and slightly wealthy relative.

This Georgian-style 1906 charmer, where hospitality reigns supreme, serves the most elegant and elaborate breakfasts imaginable—always on elegant china and always on the antique dining room table. Unless, of course, you prefer to dine somewhere else in the inn or on the grounds. Your comfort and your preferences come first here.

THE MANSAKENNING
CARRIAGE HOUSE

They say that what really sets Michelle and John Dremann's beloved Mansakenning Carriage House apart are the guest rooms. As you look over the following descriptions, you'll begin to see what they mean.

The Mansakenning Suite with eleven windows is the largest guest room in the inn. With a cathedral ceiling, French doors, private balcony, woodburning fireplace, and a king-sized bed, it's safe to say this is not your "run of the mill" inn guest room. The Huntsman's Hideaway, Fox Den, Country Covert, and Saddlery are also luxuriously appointed suites, which have been created within the inn's former stables. This meticulously renovated building, where the horses used to "bed down," now sports antiques, rare books, and fine art.

Plush bathrobes and fresh fruit trays in your beautiful room set the standard of warmth and hospitality to which others can only aspire.

Pecan & Cream Cheese-Stuffed French Toast with Peach-Apricot Sauce

One French baguette, cut into 1 ½-inch slices
One 8-ounce package cream cheese, softened
1 cup pecans
9 tablespoons Curaçao liqueur
4 – 6 tablespoons honey
⅔ cup half-and-half
2 large eggs, beaten
1 teaspoon pure vanilla extract
2 tablespoons clarified butter
1 recipe *Peach-Apricot Sauce* (see recipe below)
3 – 4 fresh peaches, pitted and sliced
Confectioners' sugar

Lay the sliced bread on a work surface and slice through almost to the end to make a slit in the center for stuffing.

In a food processor, puree the cream cheese, ½ cup of the pecans, 3 tablespoons of the liqueur, and 4 tablespoons of the honey. Taste and adjust, adding more honey if needed. Coarsely chop the remaining pecans and fold into the cream cheese mixture. Stuff the sliced bread with 1 tablespoon of the mixture. Set aside.

In a medium-sized bowl, mix together the half-and-half and eggs. Add the vanilla and remaining liqueur and blend well. Dip the reserved bread slices into the egg batter, turning to coat well. In a large skillet, heat the butter and sauté the bread over medium heat until golden brown and crisp.

Serve two to three slices of the French toast per person and top with the sauce. Garnish with a half of a peach fanned out and sprinkle with the confectioners' sugar. Serve.

Peach-Apricot Sauce

One 6-ounce can peaches in syrup
¾ cup apricot preserves or jam
3 tablespoons Curaçao liqueur

In a blender or food processor, puree the peaches with the syrup until smooth. Pour into a small saucepan and stir in the preserves and liqueur. Cook over medium heat until thickened.

Keep warm until ready to use.

Yield: 6 to 8 servings

THE MANSAKENNING CARRIAGE HOUSE
Rhinebeck, New York

Blueberry-Stuffed French Toast

12 slices thick bread, crusts removed and cubed
Two 8-ounce packages cream cheese, cubed
3 cups fresh blueberries
12 eggs
⅓ cup pure maple syrup
2 cups milk
1 cup water
1 cup granulated sugar
2 tablespoons cornstarch
1 tablespoon butter, melted

Spray a 9 x 13-inch glass baking dish with cooking spray and place half of the bread cubes in the bottom. Evenly place the cream cheese cubes over the top of the bread and scatter 1 cup of the blueberries over the cream cheese. Place the remaining bread over the blueberries.

In a large bowl, beat together the eggs, syrup, and milk. Pour the egg mixture over the bread and cheese. Cover with plastic wrap and chill overnight.

Preheat oven to 350° F. Remove plastic wrap and cover with aluminum foil and bake for 30 minutes. Remove foil and bake for 30 minutes more.

In a small saucepan, combine the water, sugar, cornstarch, and 1 cup of the blueberries and cook until the sauce thickens, stirring frequently. Mix in the remaining blueberries and butter. Keep warm.

Cut the French toast into serving pieces. Pour the warm sauce over each piece and serve immediately.

Yield: 8 servings

MAPLES INN
Bar Harbor, Maine

MAPLES INN

"There is a pleasure in the pathless woods, and a rapture on the lonely shore. There is a society where none intrudes, by the deep sea, and music in its roar." With these words Bar Harbor, Maine's Maples Inn welcomes you to the early 1900s.

Located on a quiet residential street, the Maples Inn offers six tastefully decorated guest rooms named after the trees of northern Maine: White Birch, Weeping Willow, Shore Pine, English Holly, Red Oak, and Silver Maple. An often requested breakfast favorite original of owner/innkeeper Susan Sinclair is Blueberry-Stuffed French Toast.

Dieters' Note: Fat-free cream cheese and low-calorie bread may be substituted to lower the "guilt quotient" considerably!

Stuffed French Toast ❖

4 ounces cream cheese, softened
¼ cup ricotta cheese
8 slices whole-wheat bread, crusts removed
3 tablespoons blueberry preserves
10 eggs, beaten
¼ cup whipping cream
1 tablespoon pure vanilla extract
1 – 2 tablespoons butter
Fresh blueberries, rinsed
Pure maple syrup, heated

In a small bowl, beat together both cheeses until smooth. Divide the cheese among four slices of the bread, spreading to the edges. Dot each slice with the preserves, then top each with the remaining bread slices. Cut the slices with a heart-shaped cookie cutter.

In a wide shallow baking dish, beat together the eggs, cream, and vanilla and soak the bread in the egg mixture, turning once.

In a large sauté pan, melt the butter and sauté the bread over medium heat until golden brown on both sides, turning once. Sprinkle the blueberries on each serving and serve immediately with the warm syrup.

Yield: 4 servings

GRANT CORNER INN
Santa Fe, New Mexico

Orange Sauce

2 teaspoons butter
1 ½ cups honey
2 tablespoons grated orange rind
½ cup fresh orange juice
2 teaspoons pure orange extract
French toast
Fresh peach slices
Freshly whipped cream

In a small saucepan, melt the butter with the honey. Remove from heat and stir in the orange zest, orange juice, and orange extract.

Drizzle warm over French toast. Add the peach slices and top with a dollop of the whipped cream. (The sauce can be stored in the refrigerator. Warm before serving.)

Yield: 2 cups

SUGARTREE INN
Warren, Vermont

David's Spicy Sausage⬧

2 ½ pounds pork steak, cut into 1-inch pieces
½ medium green bell pepper, finely chopped
5 cloves garlic, minced
¼ cup finely chopped fresh Italian parsley
⅛ cup finely chopped fresh oregano
⅛ cup chopped fresh chives
1 tablespoon freshly ground black pepper
½ tablespoon cayenne pepper
Salt
1 cup red table wine

In a large glass bowl, mix together all of the ingredients. Marinate overnight in the refrigerator, stirring occasionally.

Push the mixture through a sausage grinder with ¼-inch diameter holes only once. Either stuff directly into a casing or reserve for bulk sausage. (The sausage can be stored in the refrigerator until ready to serve or frozen.)

Yield: 2 ½ pounds

SHELBURNE INN
Seaview, Washington

Spicy Eggs & Cheese Soufflés

½ loaf sourdough French bread, sliced and cubed
¼ cup cooked chopped mild green chile peppers
¾ cup chopped fresh mushrooms
¾ cup chopped green onions
6 eggs
1 cup milk
1 ¼ teaspoons dry mustard

SUGARTREE INN

Close your eyes for a moment and just imagine what your typically romantic, western Vermont country inn might be . . . and your imagination will take you to the front porch of Sugartree. Located just steps away from one of Vermont's premier ski slopes, Sugarbush, the Sugartree Inn is an inn-goers delight. From the warm glow of oil lamps flickering on a snowy December evening to the thousands of vibrant flowers, which frame the inn in the spring, Sugartree lives up to the promise of a gracious retreat.

Kathy and Frank Partsch, the owners and innkeepers, have a particular affinity for brunch with guests and friends. Sugartree's Orange Sauce drizzled over French toast with fresh peaches and whipped cream is like the taste of a summer sunrise on a cold winter day.

THE GINGERBREAD MANSION

What happens when a highly successful San Francisco financial analyst with a green cameo Depression glass collection and a penchant for serving others falls in love with an 1899 picture-postcard-perfect Victorian mansion? Read on!

The Gingerbread Mansion, located in the lovingly restored Victorian village of Ferndale, California, is a nine-guest room inn featuring a unique combination of Queen Anne and Eastlake architectural styles elaborately trimmed with ornate gingerbread. Painted in pleasing and traffic-stopping yellow and peach tones and surrounded by its own colorful English garden of provocative topiaries and two-story-tall camelias, The Gingerbread Mansion is widely considered to be one of northern California's most photographed homes. This striking inn has been featured everywhere, from 1,000-piece jigsaw puzzles to the cover of *How to Open and Successfully Operate a Country Inn.*

The thoughtful extras in this very special place always include a generous and sumptuous homemade breakfast, bathrobes tucked neatly in the dresser drawer, turned down beds with delicately placed hand-dipped chocolates on the pillow, an early morning tray of coffee and juice in your room, of course, and guest bicycles painted to match the colors of the inn. Ken Torbert, your gracious host, is proud to serve you breakfast each day of your stay, and he serves it on his keepsake Depression glassware.

Dash ground cumin
1 ¼ cups cooked cubed ham
¾ cup shredded Monterey Jack cheese
¾ cup shredded cheddar cheese
Ground paprika

Grease six 8-ounce ramekins. Place enough bread cubes in each ramekin to fill the bottom. Divide, in order, the peppers, mushrooms, and green onions over the bread.

In a medium-sized bowl, beat together the eggs, milk, mustard, and cumin and pour evenly over the ramekins. Divide the ham evenly among the ramekins and top with both cheeses. Sprinkle with the paprika. Cover and chill overnight.

Preheat oven to 350° F. Bake, uncovered, for 30 minutes. Serve immediately.

Yield: 6 servings

THE GINGERBREAD MANSION
Ferndale, California

Pat's Huevos Rancheros❖

2 ½ cups *Pat's Beans* (see recipe below)
6 blue or yellow corn tortillas
¾ cup fresh salsa
6 eggs
1 cup sour cream
1 ½ cups shredded longhorn cheese

In a medium-sized saucepan, heat the beans over low heat, covered, for 10 – 15 minutes, stirring occasionally.

Preheat oven to 350° F. Wrap the tortillas in aluminum foil and place in the oven for 5 minutes.

Place each softened tortilla on the bottom of a shallow, individual baking dish and divide the warm beans, then the salsa among the tortillas.

In a large skillet, fry the eggs. Place 1 egg on each tortilla. Top with the sour cream and the cheese and bake for 5 minutes, or just until the cheese has melted. Serve immediately.

Pat's Beans

1 pound uncooked pinto beans
1/3 cup hot bacon drippings
1 pound lean ground beef
1 cup chopped onions
1 clove garlic, minced
1/4 cup oyster sauce
1 tablespoon Worcestershire sauce
1 small pickled jalapeño pepper, seeded and chopped
1 teaspoon adobo seasoning or salt
1 egg, beaten

Soak the beans in 6 cups water overnight. Drain. Add 4 cups fresh water and simmer, covered, for 1 hour 30 minutess or until very tender.

In a Dutch oven, heat the bacon drippings and cook the beef, onions, and garlic. Do not drain. Add the oyster sauce, Worcestershire sauce, jalapeño pepper, and seasoning.

Slightly mash the cooked beans. Add the mashed beans to the beef mixture and cook, uncovered, for 40 – 45 minutes, or until the mixture is very thick and most of the liquid is evaporated.

Stir about 1 cup of the hot mixture into the egg. Return to the Dutch oven and cook until bubbly, stirring constantly. Cook, stirring constantly, for 1 minute more. Makes about 7 cups.

Yield: 6 servings

GRANT CORNER INN
Santa Fe, New Mexico

Eggs Rellenos

3 medium green bell peppers, seeded and cut into 1/4-inch slices
3 medium red bell peppers, seeded and cut into 1/4-inch slices
1/3 pound medium-sharp cheddar cheese, grated
1/3 pound Monterey Jack cheese, grated
6 eggs
1 cup ricotta or cottage cheese
1/2 teaspoon seasoning salt
1/4 teaspoon white pepper
2 cups sour cream
1 cup fresh salsa

Preheat oven to 350° F. Grease a 9 x 13-inch baking pan.

Layer all of the pepper slices with both grated cheeses in the prepared pan. Set aside.

In a blender, beat the eggs. Add the ricotta cheese and blend until smooth. Add the seasonings and sour cream and blend for 5 seconds more. Stir in the salsa.

Pour the mixture over the reserved pepper and cheese mixture and bake for 1 hour or until puffed and golden and set in the middle. Remove from the oven and let stand for 10 minutes before serving. Serve.

Yield: 6 to 8 generous servings

THE BABBLING BROOK
Santa Cruz, California

THE INN AT THE TAYLOR HOUSE

Chip and Roland Schwab have created a bit of Europe in the peaceful, rural heart of the Blue Ridge Mountains. This charming farmhouse is decorated with fine antiques, oriental rugs, artwork, and European goose down comforters on all of the beds. Bright fabrics, wicker furniture, and flowering plants abound. Thoughtful touches include fluffy terry robes in each guest room and personalized glycerine soaps.

Summertime afternoon tea at the Taylor House has become so popular that reservations are encouraged. The inn also serves as home to an irresistible menagerie of farm animals and one "cock of the walk," named "Joses," who greets each new dawn with his own brand of Taylor House "cockle doodle doo."

Chilied Puffed Eggs

5 eggs, well beaten
1 cup cottage cheese
¼ cup all-purpose flour
¼ teaspoon salt
½ pound Monterey Jack cheese, grated
¼ cup (½ stick) butter, melted
½ teaspoon baking powder
One 4-ounce can diced green chilies, drained

Preheat oven to 350° F. Lightly butter a 9 x 13-inch glass baking dish.

In a large bowl, combine the first seven ingredients and mix together well. Stir in the chilies. Pour into the prepared pan and bake for 35 minutes, or until lightly browned and a knife inserted in the center comes out clean. Serve immediately.

Variations: Add slivered ham, cooked and drained sausage, sliced fresh mushrooms, or chopped artichoke hearts.

Yield: 8 generous servings

THE INN AT THE TAYLOR HOUSE
Valle Crucis, North Carolina

Chard-Sausage Eggs

1 bunch fresh swiss chard
½ pound mild Italian or turkey sausage
1 tablespoon butter
1 medium onion, chopped
6 – 8 fresh mushrooms, sliced
1 clove garlic, minced
6 – 8 eggs
2 tablespoons water
1 medium tomato, sliced
½ cup grated Monterey Jack cheese

In a large saucepan, steam the chard for 3 – 6 minutes or until tender. Chop set aside.

Remove the casing and cut the sausage into small pieces. In a medium-sized ovenproof frying pan, melt the butter. Stir in the sausage pieces, onion, mushrooms, and garlic and cook over medium heat until the vegetables are tender and the sausage is lightly browned. Stir in the reserved chard and cook for about 1 minute to allow the liquid to evaporate.

In a medium-sized bowl, beat the eggs. Add the water and continue to beat until well blended. Pour the egg mixture over the chard mixture and cook the eggs, gently lifting the cooked portion to allow uncooked portion to cook.

Preheat the broiler. When the egg mixture is softly set, remove from heat. Top with the tomato slices and cheese. Place the pan under the broiler until the cheese is melted. Cut into serving portions and serve immediately.

Yield: 4 to 6 servings

RANCHO SAN GREGORIO
San Gregorio, California

Eggs Picante❖

6 eggs
½ cup sour cream
¼ pound bulk sausage
⅛ cup finely chopped onions
¼ cup picante sauce or salsa

GARTH WOODSIDE MANSION

Mark Twain was not the only guest of John Garth, the prosperous business man of Hannibal, Missouri, who owned this splendid Victorian mansion, but Twain most certainly was one of the better known. When you first gaze upon the soaring exterior of this extensively trimmed 1870 Victorian, it is difficult not to wonder about its past. Because the mansion remained essentially a single-family residence for most of the twentieth century, before becoming a museum, the majority of the antiquities originally collected by Mr. Garth and his family during the last quarter of the nineteenth century remain together.

When Irv and Diane Feinberg purchased the Garth Woodside Mansion in 1987, they did so with a steadfast dedication to accurately restoring it to its original splendor. Everything from the authentic nineteenth-century paint colors on the exterior to the use of documentary wallpapers and rich period trim paint on the interior reflects the care and dedication of innkeepers with a mission. The end result is spectacular. The thoroughly restored interior furnishings have been complemented by the Feinbergs' own extensive collection of Victoriana.

Breakfast is serious business here. Elegant fresh fruitcups are made even more so by the addition of a smooth Lemon Cream Sauce, and Eggs Picante or Spicy Sausage Quiche typically complete the feast. Mark Twain would have been very proud.

CASTLE MARNE

Built in 1889, Castle Marne is considered by many to be the finest example of the brilliance of America's most eclectic architect, William Lang. Its history glows through the hand-rubbed woods, the renowned circular stained glass Peacock Window, and the spectacular, original ornate fireplaces.

Your stay at the Pieker family's castle combines Old World grace and Victorian charm with modern-day convenience and comfort. Each guest room is a unique experience in pampered elegance. Carefully chosen furnishings bring together authentic period antiques and family heirlooms to create the perfect mood for a romantic weekend getaway.

Relax away the pressures of everyday life in one of the luxury suites, complete with a soothing soak in your own jet whirlpool tub. You awake to the spicy aroma of brewing Marne-blend coffee and homemade breads and muffins. Linger over a complete gourmet breakfast in the extravagant cherry-paneled formal dining room, and let your spirits be swept away to another century.

¼ cup sliced fresh mushrooms
4 ounces cheddar cheese, grated
4 ounces mozzarella or Monterey Jack cheese, grated

Preheat oven to 350° F. In a blender or food processor, blend together the eggs and sour cream. Pour into a greased 9 x 13-inch baking dish and bake until set, about 15 minutes.

In a small skillet, sauté the sausage and onions for about 5 – 7 minutes, or until the sausage is lightly browned. Drain the fat and set aside.

Remove the egg mixture from the oven and cool slightly. Drizzle with ⅛ cup of the salsa. Spoon the reserved sausage mixture and the mushrooms over the salsa. In a small bowl, mix together both cheeses and sprinkle over the top. Bake for 25 – 30 minutes or until bubbly. Drizzle with the remaining salsa and serve immediately.

Yield: 6 servings

GARTH WOODSIDE MANSION
Hannibal, Missouri

Colorado Chili Casseroles

Four 7-ounce cans whole mild green chiles, drained
1 pound Monterey Jack cheese, cut into ¼-inch slices
5 eggs, beaten
1 cup milk
¼ cup all-purpose flour
½ teaspoon salt
Dash white pepper
2 cups grated mild cheddar cheese
Sour cream
8 fresh tomato slices

Slit the chiles lengthwise on one side. Remove the seeds and drain on paper towels. Place the cheese slices inside the chiles.

Preheat oven to 350° F. Divide the stuffed chiles among eight greased ramekins. In a medium-sized bowl, mix together well the eggs, milk, flour, salt, and white pepper and pour the mixture evenly over the chiles. Sprinkle the top with the grated cheese and bake, uncovered, for 45 minutes.

Garnish each serving with a dollop of the sour cream and a tomato slice. Serve.

Yield: 8 servings

CASTLE MARNE
Denver, Colorado

Baked Eggs
with Three Cheeses❖

4 eggs
½ cup milk
1 teaspoon granulated sugar
½ pound Muenster cheese, shredded
2 ounces cream cheese, cubed
1 cup small curd cottage cheese
⅓ cup butter, melted
¼ cup all-purpose flour
½ teaspoon baking powder

Preheat oven to 350° F. Spray a 2-quart baking dish with cooking spray.

In a medium-sized bowl, beat together the eggs, milk, and sugar. Add the cheeses and butter and mix well. Stir in the flour and baking powder.

Pour the mixture into the prepared dish and bake for 45 – 50 minutes, or until a knife inserted in the center comes out clean. Cut into wedges and serve immediately.

Yield: 6 servings

THE QUEEN VICTORIA
Cape May, New Jersey

Breakfast Casserole

¼ pound sharp cheddar cheese, grated
¼ teaspoon dry mustard
¼ teaspoon ground paprika
½ teaspoon salt

THE QUEEN VICTORIA

If watching the pounding surf, enjoying excellent restaurants, touring historic homes, or simply curling up with a good book by the fireplace is your idea of the perfect getaway retreat, then The Queen Victoria, located in the heart of Cape May's National Landmark Historic District, may be just your cup of tea.

Dane and Joan Wells take pride in providing royal service to their guests. From your turned-down bed in the evening with a special treat awaiting you on the pillow to a "serve yourself" popcorn popper and ice maker in the twenty-four-hour guest pantry, The Queen Victoria offers the pampering of a special retreat with all the conveniences of home. You can even enjoy breakfast in bed on a wicker tray, filled with home-baked treats, fresh juice, quiche, and hot coffee and delivered to your guest room door.

Guests who prefer to have breakfast among others often join other guests gathered at the "groaning sideboards" for a hearty breakfast of egg casserole, fresh Jersey fruits, juices, home-baked breads and muffins, the Queen Victoria's signature granola, and imported coffees and English teas. Royal indeed.

1880 SEAFIELD HOUSE

In the village of West Hampton Beach is Seafield House, a hidden 100-year-old bed and breakfast country retreat that is the perfect place for a romantic hideaway, a weekend of privacy, or just a change of pace from city life. Only ninety minutes from Manhattan, Seafield House is ideally situated on the beach's exclusive Seafield Lane.

Seafield House is not just a rural retreat, but a home, lovingly preserved by Mrs. Elsie Collins and lavishly filled with her antiques and personal touches. The house was built sometime between 1873 and 1888 and features the Victorian architectural designs of that era.

Many guests are sent away with a jar of Mrs. Collins' rhubarb-ginger jam after enjoying a delicious Breakfast Casserole and freshly baked muffins. Her guests rave about her cooking and the beautiful inn that she calls home.

½ **cup sour cream**
½ **pound bulk sausage, cooked and drained**
5 – 8 eggs

Spray a 2-quart baking dish with cooking spray.

Sprinkle half of the cheese in the bottom of the prepared dish. In a small bowl, combine the mustard, paprika, salt, and sour cream. Add the sausage and spread the mixture over the cheese. Cover with plastic wrap and chill overnight.

Preheat oven to 325° F. In a medium-sized bowl, beat the eggs and pour over the chilled sausage mixture. Sprinkle the remaining cheese over the top and bake for 25 – 30 minutes, or until the eggs are set. Serve immediately.

Yield: 4 to 6 servings

1880 SEAFIELD HOUSE
West Hampton Beach, New York

Smoked Salmon Torte

6 ounces cream cheese
½ **cup sour cream**
½ **pound smoked salmon**
1 tablespoon capers
1 ½ teaspoons Dijon mustard
1 teaspoon chopped fresh dill
⅔ **cup unbleached all-purpose flour**
⅓ **cup buckwheat flour**
Pinch salt
3 eggs, beaten
1 cup milk
2 tablespoons melted butter
Sour cream
6 – 8 sprigs fresh dill

In a food processor, blend the cream cheese and ½ cup sour cream until smooth. Add the salmon, capers, mustard, and dill and process by pulses until just blended. Do not puree, but blend carefully so the filling has some pieces of salmon and the capers are still intact. Set aside until the crêpes are made.

In a medium-sized mixing bowl, sift together both flours and salt. In a small bowl, mix together the eggs, milk, and butter.

Make a well in the center of the flour mixture and add the egg mixture. Whisk until well blended and smooth. Let stand for 15 minutes.

Heat a 10 – 12-inch nonstick sauté pan or skillet until very hot. Ladle the batter into the pan, rapidly tipping and moving the pan in a figure-eight motion so the batter is evenly and thinly covering the bottom and slightly up the sides. Brown on one side for 40 seconds. Turn and brown the other side. Remove and repeat the procedure to make four more crêpes. As each crêpe each prepared, stack and set aside. Keep warm.

Spread the reserved filling over each of four crêpes and stack, ending with a crêpe on top. Cut into wedges and top with a dollop each of the filling and sour cream. Add a dill sprig to each serving and serve.

Yield: 6 to 8 servings

TURTLEBACK FARM INN
Orcas Island, Washington

Crab Brunch Squares with Red Pepper Cream Sauce❖

4 eggs
2 ⅔ cups milk
¾ teaspoon Dijon mustard
6 ounces Brie cheese, rind removed and cut into ¼-inch cubes
½ cup sliced black olives
1 small onion, finely chopped
2 tablespoons finely chopped fresh parsley
1 teaspoon Worcestershire sauce
3 ½ cups cooked white rice
1 pound fresh lump crabmeat, picked through for shells and shredded
Ground paprika
1 recipe *Red Pepper Cream Sauce* (see recipe below)

Preheat oven to 325° F. In a medium-sized mixing bowl, beat the eggs, milk, and mustard until well blended. Stir in the remaining ingredients, except the paprika. Pour into a greased 9 x 13-inch baking pan and bake for 40 – 45 minutes, or until a knife inserted in the center comes out clean.

TURTLEBACK FARM INN

The Turtleback Farm Inn overlooks eighty acres of forest and farmland in the shadow of Turtleback Mountain and commands a spectacular view of lush meadows, duck ponds, and classic country outbuildings. Without a doubt, Orcas Island is one of the loveliest among the San Juan Archipelago in the sparkling waters of Puget Sound.

Originally constructed in the late 1800s, the farmhouse was renovated and expanded in 1985. The living room boasts a Rumford fireplace, comfortable seating, and every guest room is furnished with a blend of contemporary and antique pieces. The travel editor of the *Los Angeles Times* chose the inn as one of the dozen most romantic spots in the United States.

Innkeepers Bill and Susan Fletcher provide a zestful beginning to the day with a breakfast of fresh fruit, homemade granola, and freshly baked breads or pastries. The daily main course features farm fresh eggs and meats in delightful combinations. At the end of the day, relax with a glass of sherry by the fire. You're among friends.

Lightly sprinkle the paprika over the top and cut into squares. Serve immediately with the sauce.

Red Pepper Cream Sauce

4 tablespoons (½ stick) unsalted butter
1 large red bell pepper, seeded and cut into ¼-inch dice
¼ cup thinly sliced green onions
¼ cup all-purpose flour
¼ teaspoon salt
¼ teaspoon white pepper
1 ¾ cups milk
3 teaspoons fresh lemon juice
Fresh chives, finely chopped

In a small heavy saucepan, melt the butter and sauté the bell pepper and onions for 2 minutes. Add the flour and sauté over low heat for 3 minutes more. Blend in the salt and white pepper. Gradually whisk in the milk and lemon juice and cook for 1 minute.

Place the mixture in a blender and blend on high for 2 minutes or until thoroughly pureed. Spoon over the brunch squares and garnish with the chives. Makes about 2 cups.

Yield: 8 generous servings

GRANT CORNER INN
Santa Fe, New Mexico

Country Ham with Redeye Gravy❖

1 pound country ham
Vegetable oil
1 cup freshly brewed black coffee

Preheat oven to 350° F. Cut the ham into biscuit-sized pieces and place in a cast-iron skillet. Drizzle a small amount of oil over the ham pieces and "fry" in the oven for 10 – 15 minutes. Do not overcook.

Place the cooked ham in a shallow serving bowl and keep warm, while making the gravy.

Pour off excess fat from the skillet, leaving 1 – 2 tablespoons of the drippings. Add the hot coffee, stirring constantly, and bring to a boil. Stirring constantly, continue to cook, scraping the bottom of the skillet to include the red-colored residue that sticks to the bottom. If it boils down too much, add a little water.

Pour the gravy over the reserved ham and serve immediately.

Yield: 8 side servings

MAST FARM INN
Valle Crucis, North Carolina

Angel Biscuits with Honey-Mustard & Country Ham❖

2 ½ cups all-purpose flour
½ tablespoon baking powder
½ teaspoon baking soda
⅛ cup granulated sugar
½ tablespoon salt
½ cup vegetable shortening
½ tablespoon active dry yeast
¼ teaspoon warm water
1 cup buttermilk
⅛ cup honey
⅛ cup whole grain mustard
3 – 4 ounces country ham, thinly sliced

Preheat oven to 450° F. In a large bowl, sift together the flour, baking powder, baking soda, sugar, and salt. Cut in the shortening quickly with fingertips or a pastry blender until the mixture is the consistency of coarse meal.

In a small bowl, dissolve the yeast in the warm water. When the yeast is active, add the yeast and buttermilk to the shortening mixture and mix together until smooth.

Knead the dough for 2 – 3 minutes. Roll out the dough on a lightly floured surface to a ½-inch thickness. Cut the biscuits with a biscuit cutter and place on an ungreased baking sheet. Let rise for 30 minutes, then bake the biscuits for 10 minutes.

In a small bowl, mix together the honey and mustard and set aside.

Slice each biscuit in half and spread with the honey mixture. Add a thin slice of the ham and replace the top half of the biscuit. Serve. (Biscuits not served can be frozen.)

Yield: 15 biscuits

THE FEARRINGTON HOUSE
Pittsboro, North Carolina

Southwestern Chicken❖

6 frozen pastry shells
One 6 ½-ounce jar marinated artichokes
½ cup sour cream
One 4-ounce can chopped green chiles
½ teaspoon minced garlic
1 teaspoon fresh lemon juice
½ teaspoon salt
2 tablespoons chopped green onions
3 cups cooked diced chicken
1 cup grated Monterey Jack cheese

Bake the pastry shells according to package directions.

In a food processor, combine the remaining ingredients, except the chicken and cheese, and pulse until well blended.

In large saucepan, combine the chicken, cheese, and artichoke mixture and heat, stirring constantly, until the cheese melts and the mixture is hot. Do not let burn on the bottom.

Spoon the mixture into the pastry shells and serve immediately.

Yield: 6 servings

INTERLAKEN INN
Lake Placid, New York

Basil-Mint Frittata with Pine Nuts & Chicken❖

12 eggs
¼ cup whipping cream

Salt to taste
½ cup chopped fresh mint
½ cup chopped fresh basil
½ cup pine nuts
¼ cup olive oil
Cayenne pepper to taste
¾ cup cooked chopped chicken breast
½ cup cooked fresh-cut corn kernels
½ cup grated cheddar cheese
Fresh salsa
Crème fraîche

In a large bowl, beat together the eggs, cream, and salt. Set aside.

In a small bowl, combine the herbs, pine nuts, oil, and cayenne. Heat an 8-inch nonstick sauté pan and add one-fourth of the oil mixture to the hot pan and sauté until the pine nuts are browned. Stir in one-fourth of the chicken and and one-fourth of the corn.

Set heat to medium and add one-fourth of the reserved egg mixture to the pan. Add one-fourth of the cheese, pushing the cheese into the eggs until no longer visible. Pull in the edges of the egg mixture as the eggs firm. When the bottom of the frittata is golden, turn and continue to cook until other side is golden.

Turn the frittata onto a warmed plate and place in a warm oven. Repeat the procedure to make three more frittatas.

Garnish each frittata with the salsa and crème fraîche and serve immediately.

Yield: 4 servings

SHELBURNE INN
Seaview, Washington

Vegetarian Brunch Torte❖

8 eggs, well beaten
½ cup milk
1 ½ cups softened cream cheese
¼ cup roasted salted sunflower seeds
½ teaspoon finely chopped fresh parsley
½ teaspoon finely chopped fresh chives
½ teaspoon finely chopped fresh oregano

Fresh cherry tomatoes, halved

Preheat oven to 350° F. Grease three 9-inch pie plates.

In a medium-sized bowl, combine the eggs and milk and blend well. Divide the egg mixture equally among the prepared plates and bake for 15 minutes, or until the eggs have set. Cool for 5 minutes.

In another bowl, beat together the cream cheese, sunflower seeds, parsley, chives, and oregano. Set aside.

Unmold the three baked omelets. Place one omelet on a warmed platter and spread with half of the reserved cream cheese mixture. Top with second omelet, spreading remaining cream cheese on top. Top with the third omelet.

Cut the torte into wedges and garnish with the tomatoes. Serve immediately.

Yield: 6 servings

GRANT CORNER INN
Santa Fe, New Mexico

Fresh Winter Squash Fritters

**One 2-pound fresh winter squash, peeled, seeded, and
  shredded**
¼ cup heavy cream
4 tablespoons cornstarch
2 large eggs, beaten
Salt and pepper to taste
**4 tablespoons chopped fresh herbs: choice of oregano,
  marjoram, rosemary, chives, parsley, or winter savory**
1 tablespoon chopped garlic
½ tablespoon olive oil
Crème fraîche

In a medium-sized mixing bowl, combine the first seven ingredients and mix together until well combined.

Heat a griddle or large skillet and add the oil. Pour the batter into circles (pancake-style) and fry until golden brown, about 1 minute per side. Keep the fritters in a warm oven until all are prepared.

Dab the fritters with the crème fraîche and serve immediately.

Yield: 6 to 8 servings

CARTER HOUSE/HOTEL CARTER
Eureka, California

Southwest Breakfast Tortillas

1 ¼ cups sliced fresh mushrooms
⅓ cup chopped red onions
⅓ cup chopped red bell pepper
⅓ cup chopped green bell pepper
1 tablespoon olive oil
¼ teaspoon ground cumin
Pinch black pepper
12 large eggs, beaten
¼ cup coarsely broken unsalted tortilla chips
Six 10-inch fresh flour tortillas, heated
1 ½ cups green chile salsa

In large nonstick skillet, cook the vegetables in the oil until crisp-tender. Stir in the cumin and black pepper. Pour the eggs over the vegetables. Do not stir.

As the eggs become set around the edges, push the cooked portion to the center, allowing the uncooked portion to flow to the edges of the skillet. Break up the egg mixture and turn to complete cooking. Stir in the tortilla chips.

Spoon ¾ cup of the egg mixture across the center of each tortilla. Roll up each tortilla and place on a serving plate and top each with ¼ cup of the salsa. Serve immediately.

Yield: 6 servings

WESTWAYS RESORT INN
Phoenix, Arizona

Lemon-Broccoli Quiche

1 ¼ cups medium-dice fresh broccoli
One 8-ounce can sliced water chestnuts, drained and well
  rinsed

¾ cup mayonnaise
¾ cup half-and-half
3 eggs, slightly beaten
⅛ teaspoon ground nutmeg
2 tablespoons fresh lemon juice
¼ teaspoon soy sauce
Pinch salt
2 teaspoons cornstarch
1 ½ cups shredded Swiss cheese
1 unbaked 9-inch pastry shell
Ground paprika

In a small saucepan, steam the broccoli until crisp-tender, about 4 – 6 minutes. Add the water chestnuts and set aside.

Preheat oven to 350° F. In a medium-sized bowl, combine the next eight ingredients and mix together well.

Place the reserved broccoli mixture and the cheese evenly in the crust. Carefully pour in the egg mixture. Sprinkle with the paprika and bake for 35 – 40 minutes. Let stand for 15 minutes before serving. Serve.

Yield: 6 servings

THE OAKS HISTORIC BED & BREAKFAST COUNTRY INN
Christiansburg, Virginia

Chicken-Pecan Quiche❖

2 cups cooked finely chopped chicken
1 cup grated Monterey Jack cheese
¼ cup chopped scallions
1 tablespoon chopped fresh parsley
1 tablespoon all-purpose flour
One 9-inch unbaked pastry shell
3 eggs, beaten
1 ¼ cups half-and-half
½ teaspoon brown mustard
½ cup chopped pecans

Preheat oven to 325° F. In a medium-sized bowl, mix together the chicken, cheese, scallions, parsley, and flour and place the mixture in the pie shell.

In a small bowl, mix together the eggs, half-and-half, and

mustard and pour over the chicken mixture. Sprinkle the pecans over the top and bake for 1 hour. Let stand for 10 minutes before serving. Serve.

Yield: 6 servings

MAINSTAY INN & COTTAGE
Cape May, New Jersey

Crustless Crab Quiche❖

4 eggs
1 cup sour cream
1 cup small curd cottage cheese
¾ cup grated Parmesan cheese
¼ cup unbleached all-purpose flour
Pinch salt
4 drops Tabasco sauce, or other hot pepper sauce
Pinch freshly ground nutmeg
¾ cup diced fresh crabmeat
2 cups shredded Monterey Jack cheese

Preheat oven to 350° F. Lightly grease a 10-inch glass pie plate.

In a food processor, blend the eggs, sour cream, cottage cheese, Parmesan cheese, flour, salt, Tabasco sauce, and nutmeg. Pour the mixture into a large bowl and stir in the crabmeat and Monterey Jack cheese.

Pour the crabmeat mixture into the prepared pie plate and bake for 45 – 60 minutes, or until puffed and golden brown and a knife inserted near the center comes out clean. Let stand for 10 minutes before serving. Serve.

Yield: 8 servings

BLUEBERRY HILL
Goshen, Vermont

Macadamia-Chocolate Chip Streusel Coffee Cake❖

Streusel:
½ cup packed light brown sugar
½ cup all-purpose flour
Pinch salt
3 tablespoons chilled unsalted butter, cut into ½-inch cubes
1 cup coarsely chopped macadamia nuts
8 ounces (about 1 ⅓ cups) semisweet chocolate chips

Cake:
4 cups all-purpose flour
2 teaspoons baking powder
1 teaspoon baking soda
1 teaspoon salt
1 cup (2 sticks) unsalted butter, melted and cooled
2 cups granulated sugar
2 cups sour cream, at room temperature
2 extra-large eggs, at room temperature
2 tablespoons pure vanilla extract
Confectioners' sugar

To make the streusel, stir together the brown sugar, flour, and salt in a medium-sized bowl. Place the butter cubes evenly over the sugar mixture. Using fingertips, quickly rub the butter into the dry ingredients until the mixture resembles coarse meal. Stir in the nuts and chocolate chips and set aside.

To make the cake, position a rack in the center of the oven and preheat to 350° F. Butter a 12-cup bundt pan.

In a large bowl, sift together the flour, baking powder, baking soda, and salt. In another large bowl, whisk together the butter, sugar, sour cream, eggs, and vanilla until creamy. Make a well in the center of the flour mixture and whisk in the butter mixture just until smooth.

Spread one-third of the batter over the bottom of the prepared pan and sprinkle half of the reserved streusel evenly over the batter. Top with another one-third of the batter and sprinkle with the remaining streusel. Top with the remaining batter and spread evenly. Bake for 1 hour – 1 hour 10 minutes, or until a tester inserted in the center comes out clean.

Cool in the pan on a wire rack for 10 minutes. Invert the cake onto the rack and cool for at least 20 minutes more.

Place on a large serving dish and sift the confectioners' sugar lightly over the top. Serve warm or at room temperature. (The coffee cake can be stored in an airtight container for up to four days.)

Yield: 12 servings

STEAMBOAT INN
Steamboat, Oregon

Shoofly Coffee Cake

4 cups all-purpose flour
2 cups packed brown sugar
¾ cup vegetable shortening
1 teaspoon salt
1 teaspoon pure vanilla extract
2 cups boiling water
1 cup dark molasses
1 tablespoon baking soda

Preheat oven to 350° F. In a large mixing bowl, mix together the first five ingredients with a fork. Set aside 1 cup for the topping.

In a small mixing bowl, stir together the water, molasses, and baking soda and add to the flour mixture. Mix together well.

Pour the batter in a greased 9 x 13-inch baking pan. Sprinkle on the reserved topping and bake for 40 minutes. Cool slightly on a wire rack. Serve warm.

Yield: 8 servings

OLD FARM INN
Rockport, Massachusetts

Morning Cake Delight

1 pound butter, at room temperature
6 eggs, beaten
½ cup sour cream
½ cup milk
1 ½ teaspoons pure almond extract

OLD FARM INN

Captain Woodbury settled the Old Farm Inn property in 1702. At that time it encompassed the entire northern tip of the beautiful craggy coast area known as Cape Ann. Today, the inn lies nestled among birch trees and wildflowers on five acres of fields and woodlands. Records show the farmhouse was actually built on or before 1799.

Innkeepers Bill and Susan Balzarini have been welcoming guests to their former dairy farm since the early 1960s, when the property was thoroughly renovated. The peaceful salt-tinged breezes provide the perfect backdrop for quiet dreamy afternoons. This creaky-floored, historic old farmhouse literally overflows with antiques and colorful handmade quilts with whimsical touches at every turn.

HAWTHORNE INN

1 tablespoon baking powder
2 cups granulated sugar
1 banana, mashed
4 cups all-purpose flour
1 cup fresh berries (any type)
1 recipe *Hawthorne Inn Topping* (see recipe below)

Preheat oven to 375° F. In a large mixing bowl, mix together the first eight ingredients until very smooth. Beat in the flour until well coated. Do not overbeat.

Pour half of the batter into a buttered, floured bundt pan and sprinkle the berries over the batter. Pour the remaining batter over the berries and bake for 1 hour 15 minutes. Cool in the pan on a wire rack for 10 minutes. Invert the cake onto the rack and cool for 10 minutes more.

Place the cake on a large serving dish and serve with the topping.

Hawthorne Inn Topping

½ cup fruit yogurt (any type)
½ cup sour cream
½ cup fresh whipped cream

In a small serving bowl, fold the yogurt and sour cream into the whipped cream and serve with the cake.

Yield: 12 servings

HAWTHORNE INN
Concord, Massachusetts

Cafe Marquesa's Granola

3 cups steel-cut rolled oats
1 ¾ cups coarsely chopped almonds
2 ¼ cups sunflower seeds
⅓ cup safflower or soy oil
⅓ cup honey
⅓ cup pure maple syrup
2 ¼ teaspoons pure vanilla extract
½ teaspoon pure almond extract
½ tablespoon freshly ground cinnamon
¾ cup or more dried fruit: raisins, currants, apricots, figs, prunes, dates, cranberries, or cherries

Heavy cream

In a large bowl, combine the oats, almonds, and sunflower seeds and set aside.

Combine the oil, honey, syrup, both extracts, cinnamon, and salt in a large saucepan and heat over medium heat until the mixture becomes watery, about 5 minutes.

Preheat oven to 325° F. Pour the warm oil mixture over the reserved oat mixture and stir until the oats are coated well. Spread the mixture in a large baking pan and bake on the center rack for 30 – 50 minutes, or until the granola turns golden, stirring every 15 minutes to toast uniformly.

Remove to a large bowl and toss occasionally until thoroughly cool and dry. Add the dried fruit and toss to mix.

Serve in bowls with a pitcher of heavy cream on the side.

Yield: 8 servings

THE MARQUESA HOTEL/CAFE MARQUESA
Key West, Florida

Dutch Apple Babies❖

2 eggs
½ cup milk
1 teaspoon pure vanilla extract
1 tablespoon granulated sugar
½ cup all-purpose flour
2 teaspoons butter, divided
Confectioners' sugar

Apple Mixture:
2 medium apples, peeled, cored, and sliced
½ teaspoon ground cinnamon
3 tablespoons butter

Preheat oven to 425° F. In a blender or food processor, blend together the eggs, milk, and vanilla. Gradually add the sugar and flour while still blending. Set the batter aside.

Place ½ teaspoon of the butter into each of four individual au gratin dishes. Place the dishes on the lowest rack in the oven

THE MARQUESA HOTEL

The Marquesa Hotel is newly restored and has earned its place in the National Register of Historic Places. The pistachio-hued home with dark blue-gray shutters ranks among the island's finest. *Palm Beach Life Magazine* says, "Everything worth seeing on the island is within easy walking distance" of the hotel. Guests experience a refined elegance as soon as they enter this 1884 home. The hotel offers many amenities not often found in a small hotel, such as a full-time concierge, who kindly greets and assists guests.

Owners Richard Manley and Erik deBoer also situated the Cafe Marquesa right next door. The Cafe provides breakfast service for the hotel guests and dinner service for both guests and the general public. A creative menu features American regional dishes, which are served in a bistro-style dining room with Cantera stone floors, mahogany bar, and trompe l'oeil walls.

BLUE HARBOR HOUSE

Remember when the mere thought of breakfast in bed evoked visions of pampered decadence? If you thought that was decadent, just wait until you arrive at the Blue Harbor House breakfast table. If you're like a lot of inn-goers, who have discovered the richness of the Maine coast and the 1835 classic New England cape-designed Blue Harbor House, you'll find this breakfast treat is worth getting up for!

Innkeepers Jody Schmoll and Dennis Hayden take the concept of hospitality very seriously—even to the point of acquiring a matched set of pottery apple bakers to ensure their fresh, crisp breakfast apples are baked to perfection every time. Once baked, this memorable treat is served piping hot from the oven and topped with a scoop of vanilla ice cream. For breakfast? Yes indeed! Baked Apples is the most often requested item on the breakfast menu at this beautifully restored ten-guest room country inn.

You'll want to save time for a stroll through the village of Camden and picturesque Camden Harbor, where the mountains literally meet the sea. But don't get too carried away with souvenir shopping; dinner this evening at the Blue Harbor House is a genuine "all you can eat" Down East Lobster Bake served outside in the back patio garden. Lobsters, steamers, and corn on the cob, drenched in melted butter and freshly squeezed lemon juice, are topped off with homemade chocolate chip cookies and (you guessed it) homemade ice cream!

until the butter is melted.

In a small bowl, stir together all of the apple mixture ingredients and divide among the dishes. Pour the reserved batter over the apple mixture and bake for 10 minutes. Sift the confectioners' sugar over the tops and serve immediately.

Yield: 4 servings

THE HEARTSTONE INN
Eureka Springs, Arkansas

Baked Apples

Butter
4 Granny Smith apples, cored
1 recipe *Spiced Sugar* (see recipe below)
4 tablespoons raisins, divided
4 tablespoons chopped nuts, divided
4 tablespoons water, divided
French vanilla ice cream

Butter the skin of each apple, then roll the apples in the spiced sugar. Place each apple in an ovenproof serving bowl and fill each core with 1 tablespoon raisins and 1 tablespoon nuts.

In the bottom of each bowl, add 1 tablespoon water and bake for 45 – 60 minutes, or until the skin has opened. Serve hot with the ice cream.

Spiced Sugar

¼ cup granulated sugar
1 cup packed brown sugar
3 teaspoons ground cinnamon
1 teaspoon ground allspice
1 teaspoon ground nutmeg

In a shallow medium-sized bowl, combine all of the ingredients and mix well. Makes about 1 ½ cups.

Yield: 4 servings

BLUE HARBOR HOUSE
Camden, Maine

Stewed Winter Fruit❖

1 pound pitted dried apricots
1 pound pitted dried prunes
1 pound pitted dried dates
1 pound currants
1 pound coarsely chopped pecans or walnuts
4 medium apples, cored, and cubed
4 medium pears, cored and cubed
¾ cup pure Vermont maple syrup
1 cup apple cider
Heavy cream

Preheat oven to 375° F. In a large baking dish, layer the dried
fruits, pecans, and fresh fruits.

Pour the syrup and cider over the fruits. Cover tightly and bake
for 1 hour 15 minutes, or until the fruits are soft. Serve warm
with a pitcher of heavy cream.

Yield: 6 to 8 servings

BLUEBERRY HILL
Goshen, Vermont

Chalet Suzanne's Broiled Grapefruit

2 tablespoons ground cinnamon
½ cup granulated sugar
2 large grapefruit, at room temperature
6 tablespoons (¾ stick) butter
2 teaspoons granulated sugar, divided

In a small bowl, mix together the cinnamon and the ½ cup
sugar. Set aside.

Slice each grapefruit in half and cut the membrane around the
center of the fruit. Cut around each section half, close to the
membrane, so the fruit is completely loosened from the shell.

Fill the center of each half with 1 ½ tablespoons of the butter
and sprinkle ½ teaspoon of the sugar over each half. Sprinkle 2
tablespoons of the reserved cinnamon mixture over each half.

Preheat the broiler. Place the grapefruit in a shallow baking pan and broil until the tops are browned and bubbly. Serve immediately.

Yield: 4 servings

CHALET SUZANNE
Lake Wales, Florida

Honey Cream Fruit Skewers❖

2 fresh kiwis, peeled and each cut into 8 wedges
¼ fresh cantaloupe, cut into 8 chunks
¼ fresh honeydew melon, cut into 8 chunks
¼ fresh pineapple, cut into 8 chunks
8 large fresh strawberries, washed and hulled
1 recipe *Honey Cream Sauce* (see recipe below)

Divide the fruit among eight short bamboo skewers, threading the fruits so the kiwis are on both ends. Chill.

Serve two skewers per person with the sauce on the side.

Honey Cream Sauce

½ cup honey
¼ cup fresh lemon juice
¼ teaspoon ground paprika
½ cup heavy cream, whipped

In a small bowl, blend together the honey, lemon juice, and paprika. Fold in the whipped cream, cover, and chill until ready to serve.

Yield: 4 servings

GRANT CORNER INN
Santa Fe, New Mexico

Appendix

If you have enjoyed the recipes in this fine collection from inns throughout the country, we encourage you to write or call the innkeepers with your comments and thoughts. Even better, visit the inns and get to know these gracious and friendly people.

NORTHEAST

Asa Ransom House
10529 Main Street
Clarence, NY 14031-1684
716-759-2315
Bob and Judy Lenz, Innkeepers

Barrows House
RT 30
Dorset, VT 05251
802-867-4455
Linda and Jim McGinnis,
    Innkeepers

The Bird & Bottle Inn
Old Albany Post Road, RT 9
Garrison, NY 10524
914-424-3000
Ira Boyar, Innkeeper

Blue Harbor House
67 Elm Street
Camden, ME 04843
207-236-3196; 800-248-3196
Jody Schmoll and Dennis
    Hayden, Innkeepers

Blueberry Hill ❖
RD 3
Goshen, VT 05733
802-247-6735; 800-448-0707
Tony Clark, Innkeeper

Charles Hinckley House
Olde Kings Highway
RT 6A, PO Box 723
Barnstable, MA 02630
508-362-9924
Les and Miya Patrick,
    Innkeepers

1880 Seafield House
Two Seafield Lane
West Hampton Beach, NY
    11978
516-288-1559
Mrs. Elsie Collins, Innkeeper

The Governor's Inn ❖
86 Main Street
Ludlow, VT 05149
802-228-8830; 800-468-3766
Charlie and Deedy Marble,
    Innkeepers

Hawthorne Inn
462 Lexington Road
Concord, MA 01742
508-369-5610
Gregory Burch and Marilyn
    Mudry, Innkeepers

The Hermitage
Coldbrook Road
Wilmington, VT 05363
802-464-3511
The McGovern Family, Owners/
    Innkeepers

Inn at Sawmill Farm
Box 367
West Dover, VT 05256
802-464-8131
Rod and Ione Williams,
    Innkeepers

The Inn at Starlight Lake
Box 27
Starlight, PA 18461
717-798-2519; 800-248-2519
Judy and Jack McMahon,
    Innkeepers

The Inn at Stockbridge
RT 7 North, Box 618
Stockbridge, MA 01262
413-298-3337
Lee and Don Weitz, Innkeepers

The Inn at Weathersfield
RT 106, Box 165
Weathersfield, VT 05151
802-263-9217; 800-477-4828
Mary Louise and Ron Thorburn,
    Innkeepers

Interlaken Inn ❖
15 Interlaken Avenue
Lake Placid, NY 12946
518-523-3180; 800-428-4369
Roy and Carol Johnson,
    Innkeepers

Longfellow's Wayside Inn
Wayside Inn Road
South Sudbury, MA 01776
508-443-1776
Robert H. Purrington, Innkeeper

The Lyme Inn
On the Common
Lyme, NH 03768
603-795-4404
Mickey and Tammy Dowd,
    Owners/Innkeepers

Mainstay Inn & Cottage ❖
635 Columbia Avenue
Cape May, NJ 08204
609-884-8690
Tom and Sue Carroll,
    Innkeepers

Manor House ❖
612 Hughes Street
Cape May, NJ 08204-2318
609-884-4710
Tom and Mary Snyder,
    Innkeepers

❖ designates inns that have supplied recipes from their own cookbooks.

The Mansakenning Carriage
  House
29 Ackert Hook Road
Rhinebeck, NY 12572
914-876-3500
Michelle and John Dremann,
  Innkeepers

Maples Inn
16 Roberts Avenue
Bar Harbor, ME 04609
207-288-3443
Susan Sinclair, Owner/Innkeeper

The Newcastle Inn ❖
River Road
Newcastle, ME 04553
207-563-5685; 800-832-8669
Ted and Chris Sprague,
  Innkeepers

Old Farm Inn
291 Granite Street
Rockport, MA 01966-1028
508-546-3237
Bill and Susan Balzarini,
  Innkeepers

Oliver Loud's Inn
Richardson's Canal House
1474 Marsh Road
Pittsford, NY 14534
716-248-5200
716-248-5000
Viviene Tellier, Innkeeper

The Point
Star Route, Box 65
Saranac Lake, NY 12983
518-891-5678
David and Christie Garrett,
  Innkeepers

The Queen Victoria ❖
102 Ocean Street
Cape May, NJ 08204
609-884-8702
Dane and Joan Wells, Innkeepers

Rabbit Hill Inn
RT 18
Lower Waterford, VT 05848
802-748-5168; 800-762-8669
John and Maureen Magee,
  Innkeepers

Ralph Waldo Emerson Inn
Phillips Avenue, Box 2369
Rockport, MA 01966
508-546-6321
Gary and Diane Wemyss,
  Innkeepers

The Red Lion Inn ❖
Main Street
Stockbridge, MA 01262
413-298-5545
Jack and Jane Fitzpatrick, Owners
Betsy Holtzinger, Innkeeper

Rose Inn
RT 34 North, PO Box 6576
Ithaca, NY 14851-6576
607-533-7905
Charles and Sherry Rosemann,
  Innkeepers

Sea Crest By The Sea
19 Tuttle Avenue
Spring Lake, NJ 07762
908-449-9031
John and Carol Kirby,
  Innkeepers

The Settlers Inn ❖
Four Main Avenue
Hawley, PA 18428
717-226-2993; 800-833-8527
Jeanne Genzlinger, Innkeeper

The 1661 Inn
Hotel Manisses
Spring Street
Block Island, RI 02807
401-466-2421
401-466-2063
The Abrams Family, Innkeepers

Sugartree Inn
Sugarbush Access Road
Warren, VT 05674
802-583-3211
Kathy and Frank Partsch,
  Owners/Innkeepers

Trail's End ❖
Smith Road
Wilmington, VT 05363
802-464-2727
Bill and Mary Kilburn,
  Innkeepers

Vermont Marble Inn
On the Town Green
Fair Haven, VT 05743
802-265-8383; 800-535-2814
Bea and Richard Taube, Shirley
  Stein, Innkeepers

The Weathervane Inn
PO Box 388, RT 23
South Egremont, MA 01258
413-528-9580
The Murphy Family, Innkeepers

The White Inn
52 East Main Street
Fredonia, NY 14063
716-672-2103
Robert Contiguglia and Kathleen
  Dennison, Innkeepers

Windham Hill Inn ❖
RR 1, Box 44
West Townshend, VT 05359
802-874-4080
Ken and Linda Busteed,
  Innkeepers

NORTHCENTRAL

Old Rittenhouse Inn ❖
311 Rittenhouse Avenue
PO Box 584
Bayfield, WI 54814
715-779-5111
Jerry and Mary Phillips,
  Innkeepers

Rivertown Inn
306 West Olive Street
Stillwater, Minnesota 55082
612-430-2955
Chuck and Judy Dougherty,
    Innkeepers

Stafford's Bay View Inn
613 Woodland Avenue
PO Box 3
Petoskey, MI 49770
616-347-2771
The Stafford Smith Family,
    Innkeepers

Victorian Treasure Bed &
    Breakfast
115 Prairie Street
Lodi, WI 53555
608-592-5199
Todd and Kimberly Seidl,
    Innkeepers

The White Gull Inn
4225 Main Street
PO Box 160
Fish Creek, WI 54212
414-868-3517
Andy and Jan Coulson,
    Innkeepers

White Lace Inn
16 North 5th Avenue
Sturgeon Bay, WI 54235
414-743-1105
Dennis and Bonnie Statz,
    Innkeepers

NORTHWEST

Inn at Swifts Bay
RT 2, Box 3402
Lopez Island, WA 98261
206-468-3636
Robert Hermann and
    Christopher Brandmeir,
    Innkeepers

Shelburne Inn ❖
The Shoalwater Restaurant ❖
4415 Pacific Way, Box 250
Seaview, WA 98644
206-642-2442
David Campiche and Laurie
    Anderson, Innkeepers
Ann and Tony Kischner,
    Restaurant Owners

Steamboat Inn ❖
RT 138
Steamboat, OR 97447-9703
503-496-3495
503-498-2411
Sharon and Jim Van Loan,
    Innkeepers
Patricia Lee, Manager

Turtleback Farm Inn
Crow Valley Road, RT 1
Box 650, Eastsound
Orcas Island, WA 98245
206-376-4914
William and Susan C. Fletcher,
    Innkeepers

SOUTHEAST

Adams Edgeworth Inn
Monteagle Assembly
Monteagle, TN 37356
615-924-2669
Wendy and David Adams,
    Innkeepers

The Ashby Inn
RT 1, Box 2A
Paris, VA 22130
703-592-3900
John and Roma Sherman,
    Innkeepers

The Bailiwick Inn ❖
4023 Chain Bridge Road
Fairfax, VA 22030
703-691-2266; 800-366-7666
Anne and Ray Smith, Innkeepers

Chalet Suzanne
3800 Chalet Suzanne Drive
Lake Wales, FL 33853-7060
813-6766011; 800-433-6011
The Hinshaw Family, Innkeepers

Clifton, The Country Inn
RT 13, Box 26
Charlottesville, VA 22901
804-971-1800
Craig and Donna Hartman,
    Innkeepers

The Fearrington House ❖
2000 Fearrington
Village Center
Pittsboro, NC 27312
919-542-2121
Jenny and R.B. Fitch, Owners
Valerie Komives, Innkeeper

Glen-Ella Springs Inn ❖
Bear Gap Road
RT 3, Box 3304
Clarksville, GA 30523
706-754-7295; 800-552-3479
Bobby and Barrie Aycock,
    Innkeepers

Grandview Lodge
809 Valley View Circle
Waynesville, NC 28786-5350
800-255-7826
Stan and Linda Arnold

Grey Gables Bed & Breakfast
Highway 52, PO Box 5252
Rugby, TN 37733
615-628-5252
Bill and Linda Brooks Jones,
    Innkeepers

The Greystone Inn
Greystone Lane
Lake Toxaway, NC 28747
704-966-4700; 800-824-5766
Tim and Boo Boo Lovelace,
    Innkeepers

The Hidden Inn ❖
249 Caroline Street
Orange, VA 22960
703-672-3625; 800-841-1253
Ray and Barbara Lonick,
    Innkeepers

High Meadows ❖
RT 4, Box 6
Scottsville, VA 24590
804-286-2218; 800-232-1832
Peter Sushka and Mary Jae
    Abbitt, Innkeepers

Historic 1842 Inn
353 College Street
Macon, GA 31201
800-336-1842
Dr. Richard Meils and Phillip
    Jenkins, Owners

The Inn at Blackberry Farm
1471 West Millers Cove Road
Walland, TN 37886
615-984-8166; 800-862-7610
Gart and Bernadette Doyle,
    Innkeepers

The Inn at Buckeystown
3521 Buckeystown Pike
Buckeystown, MD 21717
301-874-5755; 800-272-1190
Daniel Pelz, Chase Barnett,
    Rebecca Shipman-Smith,
    Innkeepers

The Inn at Little Washington
Middle and Main Streets
Washington, VA 22747
703-675-3800
Patrick O'Connell and
    Reinhardt Lynch, Innkeepers

The Inn at the Taylor House
Highway 194, PO Box 713
Valle Crucis, NC 28691
704-963-5581
Chip and Roland Schwab,
    Innkeepers

Jordan Hollow Farm Inn
RT 2, Box 375
Stanley, VA 22851
703-778-2285
Marley and Jetze Beers,
    Innkeepers

L'Auberge Provençale
RT 340, PO Box 119
White Post, VA 22663
703-837-1375; 800-638-1702
Celeste and Alain Borel,
    Innkeepers

The Lords Proprietors' Inn ❖
300 North Broad Street
Edenton, NC 27932
919-482-3541; 800-348-8933
Arch and Jane Edwards,
    Innkeepers

The Marquesa Hotel
600 Fleming Street
Key West, FL 33040
305-292-1919; 800-869-4631
Richard Manley and Erik de
    Boer, Owners
Carol Wightman, Manager

Mast Farm Inn ❖
PO Box 704
Valle Crucis, NC 28691
704-963-5857
Sibyl and Francis Pressly,
    Innkeepers

McNinch House
511 North Church Street
Charlotte, NC 28203
704-332-6159
Ellen Davis, Proprietor

The Oaks Historic Bed &
    Breakfast Country Inn
311 East Main Street
Christiansburg, VA 24073
703-381-1500
Margaret and Tom Ray,
    Innkeepers

Prospect Hill Plantation Inn
RT 3, Box 430
Trevilians, VA 23093
703-967-0844
Bill, Mireille, and Michael
    Sheehan, Innkeepers

The Rhett House Inn ❖
1009 Craven Street
Beaufort, SC 29902
803-524-9030
Steve and Marianne Harrison,
    Innkeepers

Richmond Hill Inn
87 Richmond Hill Drive
Asheville, NC 28806
704-252-7313; 800-545-9238
Susan Michel-Robertson,
    Innkeeper

The Robert Morris Inn
312 North Morris Street
PO Box 70
Oxford, MD 21654
410-226-5111
Wendy and Ken Gibson, Owners
Jay Gibson, Innkeeper

Snowbird Mountain Lodge
275 Santeetlah Road
Robbinsville, NC 28771
704-479-3433
Jim and Eleanor Burbank,
    Innkeepers

SOUTHCENTRAL

The Burn
712 North Union Street
Natchez, MS 39120
601-442-1344; 800-654-8859
Loveta Byrne, Innkeeper

Dairy Hollow House ❖
515 Spring Street
Eureka Springs, AR 72632
501-253-7444; 800-562-8650
Ned Shank and Crescent
    Dragonwagon, Innkeepers

Durham House Bed & Breakfast
   Inn
921 Heights Boulevard
Houston, TX 77008
800-722-8788
Marguerite Swanson, Innkeeper

Garth Woodside Mansion ❖
RR 1
Hannibal, MO 63401
314-221-2789
Irv and Diane Feinberg,
   Innkeepers

The Heartstone Inn ❖
35 Kingshighway
Eureka Springs, AR 72632
501-253-8916
Iris and Bill Simantel, Innkeepers

SOUTHWEST

The Babbling Brook
1025 Laurel Street
Santa Cruz, CA 95060
408-427-2437; 800-866-1131
Helen King, Innkeeper

Campbell Ranch Inn ❖
1475 Canyon Road
Geyserville, CA 95441
707-857-3476
Mary Jane and Jerry Campbell,
   Innkeepers

Carter House
Hotel Carter
1033 Third Street
Eureka, CA 95501
707-445-1390
707-444-8062
Mark and Christi Carter,
   Innkeepers

Castle Marne
1572 Race Street
Denver, CO 80206
303-331-0621; 800-92-MARNE
The Peiker Family, Innkeepers

Chanel Road Inn
219 West Chanel Road
Santa Monica, CA 90402
310-459-1920
Kathy Jensen and Susan Zolla,
   Innkeepers

The Gingerbread Mansion
400 Berding Street
PO Box 40
Ferndale, CA 95536-0040
707-786-4000
Ken Torbert, Innkeeper

Grant Corner Inn ❖
122 Grant Avenue
Santa Fe, NM 87501
505-983-6678
Louise Stewart and Pat Walter,
   Innkeepers

Harbor House Inn By The Sea
PO Box 369
5600 South Highway One
Elk, CA 95432
707-877-3203
Dean and Helen Turner,
   Innkeepers

Hearthstone Inn ❖
506 North Cascade Avenue
Colorado Springs, CO 80903
719-473-4413; 800-521-1885
Dot Williams and Ruth
   Williams, Innkeepers

Madrona Manor
101 Westside Road
Healdsburg, CA 95448
707-433-4231; 800-258-4003
John and Carol Muir, Innkeepers

Old Thyme Inn
779 Main Street
Half Moon Bay, CA 94019
415-726-1616
George and Marcia Dempsey,
   Innkeepers

Rancho San Gregorio
RT 1, Box 54
San Gregorio, CA 94074
415-747-0810
Bud and Lee Raynor, Innkeepers

The Redbud Inn
402 Main Street
PO Box 716
Murphys, CA 95247
209-728-8533; 800-825-8533
Jan Drammer, Innkeeper

Westways Resort Inn
PO Box 41624
Valley of The Sun
Phoenix, AZ 85080
602-582-3868
Darrell Trapp, Innkeeper

Recipes Arranged by Inn

Index

About the Author

R. CARRIKER

C. VINCENT SHORTT is the founder and president of Shortt Stories Teleproductions, Inc., based in Winston-Salem, North Carolina. He has been a leading force in the hospitality industry and an award-winning producer of film and television programming for the past 20 years. He is an acknowledged authority on the food and beverage industry and a contributing editor and guest columnist for a variety of hospitality industry publications. Mr. Shortt is the only four-time recipient of the Pepsi MVP Award in the United States and has been honored by the National Restaurant Association with bronze, silver, and gold awards for menu design excellence.

Mr. Shortt is the creator of the cable television series "Great Country Inns," and executive producer of the PBS series "Inn Country USA." He is the author of the newly published, revised edition of *How to Open and Successfully Operate a Country Inn*, published by Berkshire House Publishers, Stockbridge, Massachusetts. He and his wife, Ann, live in Advance, North Carolina.